Praise for
THE HOTEL ON THE ROOF OF THE WORLD:

'One of the most strangely seductive places I've been to...
Thank you to Alec Le Sueur for bringing it to life'
Michael Palin

'A comparison with Fawlty Towers is inevitable, but this is
funnier'
THE MAIL ON SUNDAY

'Le Sueur... provides us with the means of improving our
knowledge of a far-away country about which we know little'
THE GUARDIAN

'Horribly funny and worthy of any hotel sitcom'
SOUTH CHINA MORNING POST

'Imagine moving Fawlty Towers from Torquay to Tibet...
Le Sueur has distilled five years of real anecdotes into one
hilarious volume'
FOCUS magazine

'This is a rip-roaring comedy of a book... Underlying the
story is a heart-warming and sensitive understanding of the
Tibetan people'
THE HIMALAYAN CLUB

D0183180

BOTTOMS UP IN BELGIUM

Copyright © Alec Le Sueur, 2014

All rights reserved.

No part of this book may be reproduced by any means, nor transmitted, nor translated into a machine language, without the written permission of the publishers.

Alec Le Sueur has asserted his right to be identified as the author of this work in accordance with sections 77 and 78 of the Copyright, Designs and Patents Act 1988.

Condition of Sale
This book is sold subject to the condition that it shall not, by way of trade or otherwise, be lent, re-sold, hired out or otherwise circulated in any form of binding or cover other than that in which it is published and without a similar condition including this condition being imposed on the subsequent purchaser.

Summersdale Publishers Ltd
46 West Street
Chichester
West Sussex
PO19 1RP
UK

www.summersdale.com

Printed and bound by CPI Group (UK) Ltd, Croydon, CR0 4YY

ISBN: 978-1-84953-247-1

p.12/13 image of the Atomium is reproduced by kind permission of www.atomium.be Saban 2013.
p.200 beer description reproduced by kind permission of CAMRA.

Substantial discounts on bulk quantities of Summersdale books are available to corporations, professional associations and other organisations. For details contact Nicky Douglas by telephone: +44 (0) 1243 756902, fax: +44 (0) 1243 786300 or email: nicky@summersdale.com.

ALEC LE SUEUR

BOTTOMS UP IN BELGIUM

Seeking the High Points of the Low Lands

summersdale

To Conny
8/7/1965–8/7/2011

NOTE FROM THE AUTHOR

When Julius Caesar passed through the low lands on his way to conquer Britain, he reported back to Rome that the tiresome *Belgae* were 'endlessly fighting amongst themselves and especially with the people from across the Rhine'. This tradition seems to have carried on for much of the next 2,000 years, and ownership of the land that we now call Belgium has been contested more times than practically any other piece of European soil. Whether by invasion, handed out as post-war spoils or wedding presents or through inheritance carve-ups, the 'under new management' sign has been hung up by the Vikings, Franks, the Holy Roman Emperor, the Burgundians, Hapsburgs, Spanish, Austrians, French and Dutch before the Belgians finally declared their independence in 1830. Even after independence, the Germans have had a go – twice – at running the country.

In between being wiped flat by invading armies, Belgium has been remarkably prosperous, with trade, textiles and the industrial revolution all bringing vast wealth to various parts of the country. This extraordinary history of continually shifting cultural, political, linguistic and economic power has led to Belgium's peculiar and complex make-up today. If you take a ruler to the map of Belgium and draw a horizontal line from left to right across the country, just beneath Brussels, this will give you the approximate language divide between north and south. Above the line is Flanders, inhabited by the Flemings whose language is Flemish. My wife Conny described the difference between Flemish and Dutch as that between English and American English, i.e. basically the same but with a different accent and some unique expressions. Below the line is Wallonia, inhabited by the Walloons, whose language is Belgian French, which again is really just French with a few twists, such as the simplification of the way the French say ninety-nine – *quatre-vingt-dix-neuf* – to the much easier, if childish sounding *nonante-neuf*.

But it's not that simple: above the line in the language divide is the Brussels region which stands out in a sea of Flemish speakers as an official bilingual island of French and Flemish. And then to the east of the country, if you take your ruler and draw a line vertically cutting off the small bulge in the middle-right of the map, is the home of Belgium's third official language – the German speakers. Approximately 70,000 German-speaking Belgians live in nine municipalities along the Belgian–German border with their own regional parliament and German language television, radio and newspaper. It's a 'little Germany' within the Walloon, French-speaking province of Liège, a glorious example of Belgian federalism; a state within a state within a state. To be more precise, it is two 'little Germanys': much like Sumatran orang-utans living in isolated pockets of rainforest separated by palm oil plantations, the two groups of German-speaking Belgians are separated from one another by a large swathe of French-speaking Liège, which cuts between the two cantons through the pine forests of the Ardennes to the east of Spa. The pockets of German-speaking Belgians have an official listing in UNCHR's *World Directory of Minorities and Indigenous Peoples*, the first step towards recognition as an endangered species.

French was once the language of the Belgian ruling class, with Flemish-speakers looked down upon as peasants, and the German-speakers dismissed out of hand as being German. Tensions, particularly between the Franco–Flemish language divide, still flare up every so often, usually around the boundaries of bilingual Brussels where heated debates over language rights periodically lead to constitutional crises and the toppling, or non-forming of governments. But do not worry; politics and language boundaries are not the subject matter of this book. I have included this explanatory note at the start merely to give readers who may otherwise not be aware a glimpse of the complexities and tensions that lie beneath the surface of this outwardly very ordinary-appearing country and to set the scene for references to Wallonia, Flanders and the Germans in the chapters ahead.

CONTENTS

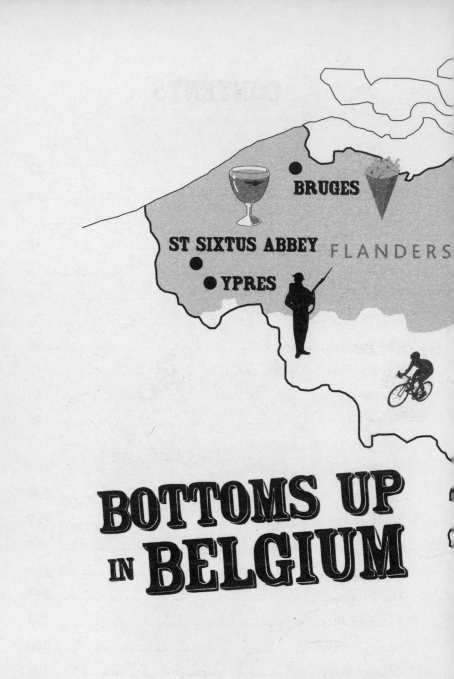

BRUGES

ST SIXTUS ABBEY

YPRES

FLANDERS

BOTTOMS UP
IN BELGIUM

HASSELT

GROOTLOON

BRUSSELS   BOMMERSHOVEN

WATERLOO

WALLONIA   SPA-FRANCORCHAMPS

ARDENNES

INTRODUCTION

Until 1993 I had never been to Belgium. I think I must have been *through* it at least once judging by the evidence of a Belgian tank driver's glove in our garden shed, but I had certainly never been *to* it. My father had picked up the glove from a Belgian roundabout on the way to our summer holiday in the Netherlands in 1969, collecting it as some kind of recompense for being stuck behind Belgian military manoeuvres for hours on end in a traffic jam that seemed to stretch the entire length of the Belgian coast. I was only six, so I don't remember much of the holiday apart from the sore point of missing one of civilisation's greatest historic moments. My older brother was very unfairly allowed to watch the first moon landing, live on a new colour TV set in the campsite games room, while I was sent to bed in the caravan in a serious strop, apparently being 'too young' to stay up. I also caught chicken pox that holiday, which I am sure was my brother's fault too, but I think that was in the Netherlands.

For over twenty years the tank driver's glove was about the sum total of my contact with Belgium, so it came as some surprise when at 2 p.m. on Saturday 7 August 1993 I found myself at the altar of a small Catholic church in Flanders, reciting my wedding vows in Flemish. I'm still not sure exactly what I said on that day, Flemish not being a language I was overly familiar with at the time, but it was the start, for better or for worse, of a long relationship with this unassuming little country. Having previously not cared, or ever really spared a single thought for Belgium, I now found myself and Belgium inextricably linked. I couldn't escape the fact that Conny, my wife, was Belgian. My in-laws: Belgian. My children would be half-Belgian. The answer to the question, 'Where did you go for your summer holidays?' would be 'Belgium'. 'Where did you go for Christmas?' 'Belgium.' 'Half-term?' 'Belgium.' 'Skiing this year?' 'No. Belgium.' I started to make half-apologetic answers: 'Just to Belgium this time,' or, 'Oh, nothing exciting really, only to Belgium.'

I had become accustomed to the fact that no one was going to reply, 'Belgium? Wow, that's amazing!' or, 'Belgium? Did you know that CNN has placed Belgium as the thirteenth coolest nation on earth and that the Belgian Adolphe Sax invented the saxophone in 1844?' No, at best, the mention of the B-word would illicit the response, 'Oh.' Just, 'Oh.' And then a long silence. Sometimes there would just be silence, or silence followed by an insincere, 'That's nice,' followed by more silence as the respondent's eyes darted around the room, looking for someone else to start a conversation with. On the occasions when the copious consumption of Chardonnay had preceded the response, the polite facade of 'Oh' would be done away with, and they would just come straight out with what everyone was really thinking:

INTRODUCTION

'*Belgium*?! Brussels and all those Eurocrats on the gravy train? It's just so *boring*. Why, you can't even name ten famous Belgians! What do you want to go *there* for?'

It is true that Belgium faces a serious image problem. The entire nationality is written off as the butt of 'thick' jokes by their northern and southern neighbours. The French even refer to a story of utter stupidity as *'une histoire Belge'*. 'Did you hear the one about the Belgian water skier who had to give up because he couldn't find a lake with a slope on it?'

British humour is no kinder to the Belgians. An early Monty Python sketch has Michael Palin hosting an episode of a show called *Prejudice* in which viewers have been asked to enter a competition in search of the most derogatory term for the Belgians, with the winning entry being 'miserable fat Belgian bastards'.

It doesn't get any better as Rowan Atkinson takes up the baton of Belgian-bashing in a Comic Relief sketch in which the Belgians are confused with aerosols and blamed for causing the hole in the ozone layer. John Cleese has a go in a more recent online rant, referring to the Belgians, or half of them at least, as 'pseudo-French bastards' but no one can touch Douglas Adams, author of *The Hitchhiker's Guide to the Galaxy*, when it comes to unprovoked Belgian-baiting. In the *Guide*, he tells us of the existence of a word that is so revolting, so offensive and so repulsive that no organism in the entire galaxy is permitted to speak it. And yes, you have guessed it, the word is: Belgium.

As if hurling specific insults at Belgians wasn't enough, they are also written off as total nonentities, hence the denigrating, 'Can you name ten famous Belgians?' question and accompanying snigger. I tried to learn a stock answer to this, but no one really wanted to listen and I didn't even know who half the people were who I claimed to be famous Belgians. For a long while, during the many family visits and enforced excursions to places of apparent touristic merit (for Belgians), I resigned myself to this outsiders' view of the country. It was flat and boring and I would just have to accept it. The most famous Belgian I could name, Hercule Poirot, wasn't even a real person.

It was on one of the family trips to Belgium, as I ordered yet another Stella Artois, the UK's most popular and therefore predictably boring beer, that it dawned on me that something was not right. What was I doing asking for a Stella when there were over a hundred locally produced beers on the menu in this little cafe? I had been seduced back in 1982, in my formative student years, when the brilliant Stella Artois advertising campaign was launched in the UK with the now legendary 'Reassuringly Expensive' tag line. I had no idea at the time that the high cost was merely a reflection of the extra duty payable in the UK on the lager's relatively high alcohol content. And I had stuck loyally, stupidly, to this beer ever since. What a marketer's dream I was – one advertising campaign leading to a thirty-year continuous purchase. When I met Conny, I ignored her comments that in Belgium, Stella Artois was just a cheap, run-of-the-mill lager that came over the counter if you ordered a *pintje* in Flanders or a *demie* in Wallonia. I ignored the fact that in the UK, Stella had become a heavily discounted line and that the brand had been devalued, nearly to the point of no return, with an alleged association with binge drinking, lager louts, aggressive behaviour and a very unflattering nickname.

From that moment, I took a vow: I would not have another Stella Artois in Belgium without first trying every other Belgian beer that I could find. Before you get the wrong impression about this, I'm not talking about a suicidal attempt to drink as many beers as I could in one session, as many of the Brits who flock to the Munich-style Belgian beer festivals attempt to do. No, this would be a lifelong vow:

No beer shall be consumed for a second time, until all other Belgian beers available have been tried.

According to the official Belgian Tourist Board website, there are over 450 different varieties of Belgian beer. Tim Webb and Joe Strange's *Good Beer Guide Belgium* (CAMRA Books), an essential accompaniment for any trip to Belgium, lists over 1,000 varieties and a strange article on Wikipedia lists over 8,700 beers. Whichever number is correct, it looks like it is going to be a while before I have another Stella.

I would encourage every reader to do the same and leave the comfort zone of your favourite tipple behind – be brave and try something new. When you are in Belgium, ask for a Delirium Tremens, a Black Albert or a Merveilleuse de Chèvremont. You might even want to go for a Coq Hardi, if that's what takes your fancy. In order to help those who take the vow I have included a checklist of Belgian beers at the end of this book, with space for you to write the date, location and score for each one. Keep this for future reference, as if you do take the vow, you certainly won't remember what you drank at the beginning when you get to number 500. And by keeping score, should you ever reach the end of the list, you will know which ones to try again, and which to avoid. The checklist is built up from various sources: cafe menus, brewery websites, gifts from friends and family and the shelves in speciality beer shops, but it is by no means exhaustive and you will be able to add many more to make the list your own.

I have also included a section of tasting notes of various beers that I have tried along the way since taking my vow. From reading these notes, beer connoisseurs and members of CAMRA will soon realise that I know very little about beer, so I might as well come clean about that at the start. Before undertaking my research, I didn't know my bottom fermentation from my filtered *gueuze*, or my Aarshot from my Eeklo. (OK, those last two are nothing to do with beer, they are just two random Flemish towns with funny names.) Bearing that in mind, the observations on the beers that I offer in this book are honest descriptions in layman's terms. I am not a fan of the Jilly Goolden school of pompous oenology, and will not be offering you suggestions that a beer 'promises hints of fresh-baked bread on a summer's day, mmm, I'm getting an Alpine meadow with the tinkling of cow bells...'

On taking my vow, another more serious thought came to mind. If I could have been so wrong about Belgian beer, what about Belgium as a whole? Had I succumbed to a narrow-minded, xenophobic, English middle-class attitude... had I become the profile of a *Daily Express* reader? This was a horrifying thought. Could there be more to the 'miserable fat Belgian bastards' than meets the eye? I would not rest until I had found the answer, and I made the solemn undertaking to set out on a quest: to challenge worldwide opinion by seeking out all that is interesting about Belgium. The following chapters contain the findings of my quest – is there anything of interest, or was Douglas Adams right, and the word 'Belgium' should never be uttered again?

The vow:
No beer shall be consumed for a second time, until all other Belgian beers available have been tried.

The quest:
To seek out all that is interesting about Belgium.

CHAPTER 1
HANENZANG

After a fine Christmas dinner around the family's Belgian dining table, I asked if anyone had any contacts in the pigeon-fancying world. Belgium is the birthplace of modern-day pigeon racing and a quick Google search had revealed a mine of information on lofts, owners and breeders, much of which centred on the small Flemish town of Arendonk, famous for the Janssen brothers' pigeon loft and a statue of a man licking a plate.

'*Duiven* (pigeons)?' they replied. No, they didn't know anyone directly and had never been to Arendonk. Cousin Frank knew someone who lived next door to a hotel with a giant sign of a pigeon on top. He could give her a call. Brother-in-law Jan's father did '*hanenzang*' but he didn't know any pigeon-racers. Conny thought her dad's friend Ludo used to race pigeons and might know someone who could help.

Wait, what did Jan's father say he did? '*Hanenzang?*' That sounded like a strange combination of words. In my limited Flemish I understood '*hanen*' to mean 'chickens' and '*zang*' to mean 'song'.

'That was funny,' I said to Conny, 'I thought Jan's father said he did "chicken-singing"!'

'Don't be stupid,' she replied. 'Chickens don't sing.' As usual, my knowledge of Flemish had let me down. When Conny and her generation spoke English it was always word-perfect, albeit with the slight Dutch accent of the man in the Grolsch ad, combined with an American twang picked up from a teenage diet of subtitled US soaps. My occasional attempts at Flemish conversation inevitably led to awkward or embarrassing situations, where I would inadvertently call someone a 'twat', or laugh out loud at what I thought was the punch-line of a joke when in fact I had just been told that an elderly uncle or aunt had died.

'And anyway, the Flemish for "chicken" is *"kip"*,' Conny corrected me. This dislodged a Belgian memory which had been stored in the depths of my mind for over forty years. While in the traffic jam on the Belgian coast road in that summer of 1969, we hadn't stopped to eat, as my mother kept seeing restaurants with menus offering a very pricey *'halve kip'*, which she very reasonably translated to us as 'half a kipper'. When you are six years old, the thought of eating half a kipper for lunch is quite nauseating, and my brother and I made sure we pushed on into the Netherlands before eventually giving in to the hunger. In those hours in the Belgian traffic, my father had picked up his trophy glove and I had gained my first two misconceptions about the Belgians: 1) that they like eating small portions of kipper for lunch; and 2) that kippers are very expensive in Belgium – in fact for the price of just half a kipper, you could purchase, say, half a chicken and chips.

'So it's not "chicken-singing" then?' I confirmed.

'Of course it's not chicken-singing,' Conny continued. 'It's cockerels. Roosters. Jan's father goes rooster-singing. It's a well-known sport here.'

'A what? A *sport*? Did you just say *"rooster-singing"*?' Pigeon-racing could wait; I had to find out more about this Belgian sporting event. Could it be the first tick on the 'interesting' tally as yet unknown to the outside world?

'When does this happen? Is it some kind of weird Belgian festival taking place once every five years?' I enquired.

'No, it's every Sunday. Pa will be going tomorrow morning. I'm sure he'll take you.'

'Pa', as Jan's father is known, lives in the south of Limburg about 70 km from the Belgian ski resorts of the Ardennes. It was a cold Boxing Day morning at his house and there had been a fresh snowfall overnight. Chicken-singing appears to be a predominantly male-orientated sport as I was only able to persuade Ruben, our twelve-year-old son, to come out with me to see the action. We followed Pa outside, through a path cut in the snow to his hen hutch at the end of the garden where his prime cockerel was waiting for us. 'Does he have a name?' I asked. He didn't. Names don't seem to be a feature on the cockerel-singing circuit. The bird didn't make a sound as Pa picked him up and placed him in a wooden container, about the size of a shoebox, with a hole at one end for his tail feathers to stick out. For a bird that was about to enter a singing competition, it was remarkably quiet. Pa has several cockerels but was only entering one in the competition today. His brother, Swa, who we would meet at the cafe in Bommershoven, was bringing another three birds. They always entered the competition together, and liked to field four birds at a time.

This corner of Limburg is mercifully free of the ribbon development, motorways and power cables that blight much of the rest of the country and the route to Bommershoven, while rather scary in the snow, was certainly very picturesque. The small country lanes took us through apple and pear orchards where the fruit-packing depots, under wraps for the winter, had stacks of wooden fruit crates piled as high as houses. Between the fields, rows of tall poplar trees stood bare against the grey sky, with balls of mistletoe dotted amongst the branches. The houses that we came across were brick-built, and while the setting was rural, their immaculate gardens with trimmed box hedges and rococo-style mail boxes were typical of the suburban neatness found across Belgium.

We passed the church at Groot-Loon which my father-in-law tells me is famous for its toads. I didn't pick up any religious connotation in this – I don't think there has been a holy apparition involving toads at Groot-Loon, or that these toads perform any specific religious function. No, apparently the toads just like to overwinter in the church grounds and the local Green Party has built them special hibernation houses. In case, like me, you are one of those people who like to believe what they read in books, or are a biology student who is now thinking of writing a dissertation on the toads of Groot-Loon, I must point out that this Belgian toad 'fact' comes with some warnings: 1) I received this information from my father-in-law during a conversation completely in Flemish when no one else was around; 2) my father-in-law does not commonly talk about toads or the Green Party, holding neither in high regard; 3) I haven't been able to check the Groot-Loon fact with anyone; and 4) I can't find anything about this on the Internet. So the

Groot-Loon church toads may be another 'lost in translation' moment and he may actually have misunderstood what I said and replied that the tarts at Van Grootloon (a cafe that he frequents) are very good. Which they are.

At the small village of Bommershoven, opposite the war memorial, we pulled in to a packed car park outside *de Ware Vrienden* ('The True Friends') cafe. I wasn't sure what we would find inside the cafe, but one thing for certain that I wasn't expecting was the wall of tobacco smoke that hit me as I opened the door. A common misconception about Belgium is that the country is at the forefront of European legislation. We are bombarded with press headlines such as, 'Brussels wants smoking ban across Europe' and 'Brussels weighs in on smoking laws' and we (OK, perhaps it's just me) quickly forget that these headlines refer to *European* legislators, not *Belgian* ones. So to my great surprise I found that the restrictive laws on smoking, much heralded by 'Brussels' and ensuring smoke-free cafes across most of the rest of Europe, did not yet exist in Belgium. The Belgium anti-smoking law only covered restaurants and cafes where food was being served. If no food were served, the punters could puff away to their hearts' and lungs' content. Fortunately, Belgium has now caught up with Brussels and the rest of Europe and you can now enter a Belgian cafe without being gassed.

While on the subject of cafes, pubs and bars, and as I have already made reference to language in this chapter, I feel I must warn readers about the potential confusion that can occur if the wrong term is used. If you say in Flanders that you want to go to a 'pub' they will understand you, as due to the good work of the British Tourist Authority, stereotypical TV programming and English lager louts, they are largely familiar with the concept of the traditional British pub. If you say that you are looking for a 'cafe', this too will be understood, as this is the word the Flemish use to describe what could also be referred to in English as a 'pub' or a 'bar'. However, should you choose to say that you are really looking forward to spending your evening in a 'bar' sampling what the locals have to offer, as I once announced to Conny, it may be useful to know that the word 'bar' generally denotes a 'brothel' in Flemish.

De Ware Vrienden was no bar, or if it was it was very well disguised. I sat next to Pa, his brother Swa and a fellow cockerel-singing punter named Ber. Looking around the cafe, from what I could see through the smoke, it was occupied by about thirty people. All men, mostly of advanced years and wearing flat caps. Pa, Swa and Ber tried to explain the rules to me.

The 'singing' element of the competition is to do with quantity, not quality. There is no judge of vocal merit and the only scoring relates to the number of times the bird sings. The premise of the 'sport', if that is the correct word for it, is based on the number of times your cockerel crows in an hour and as the owner of the bird, you place a bet on how often you think it is going to crow. To enter the competition it must crow a minimum of forty times and you can only place your bets on increments of ten crows. So you can bet that your bird will sing forty, fifty, sixty, seventy or eighty or more times, always increasing by ten. I understood these rules quite clearly but the betting combinations, explained to me by Ber in some detail in a heavy local dialect, defeated me. I could discern that, like lottery winners, the winnings were shared out by those who had guessed the correct numbers. Unlike lottery winners, if no one guessed correctly, those who were closest to the number they had predicted would receive a share of the takings. Bets were limited to a maximum amount, if I understood correctly, of €16, so no one was going to be getting rich quick on the proceeds of cockerel-singing. At least not unless they did it a lot, which my new friend Ber pointed out to me was possible. Here at *de Ware Vrienden* there was cockerel-singing on Saturday and Sunday mornings and Monday evenings. Other villages had establishments which catered for Tuesday, Wednesday, Thursday and Friday evenings, so theoretically it was possible to spend the entire week on the cockerel-singing circuit. Ber was a Sunday morning man. 'It's a beautiful sport,' he told me, adding in a booming voice broadcast to the tables near us: 'Beautiful to be without the wife!' With this the whole cafe descended into laughter. It occurred to me that the Sunday morning sessions were also useful for church-dodgers.

The landlord was very active, making sure that everyone was served promptly. He had a sheet of hand-written scores on the wall where a record of the birds which had called out the most was kept. This was an additional monthly competition, with prizes ranging from €30 for the winner down to €2 for tenth place. The landlord, seeing his cafe filled at these normally quiet times three days a week, was keen to make sure that everyone's a winner at *de Ware Vrienden*. I noticed that he too was hurriedly filling out a betting form, so must have had a cockerel or two of his own in the competition.

At 9.15 a.m. in a surprising display of agility considering the average age in the cafe, everyone jumped up and ran outside. Car boots were flung open and in a scene reminiscent of a 1960s Le Mans start, the punters collected their precious cockerel-stuffed shoeboxes and sprinted off to a building at the far corner of the car park.

Gulping down the rest of my coffee, I ran outside to keep up with Pa and Swa. I lost them in the commotion and was called over by a man standing by his car boot with too many boxes to fit under his arms. I was about to explain to him that I was an English-speaker, unfamiliar with his sport, and that I was looking for my Belgian wife's sister's husband's father who I knew only as 'Pa' and his brother who was called Swa. However, taking a quick check on the situation, instead of attempting to strike up a conversation, I simply nodded to the man, picked up his two extra boxes and ran after him to the back of the parking lot. A strange sight met my eyes. There was a row of over a hundred cages, approximately one metre off the ground, each one cockerel wide by one standing cockerel high. The cockerels were being liberated from the peace and quiet of their travelling boxes and placed in their individual singing enclosures where they faced a two-way mirror, which ran the entire length of a long concrete shed. The owners split into two groups: one ran back to the cafe while the other, the scorers, entered the shed taking up their positions on a bench, each facing a set of four birds. Behind the scorers, on high stools, sat the controllers. The controllers, one per twelve birds, have the task of looking over the shoulders of the scorers to make sure that no cheating goes on. Scorers score their own birds and anyone else's that is sitting in their set of four. Behind the controllers is a wooden screen and behind the screen is the spectator gallery. I say 'spectator gallery' but it's more of a dusty corridor, one person wide, with the wooden screen on one side and the outer concrete wall of the shed on the other. There is a narrow horizontal slit along the wooden screen, through which you can see the back of the controller's head, the backs of the scorers sitting on their bench, the score sheets in front of them, and the magnificent cockerels lined up opposite.

All hell had been let loose when the birds had been placed in their 'singing' positions. Eighty-two birds were in the competition today and each one was crowing at the top of its voice. A small brass horn, similar to an English hunting horn, was sounded, and the competition began. I shuffled along the spectator gallery, peering through the narrow slit in the wooden screen, until I recognised the back of Pa's head. He was sitting in front of his birds in cages 65 to 68. Swa was back in the cafe.

Pa and Swa had spent much time in the cafe deliberating over the scores to predict for each bird. The conditions were tricky. Would the snow-laden sky be darker than usual, leading to a low call rate, or brighter, with more calls? Previous form was studied in detail. Pa's bird, number 65, had been steady with fifty-nine, sixty-one and sixty-two calls in previous weeks, but had dropped to a disappointing forty-four crows at its last outing. After much discussion, they decided number 65 would be back on form and they put him down for sixty crows.

Ruben, who had waited outside the mustard gas-filled cafe until now, joined me in the spectator gallery. We were under strict instructions not to make a sound. At this point in the game I could not see why they had such a heavy-handed ban on making any noise in the spectator gallery, as the combined din of eighty-two cockerels crowing in unison was deafening.

At least it was for the first five minutes, until it fell ominously silent. For half a second. Then one started and they were all off again, like a Mexican wave, standing up proud and crowing, from number 1 to number 82.

I had never seen so many cockerels in one place before and was struck by the variety of shapes, size and colours that they come in. Some had golden manes over their black necks and great jowly wattles hanging down like rashers of bacon. Others had skinny little vulture heads with bare beaks and beady eyes. Number 59 looked like he had a goatee beard and number 72 tilted its head back and fluffed out like a sunflower when it crowed. One thing they had in common is that they all looked in prime condition. Pa had explained to me in the cafe that the birds have to be healthy. A bird pecking lice is not going to be crowing, and he told me that he checked their bottoms frequently. 'What do you want to look there for?' I asked him. 'This is where the lice will be, because this is where they can't peck,' he replied rather matter-of-factly. Ah, the glamour of the *hanenzang* trainer.

Every fifteen minutes, we had to squeeze up in the spectator gallery to allow half a dozen or so owners in. They were taking a break from the cafe to see if their birds were on target. Beer mats with scribbled notes were slipped under the wooden screen and messages passed between scorers and owners. Not a word was spoken. It was like Abramovich coming to check on his team, getting the score written on the back of a packet of pork scratchings and heading back to the pub until the final whistle.

After twenty-five minutes, the half-second periods of silence became more frequent. This was worrying for Pa, but I could see that his bird was right on track. Twenty-five minutes in and twenty-five crows. Rather alarmingly, I started to find myself being drawn in to the sport. There was a definite frisson of excitement as we neared the halfway mark. Could number 65 hold the line and keep his pace for a whole hour?

A minute later and number 65 stopped to preen itself. Pa had explained to me beforehand that you don't want your bird to be distracted in any way. This wasn't good. 'Come on number 65! Focus! Sing!' I thought as hard as I could, not daring to say anything out loud. It occurred to me that in any case, 'sing' was not really the right word to describe the noise these birds were making. They certainly don't 'cock-a-doodle-doo' as English language children's books would have you believe. The Belgian languages, using a similarly quaint combination of onomatopoeia and alliteration at least have the correct number of syllables but I'm sure these cockerels were not saying 'kukeleku' (Flemish), 'cocorico' (French), or 'kikeriki' (German). There was nothing remotely musical or quaint about this noise. More strangled cat than song. Some of them barely managed to retch the noise out, while others just grunted. One thing was for certain – you would not want to live next door to one of these places.

At least number 65 was doing better than its near neighbour down at 63, who was starting to peck around the floor, looking for food in the bottom of its cage. I wondered if there had ever been a case of sabotage – it would be easy enough to throw a few grains of corn into the bottom of a rival's cage. I had heard stories of scorers wearing red shirts which they revealed to their cockerels by subtly unzipping their jackets in the last few minutes of the competition in order to coax out a few more calls. I assume that this underhand behaviour is what had led to the installation of the two-way mirror that now separated the birds from the scorers. I didn't have the opportunity to inspect the facilities at the other *hanenzang* establishments, but there was to be no cockerel-rousing scandal at *de Ware Vrienden*.

Number 77 had sat down. That was one less competitor to contend with, but no, what was number 65 doing? He had turned around and was facing the back of the cage! Would he be disqualified? Could Pa count his crows? The tension was getting to me; number 65 was falling behind his crow-a-minute target and this unorthodox 360-degree move could spell disaster. Another Mexican wave began at the far end of the cages, and number 65 started stretching, turned around, stuck his chest out, strutted his stuff, head up proudly, and yes, there it was: another crow.

Caught up in the excitement, I failed to notice that Ruben had taken a handkerchief out of his pocket. It just caught my eye as he raised it to his nose, but it was too late. Bound by the rule of silence I could not call out to him and I watched helplessly as he took a deep breath and blew his nose at full blast. I signalled for him to stop but his head was buried in the handkerchief. It was a real trumpet of a blow, echoing down to the end of the spectator gallery and back, the sound reverberating around the concrete shed. The controller in front of us spun round and glared at him through the slit in the wood.

'I didn't say anything,' Ruben said to me, bringing a second glare from the controller.

It was time for us to leave the shed. Number 65 still needed nineteen crows and he had just fifteen minutes left. No spectators were allowed inside for the remaining quarter of an hour so that there could be no attempts at result-fixing from the gallery. We stood out in the cold, waiting for Pa to come out with the news. There were only Belgian-registered cars in the car park, so the sport doesn't appear to have a great international following. Perhaps lucrative television rights could be secured to bring the sport to a larger market. Would Mumm champagne like to supply a bottle or two to the winners?

With a final blow of the hunting horn, Pa and the fellow scorers emerged from the shed. He had mixed news. Swa's birds had been thirteen, ten and eight crows away from the predictions. These scores wouldn't be enough to get on the podium. But number 65 had crept back up again and managed fifty-eight crows, so just two short of the target of sixty. Would this be enough to get into the prizes?

I wish I could say that I hung around to find out, but I am afraid that with the prospect of a second round of cockerel-singing looming (*de Ware Vrienden* runs an additional half-hour competition after the main event on a Sunday morning), Ruben and I decided that we had experienced enough cockerel-induced excitement for one day. I heard later from Pa that number 65 just scraped into the winnings, but not enough to cover the losses from the other three birds. And this being Belgium, the small payout earned by number 65 had of course been subject to a large tax bill. Oh well, there's always next Sunday.

Hanenzang is certainly a different pastime and I am very pleased to have come across it on my quest. It is unusual. Very unusual. But is it materially very different from sitting in a concrete shed, placing bets on how long it is going to take patches of paint to dry? Not really. Pa, I want to say that *hanenzang* is interesting. I really do. But I'm afraid it's not.

Having seen enough of Belgian bird sports for one lifetime, I decided to cut my losses in this area and give the pigeon-fanciers of Arendonk and their dish-licking statue a miss. Pigeon-racing wasn't going to get on the interesting list any more than chicken-singing, but there is another sport, followed keenly by Belgian men in overalls, that could well help me with my quest. It takes place in Belgium once a year, in late August, deep in the forests of the Ardennes. Perhaps the very antithesis of cockerel-singing – the Formula One Belgian Grand Prix at Spa-Francorchamps.

CHAPTER 2
FORMULA ONE

It would be hard to say that Formula One is boring. It could be said that it is a fatuous waste of time, burning up the world's precious natural resources while pumping pollutants into the atmosphere and profits into certain people's pockets. But it's not boring. At least not according to Formula One fans, who appear to be particularly excited about the Spa-Francorchamps circuit, home to the Belgian Grand Prix since 1925. The BBC Sport website even goes so far as to say, 'Superlatives seem inadequate to describe the wonders of Spa-Francorchamps, the greatest modern motor racing circuit in the world.'

'Greatest in the world' and 'inadequate superlatives' are not phrases commonly associated with Belgium and I soon convinced myself that no quest into the state of Belgium's boringness would be complete without first-hand experience of the Belgian Grand Prix. This was until I found out the price of a ticket: €550 per person! It was my introduction to the first rule of Formula One: it's all about the money. I am being a bit unfair, as €550 is for a 'gold' ticket which gets you a hard plastic seat and a roof, whereas you could get a 'bronze' ticket without a seat, or cover, or decent view, for the bargain price of €160.

You still have to pay for travel and accommodation and parking and eating and drinking and ear plugs and a programme, but you are allowed to breathe and stand up, or sit in the woods. I wasn't sure if the ticket price included going to the toilet – this important information is missing from the official ticket website. I doubted it, as you have to pay to pee at a surprising variety of conveniences in Belgium. No matter whether you are in a cinema, restaurant or department store, there is always the very real threat that after a visit to the gents a 'Madame Pipi' will appear from nowhere and chase you down the street for your small change. This explains the common Belgian habit, thoroughly endorsed and enacted by my father-in-law, of relieving yourself wherever you see fit to avoid parting with the little cash that is left in your pocket after the government has stripped everything else out for tax.

I have tried telling my father-in-law that this quaint Belgian custom is not one that needs to be exported. Our house does possess a perfectly decent toilet: two of them in fact, and both free of charge for house visitors, so going off into the garden to 'look for a quiet corner' really isn't necessary. Walking around one of Conny's uncles' gardens I once made the surprise discovery of an outdoor porcelain *urinoir*, fully plumbed, attached to a tree. Perhaps he was looking for one of these, although this doesn't explain his fondness of the roadside verge, in full view of passing traffic, which should really be used for other things. Whenever I try to explain this to him, it is invariably too late. With the unfortunate combination of his hearing deficiency and lack of English together with my poor Flemish, I find myself pointing, shouting and gesticulating wildly by the side of the road, which only helps to draw the passing motorists' attention to what is going on.

It was looking as though I would never find out if peeing is included in the ticket price for the Belgian Grand Prix until my well-connected sister-in-law came to the rescue. Belgium is a small and friendly enough country that there is always a chance that someone you know will know someone who can help. And in this wonderful Belgian way, Conny's sister Betty suddenly appeared with five tickets for the practice day at Spa – two gold and three bronze. The tickets are generally sold for the entire three-day weekend (why should Formula One just sell tickets for Saturday and Sunday when it makes more money to sell them in blocks of three days?) which invariably leads to some 'unused' portions of the tickets for the practice day, which is on the Friday. If you are a Formula One devotee you will now be screaming *of course the practice day is on the Friday – didn't you know that?* Well I do now. For any readers as yet uninitiated in the world of Formula One, the season's races all follow the same pattern. Friday is the practice day, Saturday is the qualifying round which determines which position they will start at on the grid and on Sunday they have the full forty-four laps which will result in some of them throwing the champagne around.

For my Belgian father-in-law the spraying of the champagne is the lowest point of any sporting event. It spoils the end of his beloved cycle races and it epitomises the wastefulness of the world of Formula One. *'Belachelijk!'* he calls out at the TV screen as the winners cavort about the podium, laughing as they drench each other in fine wine. He's not a man of many words but *'belachelijk!'*, which my online dictionary informs me is loosely translated as 'outrageous', is a favourite and you can expect to hear it emanating from the armchair as soon as the TV highlights show the winners of a race nearing the podium, bottles in hand.

I was contemplating whether it would be better to buy a weekend gold ticket or, for the same price, sit at home in front of the TV with three cases of Mumm Champagne, all of which could be consumed without spilling a drop, when the doorbell rang. Perhaps after two and a half cases you might just want to spray the last few bottles out of the window to join in with the celebrations. It was Jan, my Belgian brother-in-law, at the door, picking us up from my Belgian family's home in Hasselt for the drive down to Spa. The five precious tickets to the practice day had been carefully shared out: three for Jan and his fellow petrolhead friends Joel and Herman, and two for the Formula One novices: me and my twelve-year-old son Ruben.

We crossed the canal to collect Joel and drove on through the fine drizzle in search of Herman's house in a village to the south of Hasselt. They told me it was in a different village, but with the gratuitous ribbon development that morphs Belgian towns and villages into one, it was very hard to tell where Hasselt ended and Herman's village began. The detached brick houses began to look very familiar and after a while you start to ask yourself if you are making any progress at all, or if you are stuck in a Hawkings-esque time–space continuum where you will circle little brick buildings with their perfectly trimmed lawns and dwarf 1970s conifers for eternity. The car windows had steamed up with condensation and the rain continued to spatter outside when Jan called out that he had spotted Herman's house. With Herman onboard, and taking over the navigation, we managed to break free from the endless circles of back roads and brick houses, and on coming across the E313 motorway, we headed south for Spa.

The town of Spa merits attention on its own as a useful riposte to the, 'But there isn't anything famous in Belgium!' rebuke. Where do these put-down people think that the word 'spa' came from? The Romans, always up for a hot bath, called the town 'Aqua Spadanae' and by the Middle Ages it had become known in Walloon as 'Espa', meaning 'spring fountain'. A visiting Englishman in the sixteenth century liked what he saw and returned home to open the first 'English Spaw' in Harrogate. From then on, the word 'spa' took over.

No one in our car made any observation on the historical importance of Spa and its contribution to the language of health and beauty resorts around the world. Conversation amongst the Flemish passengers centred instead around the make and model of any car that overtook us:

'That was a Targa 4.'
'No, it was a Targa 4S.'
'Has anyone seen the GT2 RS?'
'There goes an R8.'

Ruben played on his iPod Touch. I looked out of the window at the countryside. As we ventured south out of Limburg, the apple and pear orchards gave way to maize fields, stretching to the horizon in every direction. Brick farmsteads, their land now bisected by the motorway, appeared out of the drizzle every now and again, and giant power lines carrying electricity from the nuclear reactor in Wallonia criss-crossed the sky. After half an hour or so I realised that the signposts I was seeing as we motored by were now in French instead of Flemish, and that the town of 'Luik' that we had been heading for had suddenly turned into 'Liège'. Very confusing. The usual monotony of the flat Belgian motorway system (now there is something that is truly boring) started to change, with minor inclines, perhaps what could nearly be described as 'small hills' appearing as we continued towards the Ardennes. The pitch of the roofs of the brick houses became steeper, indicating the snow that would be falling here in a few months' time. The occasional stone-built house started to show up, as well as some stone-brick combos, a typical Belgian compromise for those in the middle who neither wanted to offend the brick builders or stone builders, or perhaps just couldn't make up their minds:

'That was a Mercedes McLaren.'
'Yes, all carbon fibre and 0–100 in 3.8.'
'Did you see Clarkson when the caravan caught fire?'

After another half hour of listening to car-talk the countryside started to change again. The fields of maize were now thinning out, being replaced by meadows for cattle and mixed woods of pine and birch. It was getting seriously hilly, with some roller coaster up and downs, as the road headed in a straight line, Roman-style, regardless of the contour.

We didn't see any signs to Spa-Francorchamps, which is a surprise considering it is so high on the Belgian 'must do' activities list, and apart from the few who will drop in by helicopter, the vast majority of fans will be looking for it from their beloved cars.

A dispute between the posh lady on the satnav and the three Belgians in the car led us to making a non-satnav authorised turn off the motorway, followed by a prompt U-turn to get us back on the motorway and a repetition of the last 10 km that we had just done. We scared lorry drivers by overtaking them for a second time. Their worried 'Haven't you already overtaken me?' expressions lingered in the rear view mirror as we ignored satnav lady again, turning off at a different side road in search of a village where Herman assured us we would be able to park. We found this route blocked by a policeman who waved us to the end of a long line of nearly stationary cars queuing to enter one of many hillside cow pastures which had been turned over to official Formula One '€10 a day thank you very much' parking.

We pulled into field 112A, on the top of a hill, in the mist. It felt like we had parked in a cloud. A line of shadowy figures in plastic raincoats clutching heavy cool boxes were just visible, descending into the pine forest at the end of the enclosure. All of a sudden an almighty roar came screaming up from beneath us somewhere in the pine trees. It was as if a Tornado fighter jet was about to come out of the undergrowth. The Formula One practice had started! But where was the noise coming from? It bounced off the hills all around us, through the trees and mist. We followed the rain macs further down the hill, assuming they knew where they were going and a trail of new arrivals squelched through the mud behind us, assuming we knew where we were going. The man in front of me, wrapped in see-through plastic like a cling-filmed turkey, put down his cool box to eat one of the toadstools by the side of the track. I hoped he knew what he was doing.

We crossed a road and through more forest, now without any path to follow, until we came to the perimeter fence outside the Formula One village. Following the advance party turning right at the fence, we passed a security guard and his Alsatian lurking in the bushes. They snarled at us as we went by. There was still no sign of a track and the last 200 metres were spent clinging on to the fence while trying to maintain balance as we picked our way along a ditch, splattering mud up to our knees. It wasn't the kind of mud that you find in spas and the water wasn't hot. It was an inauspicious entry to the 'greatest modern racing circuit in the world'.

Once inside we joined an altogether cleaner and drier-looking crowd, who had found the official entrance along the main road without having to clamber along a ditch. A lot of intense-looking young men, with the occasional long-suffering wife or girlfriend in tow, were making their way to the seated areas around the circuit. Jeans and biker jackets or racing overalls were *de rigueur*. As long as a car logo, oil manufacturer or spark plug brand appeared somewhere on your garments, you were in the in-crowd. So that was everyone there, except for me and Ruben.

The race track, designed in the 1920s, had originally joined the three Walloon towns of Francorchamps, Malmedy and Stavelot using 15 km of public roads. It was a fast track, and without modern safety measures accidents and even fatalities were commonplace. It is hard to imagine these days that crash barriers were few and far between and that seatbelts were a rarity in Formula One. Being flung out of your car at 250 km per hour was a very real possibility, and unsurprisingly the outcome for the driver in these early Grand Prix races was often fatal. During the notorious Belgian Grand Prix of 1960, three British drivers were thrown from their cars in separate incidents. Sterling Moss was lucky to escape with broken legs, while Chris Bristow and Alan Stacey, who had lost control of his car due to a bird strike, both lost their lives. A fourth British driver at the same race, Mike Taylor, drove in his first and last Grand Prix that weekend, as a crash into the trees when his steering failed on the practice day led to multiple injuries, putting an end to his racing career.

Notwithstanding the fatalities, safety improvements were slow to take on. In 1966 Jackie Stewart spun off the track at Malmedy, through a telegraph pole, a shed and into a farmhouse where he hung upside down with broken ribs while motor fuel dripped down his body until the stewards could release him. Following this incident Stewart became a champion of improved safety conditions for Formula One in general and for Spa-Francorchamps in particular. He led a drivers' boycott of the Belgian Grand Prix in 1969 and the last Formula One race to take place at Spa for more than a decade was held in 1970.

Seatbelts were finally made compulsory in Formula One in 1972, and after yet more fatalities on the track during the gruelling 24 Heures de Francorchamps in the 1970s the circuit was shortened to the safer 7.004 km and full safety barriers erected, leading to the return of Formula One to Spa in 1983. The three towns are no longer visible from the shortened circuit and the public has not been able to drive on the roads between races since 2000.

Having made our way to the edge of the track Jan, Joel and Herman installed themselves at the first beer, *frites* and waffles stand, with a view of the cars as they raced out of *La Source*: the first hairpin bend after the pits. All the stands serve the same fare, so it really doesn't make any difference which one you decide to frequent. If you like sausages, onions, burgers, *frites*, waffles and Jupiler beer, you will be OK for food and drink. Seeing as the ticket price is the same as for an all-in Mediterranean holiday, you might expect to have some of this finery included. An all-you-can-eat buffet at lunch time perhaps? Free cocktails at happy hour? But no, this would be forgetting the first rule of Formula One, and a really small bottle of water starts at €3.00.

Ruben and I went exploring, following the trail around to the Formula One village, which is less of a 'village' and more of a collection of caravans selling official, i.e. 'Formula One price', merchandise. For the cost of a mortgage on a small Belgian apartment we bought a pair of earplugs each, a necessity for which I would gladly have paid double the bargain Formula One price. We left the village as the rain intensified, heading for a small tunnel under the race track at Eau Rouge. Formula One pundits agree that this is one of the most exciting parts of the course. It was lost on Ruben and me as we were standing underneath it, sheltering from the rain with many other now equally wet, if not quite so muddy, spectators. Jan, Joel and Herman had explained to me that Eau Rouge sorts the men from the boys. Apparently only the drivers with the real *cojones* (I don't think that's a Flemish word) press the accelerator to the floor as they fly downhill at 300 km per hour into the left-handed Eau Rouge corner, keeping it flat to the floor as they hit the steep uphill, right–left turns of Radillon before screaming into the long Kemmel straight where they can hit 330 km per hour. There had been much debate at the beer and waffle stand as to which of the drivers today would have the requisite-sized *cojones* to do this. It was agreed that Hamilton would, and Joel reckoned that Massa for Ferrari would or it might have been that Herman thought Webber would. It was quite a long conversation and I think my concentration may have lapsed quite early on.

Squeezing our way through the tightly-packed tunnel, Ruben and I emerged back out in to the daylight on the other side of the race track and followed a concrete path through the midst of the pristine pine forest, which inhabits the inner grounds of the course. It was a surreal scene – like going on a nature walk but with the noise of Formula One cars reverberating all around, with passing hikers dressed as maintenance men. Instead of carrying backpacks, their arms stretched to the ground as they scraped cool boxes laden with beer along the path. One had a strap of beer cans over his shoulder strung out like an ammunition belt. We walked through this strange world for over a kilometre before reaching the far side of the circuit at Pouhon corner. There was just one kiosk serving food here. No happy hour, no warming mulled wine for us after our forest trek, just the same *frites*, waffle and burger selection as everywhere else in Belgian Formula One land.

An Internet 'fact' about the Belgian Grand Prix, often repeated by the Formula One bloggers, is that despite the Grand Prix taking place in the summer time, there was once a twenty-year period when it rained on the race every year in a row. I can't find out if this fact is true, but if our experience was anything to go by it is certainly very plausible. And it wasn't just any rain that was falling. It wasn't picture book rain with rainbows and fluffy clouds. There wasn't the excitement of a tropical downpour, or the challenge of a battle against the elements. No, this was a dull, suffocating wetness that wrapped around you like a soggy blanket. An oppressive, penetrating drizzle that soaked through all your clothing, irrespective of whether you had just purchased an official Formula One merchandise umbrella or not.

We looked inside the forest for a seat and shelter, choosing a moss-covered stone where we shared a pack of *frites* (bargain €5.00 + €1.00 for the obligatory mayonnaise) from a cardboard cone with two little plastic forks. The barrage of drizzle that we had endured in the open by the *frites* stand was now exchanged for large, random drops of water falling from the pine branches above, occasionally knocking a *frite* right off the fork. Sitting on the moss had the same effect as sitting on a wet sponge and water oozed down the back of our trousers and into our socks. It was hard to make ourselves heard above the roar of the Formula One engines. We couldn't see anything of them from our stone in the forest – there was just mist and rain and moss and tree trunks – but we could feel them as they thundered around Pouhon, just metres away. Ruben leant over to me, pulled his rain hood away from his mouth so that he could speak, looked up and shouted, 'Dad, this is the best day ever!' And surprisingly, he was right. It was.

We headed back through the woods, noting that they served a very useful purpose as a free open-air urinal for lagered-up bronze ticket holders, and collected our party's two gold tickets, generously passed over to us by Jan, Joel and Herman, to take our seats in 'Gold 8'. This is the grandstand right on the corner of the U-bend of La Source, looking down to the pit lane and to the starting line for the race. Whoever had these seats on Sunday would be in for a treat. It was a different experience to sitting in the woods: much drier for a start and the fans, instead of having the primary concern of consuming beer and *frites*, were pre-occupied with the little portable TV screens that they had hired from the Formula One village. The portable TVs allowed them to follow individual drivers, selecting a car and following its trajectory around the course while tuned in to the video footage being taken from the camera mounted above the driver's head. Some didn't appear to watch the 'real' race at all, instead spending the whole time glued to the little screen. One such fan, sitting in front of us, had conveniently left his programme open on the empty seat in front of Ruben, on a helpful page which had the colourings of each driver's helmet and car. This was a revelation for us. Instead of just seeing a blur and feeling the noise, we could now identify which driver was flying past, putting famous names to the flashes of metal. Like twitchers with a new identification guide we excitedly ticked off the names as they shot past. We saw Hamilton in his distinctive yellow helmet and Button in his red, white and blue. Michael Schumacher, with a shiny red helmet, was an easy tick. Spa is a nostalgic course for Schumacher and he would have been looking forward to a victory here in his comeback year. His first Formula One race had been at Spa in 1991 and his first Formula One victory at Spa in 1992. He still holds the record for wins at Spa, with six podium-topping races. The Red Bull guys, Webber and Vettel, would be looking to keep Schumacher off the podium this year with their swanky new cars. They were harder to tell apart as it looked like their helmets were made up of recycled Red Bull cans – Webber slightly more distinctive with a 'male pattern baldness' circle of yellow crowning his helmet. We saw Rubens Barrichello, in his 300th Grand Prix, spin his car round at La Source and an 'Ooh' went up from the stand, audible even above the engine noise.

Just before the practice was due to finish red lights started to flash around the track, indicating there had been a crash somewhere. There was a moment of excitement in the stands, presumably at the prospect of seeing millions of pounds of car reduced to a pile of scrap, but the murmur died down as the TV screens failed to reveal any wreckage. It transpired that race control had closed the track due to 'spectators in a dangerous area' – no doubt some bronze ticket holders trying to get a better view through the woods. As it was nearing 3.30 p.m. the Formula One cars were called in. It was the end of the practice session for Formula One, and the stands emptied as the GP2 Series cars came out to play.

We collected Jan, Joel and Herman from the beer and waffles stall and left the course by the main entrance. None of us had the appetite for retracing our steps through the woods and we followed the road, up the hill, passing more Formula One merchandise stalls. We enquired *'Où est le Parking 112A?'* of everyone we met, but no one, not even the traffic-directing policemen, had heard of our field.

We passed Parking 28 followed by Parking 98, which didn't inspire confidence that Parking 112A would be next. It was still raining. Some of the fields were designated as joint 'Parking/Camping' fields and we passed a group of English fans hunched up in the rain, struggling with wet canvas and tent poles. In contrast, the next camping field was host to a gathering of luxurious-looking German motor homes, whose jolly, and dry, inhabitants were busy unpacking crates of beer and rigging up the satellite porn.

Joel pointed out to me that the roads were full of potholes, 'Not like Flanders', where in the local village even the cycle track seems to get a fresh surface as soon as a chip of gravel is missing. Field 112A was still nowhere in sight and I was wondering whether we would later be asking the Germans or the English for a patch of floor to sleep on, when Jan announced that he had spotted Field 112A on the brow of the hill ahead.

Due to the various levels of *frites* and beer consumption of the car's occupants, driving back was going to be by either me or Ruben. On pulling out of the parking we were confronted by a policeman, who I thought was stopping me to give me directions to the motorway. He motioned for me to wind down my window.

'*Vos phares!*' he shouted.

'Yes, I would like to turn right please,' I replied.

'*Vos phares!*' he repeated.

'*Où est le* way to Hasselt?' I tried. 'Could it be to the right do you think? Over there?' I pointed down the road to the right.

He was getting impatient now, and that's never a good thing for a French-speaking policeman with a gun dangling from his belt.

'*Vos phares!*' – this time his irritation clearly evident.

'It's your lights,' said Herman from the back. 'You need to put the headlights on.'

I fumbled with the unfamiliar switches and levers, setting the back windscreen wiper on, dialling someone's number on the hands-free phone and switching the radio on, all under the glare of Mr 'I'm getting very cross with you' Belgian policeman, before finally finding the lights.

On Sunday, safely ensconced on the sofa at the in-laws' house, we watched the race itself. Ruben and I called out 'We were there!' every time a car passed La Source or Pouhon corner, and 'We saw him!' whenever we saw a helmet we recognised. Apparently this wasn't very interesting for the other viewers, who started to drift away after the first couple of laps. My father-in-law slept in his armchair.

Despite it being his favourite course, Schumacher failed to make an impression. Button was shunted off by Vettel on the sixteenth lap and Hamilton, who had led from the start, cruised to an easy-looking victory having judged correctly the wet–dry–wet conditions of the famously mixed-weather course, and apparently having the correctly sized *cojones* for Eau Rouge and Radillon. Webber, with his shiny yellow patch came in second and Kubica, who until now I had thought was a brand of Korean photocopier, made it into third place. The commentator announced their arrival on the podium, and as the Mumm was handed out, my father-in-law woke up, just in time to shout *'Belachelijk!'* from his armchair.

After the failure of cockerel-signing, this was a good start for my quest. Whatever you want to shout at the race winners, however much it rains, no matter how much the *frites* cost, there is nothing boring about Formula One at Spa-Francorchamps. This is definitely one for the interesting list. And the spectators at the race track gave me the idea for my next piece of research: Manneken-Pis, the statue of a small boy in Brussels participating in a national pastime – taking a pee by the side of the road. It's hardly Rodin's *The Thinker*, or Michelangelo's *David* – how did this urinating little urchin come to be and why have the Belgians adopted him as their unofficial national mascot? In terms of my quest, is he interesting, or just over-hyped tourist fodder?

CHAPTER 3
MANNEKEN-PIS

Manneken-Pis (literally translated as 'small boy peeing') is arguably the most famous symbol of Belgium. He pees gratuitously in the form of millions of kitsch souvenirs, garden statues, novelty bottle openers and corkscrews; on postcards, posters, T-shirts and the covers of practically every brochure advertising any product from Belgium. He even appears on the label of a special Manneken-Pis beer brewed by Brasserie Lefebvre and on the side of Belgian Coca-Cola dispensing machines. Drinks companies normally try to associate their products with the imagery of beautiful people quenching their thirst and generally being very cool (as with our friends at Chateau Mumm and their sponsorship of Formula One), so the picture of a small dumpy boy peeing down the front of their product is an odd image for Lefebvre and Coke to have chosen. They could of course be targeting my father-in-law, but I think he would see the Manneken-Pis effect as a natural by-product of consuming the drink, not as the compelling reason to purchase it.

Manneken-Pis doesn't seem to have done Coke and Brasserie Lefebvre any favours, who coincidentally both had a bad year in 1999. In June the Belgian government banned the sale of Coca Cola after more than a hundred school children fell ill due to an 'unpleasant odour on the outside of the canned products'. This was later attributed to mass hysteria following the Belgian dioxin-in-the-food-chain scandal of 1999, but I wouldn't have thought that putting a picture of a small boy peeing over your vending machines was such a good move after having to recall 15 million cans from the market for having an unpleasant odour.

And in November Brasserie Lefebvre received the surprise news from their US distributor that Manneken-Pis beer had been banned from entering Ohio by the State's Division of Liquor Control. A spokesman for the Department of Commerce, a Mr Bill Teets, commented that Ohio did not allow anything vulgar, sensuous or to do with children to appear on the label of a beer bottle. Hopefully Manneken-Pis just ticks two of those boxes, but that was two too many for Mr Teets.

Mr Teets would have strongly disapproved of fifteenth-century Europe. Depictions of peeing boys were in high demand, from the Belgian nobility to the fashionistas of Renaissance Italy. The first reference to a Manneken-Pis statue in Brussels is contained in a document held in the city archives which records 'dManneken pist' as a boundary marker, on the corner of Rue du Chêne and Rue de l'Étuve in 1452. Two years later a Manneken-Pis fountain makes an appearance at a party hosted by the crusading Philip 'the Good' to celebrate the rather rash promise he had made to the Pope regarding reconquering Constantinople from the Turks before the year was out. Philip's Manneken-Pis stood proudly as a table centre-piece, surrounded by the finest banqueting fare as it peed rose-water throughout the night.

A Manneken-Pis also featured in the best-selling manuscript of the day, having a cameo appearance in *The Dream of Poliphilus,* a racy romantic drama published in Venice in 1499. The hero of the tale, Poliphilus, falls asleep and searches for his true love through a series of dreams. He faces many challenges in the dreams, none more difficult than coming across a bathing pool bedecked with scantily clad nymphs: 'The maidens disrobed and placed their clothes on the last step above the water, covering their fair hair with fine gilt mesh caps. And without shame they permitted me freely to see their naked, white, and delicate persons, saving their pudenda, which they always guarded.' As Poliphilus approached the maidens, presumably diverted from his quest by the mystery of those hidden 'pudendas', a statue of a small naked boy – a Manneken-Pis – sprang to life and peed in his face. (Seriously, what kind of stories made it on to the fifteenth-century Venetian bestseller lists?) This distraction apparently caused Poliphilus and the naked nymphs to burst into laughter, allowing Poliphilus to continue on his quest and the 'pudendas' to stay under wraps.

Following this incident, depictions of peeing boys, or *putto pisciatore* as those in the know referred to them, made frequent appearances in the leading art and literature of the next 200 years. Titian occasionally popped a *putto pisciatore* in the corner of his masterpieces, normally to pee over some reclining nymph, and in the mid-seventeenth century the finely named Eustache Le Sueur (no relation) left us with a magnificent, near-photographic depiction of the *putto pisciatore* scene from

The Dream of Poliphilus. It was the golden age of Manneken-Pis with the literati of the Renaissance period bestowing multi-layered meanings on him that could only be interpreted by the smartest intellectuals of the day. According to a very informative booklet I picked up at the Manneken-Pis clothes museum (yes, there is a museum devoted to the clothes of Manneken-Pis) levels of interpretation included literal, figurative, moral, meta-physical, comic, carnal, erotic, Bacchic, sacred and profane. I shall leave it up to the reader to decide which one of these interpretations Pope Leo X was after when he commissioned a personal tapestry of naked, frolicking children incorporating a *putto pisciatore*. All I can guess is that it must have been a job to stuff the tapestry under a pew whenever the Church Commission came to visit.

Fortunately, the arrival of the Age of Enlightenment in the mid-eighteenth century finished off the pretentious nonsense of the Renaissance, and the Bruxellois were free to ponder the origins of their statue without the use of academic treatises. Instead of fancy multi-layered theories, the people of Brussels invented their own simple legends to explain the statue of the little boy taking a pee.

Depending on which guide book you read, or which tour guide you overhear giving an explanation to a group of bemused tourists standing by the statue, any one of the following legends may, or may not, be true. Please take your pick:

Legend 1 – The Wicked Witch
In 1450 a small boy finding himself in need of a pee used a doorway on the corner of Rue du Chêne and Rue de l'Étuve. Fed up with the whiff of urine on her doorstep, the owner of

the property, a wicked witch, punished him by casting a spell that would ensure he would have to stay at the doorway peeing for eternity. (This sort of misses the point. If she didn't want anyone peeing on her doorstep, why would she make the little boy pee there for eternity?) Luckily for the little boy, a kind old man who lived nearby had seen it all happen, and broke the witch's spell by putting up the Manneken-Pis statue. Thanks to the elderly gentleman, the small boy and the Bruxellois were free to pee in doorways once more.

Legend 2 – Godefroid and the Crusades

Weary Crusaders returning from the wars would stop to rest outside the house of the Count of Hoves in Brussels. One day the Count sent his young son, Godefroid, to greet the soldiers. For some unknown reason, Godefroid peed on them. To make up for the embarrassment, the Count erected a statue of a small boy peeing. (But if you were embarrassed by the peeing incident, it doesn't seem very likely that you would put up a statue so that it can be immortalised and eventually become the national symbol of your country.) I don't know about you, but so far I'm not buying into legends one or two.

Legend 3 – The Bloemardine Movement

According to the informative leaflet at the Manneken-Pis costume museum in Brussels, members of the Bloemardine 'mystic movement' were fifteenth-century 'defenders of earthly pleasures' in Brussels. During one of their parades around the city, the son of Duke John relieved himself and was held aloft in triumph, presumably for having performed an earthly pleasure. The clergy of the day found this scandalous, and to apologise Duke John erected the statue of Manneken-Pis. (Again, immortalising an embarrassing act? These legends really need to get a bit more credible.)

Legend 4 – Godefroid III and the battle of Ransbeek

Now this one is more like it. Upon the death of a duke in 1142, two of his subjects, Gauthier Berthout and Gerard de Grimbergen mounted an uprising to take over his lands. The duke's widow called on the help of the Count of Flanders to see them off. The count insisted that the duke's infant son, Godefroid III, witness the action, and placed the toddler in a cradle hanging from an oak tree in the middle of the battlefield. (EU Health and Safety regulations do not feature highly in this legend.) The battle did not go well for the count and he was losing ground until his troops were roused into action by the sight of the infant Godefroid peeing from his cradle. From that moment on the battle turned and the count's men won the day. To celebrate the part played by the young Godefroid, the men dug up the oak tree, planted it in Rue du Chêne and built a statue of their young duke in action.

Legend 5 – The Gunpowder Plot

After a lengthy siege of Brussels, the invading force appeared to withdraw from their positions and the Bruxellois could once more relax. However, the invaders had tricked the city dwellers and had piled gunpowder into a tunnel under the City Hall. As the Bruxellois celebrated the end of the siege, only a small boy noticed the burning fuse. He quickly did what any fast-thinking Belgian would do – he peed on it – and the fuse was put out, saving the city of Brussels. To honour the boy, a statue was erected. (At least this is a reason for a statue.) Another version of this legend has Manneken-Pis saving the city by peeing on a fire. Presumably a rather small fire.

Legend 6 – Ham and Adultery

Again, I am afraid we are veering off into the realms of improbability here. In the eighth century, a local lord was having difficulty in producing an heir. He called on the services of Vindicien, Bishop of Arras, who performed some sort of service for the lord's wife (there is no record as to what this was exactly) which resulted in the birth of a son nine months later. We learn that upon being introduced to Vindicien, the baby 'peed so high that he splashed his beard'. The local lord invited the glamorous Lady Gudula, from the Château de Ham (I'm not making this up) to the baptism and promptly left his wife to shack up with Gudula in Ham. Vindicien later became a saint but at this time he had a mean, some might even say a 'vindictive' streak, and being so incensed by the behaviour of the lord, he used his powers to ensure that the boy would never grow any bigger and would pee for eternity. Just who made the statue after that is anyone's guess.

Legend 7 – Little Boy Lost

A wealthy nobleman lost his son in the crowds in the city centre. His family searched far and wide but to no avail and after five long days they were giving up hope, when the young lad was found taking a pee at the corner of Rue du Chêne and Rue de l'Étuve. To commemorate his safe return, his father commissioned a statue to be built on the spot where he was found.

Legend 8 – In the Face of the Spanish

During the tenancy of the Spanish as overlords of Belgium in the sixteenth century, a small boy would pee out of his first floor window onto the hated Spanish troops as they marched below. To commemorate this act of defiance, the patriotic Bruxellois built a statue. We can guess where.

Legend 9 – The Miracle During the Procession

A small boy taking part in one of the city's lengthy processions answered the call of nature, only to find that a miracle had occurred and he could not stop peeing, and yes, the good citizens of Brussels built a statue to commemorate this. I don't wish to belittle this miraculous event but surely miracles involve turning water into wine, or feeding multitudes of fishermen, or restoring the lame to good health. I wouldn't describe the affliction of constant urination as much of a 'miracle'.

Legend 10 – The Mole Whisperer

Brussels was plagued with an infestation of moles. The royal palaces and all the city's parks and gardens were blighted with unsightly mounds of earth. The Bruxellois could do nothing to rid the land of the unholy beast until one day a small boy peed on one, and miraculously, from that day forth, the moles were never seen again. The Burgemeester of Brussels was so pleased with the boy that he made a statue of him at the place where it had occurred.

OK, I made that last one up, but judging by the credibility of some of the other legends I think this one about the moles has a pretty good chance of making it. Let's see if we can get this legend going. Wikipedia is a good starting point and if anyone would like to make a YouTube video, preferably using Lego, please do so.

Whichever legend has the closest bearing on the truth, the real purpose of the statue was to provide clean drinking water to the Bruxellois, joining a network of drinking fountains around the Grand Place. He was not the only fountain in the area to use a bodily function to discharge water: the statue of *The Three Maidens* gushed water from a nipple each, and if you speak French or Flemish you can work out where the water from the fountain known as *Le Cracheur*, or *de Spuwer* comes from. In case these words are not in your daily vocabulary, they translate into English as 'The Spitter'. *De Spuwer* is allegedly even older than Manneken-Pis and is a rather miserable-looking chap, permanently dribbling down his bare chest and folded arms, which may explain why he has stayed in relative obscurity, while the jolly little peeing boy has become a national hero. As with Manneken-Pis, an assortment of legends has grown up around *de Spuwer*. Given that he now spits between two gay bars, I am sure there would be room in Brussels folklore for one more.

Over the years, the Brussels Manneken-Pis has had to cope with rivals to his claim to be the most important and lovable peeing statue of Belgium. The oldest of these rivals is a Manneken-Pis in East Flanders. The good people of Geraardsbergen are very put out by the claims of the Bruxellois that the Brussels Manneken-Pis is older. The brotherhood of the Geraardsbergen Manneken-Pis will tell you that their statue, from 1459, pre-dates the Brussels Manneken-Pis (although the original Brussels statue dates from at least 1452, so this isn't a very good claim). He does look remarkably similar to the Brussels one, just a bit flabbier and with a hint of the early development of man-boobs. In fact it could be said that the Manneken-Pis statues are really small statues of men, or statues of small men, rather than statues of boys. The Geraardsbergers are so proud of their statue that instead of tucking him away around a side road, as the Bruxellois do, they display him in pride of place, right in front of the town hall. The Geraardsbergers were so incensed by a television programme claiming that the Bruxellois had the older statue, that on a Monday morning in February 2011, a group calling themselves the 'Liberation Front' kidnapped the Geraardsberger statue. They sent a ransom note to the mayor, complaining that he had not defended their statue against the outrageous claims of the Bruxellois. There are a few obvious flaws to this plan of the Liberation Front. First of all, they appear to have chosen the wrong name for their group as they are not aiming to 'liberate' anything. The 'Our Statue Is Older Than Yours Front' would seem more appropriate. Secondly, writing in the demand note that you will look after the statue very carefully, doesn't sound very kidnapper-like. Shouldn't the Liberation Front threaten to melt it down, or snap bits off and send them back one by one until their demands are met? And thirdly, if you are going to make demands and write ransom notes after kidnapping a statue, wouldn't you capture the other side's statue and not your own? Perhaps they spotted these flaws, as they returned the statue, unharmed, on the Thursday.

The more recent rival for attention is not a fellow Manneken-Pis but the statue of a small girl, known as Jeanneke Pis. Some guide books claim that Jeanneke Pis was put up by feminists fed up with the attention given to the male Manneken-Pis, but Jeanneke Pis's caretaker, Foued Hamza – who I bumped into at the Jeanneke Pis statue holding a large canister of carbon dioxide, told me this was nonsense. Foued has been looking after Jeanneke Pis for the last twenty years and runs one of the many restaurants in the Rue des Bouchers area of Brussels. It was his landlord, who seems to have owned most of the restaurants in Rue des Bouchers until he was murdered in 1998, who commissioned the statue as a gimmick to bring tourists to his area. As a small but steady trickle of Japanese tourists made their way up the cul-de-sac off the Rue des Bouchers to take a picture of her, I could see that it had been a shrewd move.

'What are you going to do with the carbon dioxide?' I asked.

'She gets blocked. You need to use gas,' Foued replied as he connected a hose from the canister up a back passage and blasted carbon dioxide through her tubes.

'I've seen that Manneken-Pis has costumes. Does Jeanneke Pis have any?' I asked him, still rather troubled by the sight of the colonic irrigation taking place in front of my eyes.

'No, this is private. It's just me. No one else helps,' he said, giving her a final blast of gas and waving a hand disparagingly at the obvious benefactors of the passing Jeanneke Pis trade at the Delirium Tremens bar next door.

At his restaurant, La Petite Fountaine, with his carbon dioxide canister back behind the counter, Foued told me that he donates the coins dropped in the fountain to a local hospital for 'medical research'. He also hands over any proceeds from the sale of a postcard of the small girl taking a pee. I would like to think positively about Jeanneke Pis in some way, but despite Foued's hard work and devotion, I can't help think that Jeanneke Pis is gross, slightly pervy and just wrong.

A third fountain completes the trinity of peeing statues in Brussels: Zinneke-Pis, a mongrel dog who has been cocking his leg on a bollard in Rue des Chartreux since 1998. Again gross, but at least fairly amusing. It is quite hard to find and doesn't have the water connected, allegedly due to a complaint from local officials. Hopefully the Bruxellois will call it a day at three.

Many of the original Brussels fountains were upgraded in the seventeenth century, and in 1619 the stone statue of Manneken-Pis was replaced by a 55 cm bronze, cast by Jérôme Duquesnoy the Elder. Being small and eminently portable, the statue lent itself to being kidnapped and it has gone missing at least six times in the last 300 years. The English are alleged to have taken him 'for a laugh' at one point and a group of French soldiers pocketed him in 1747, dropping him off outside a brothel a few days later. King Louis XV, who was visiting Brussels at the time, was not amused with this political embarrassment and in order to make amends with the Bruxellois presented Manneken-Pis with a costume of a marquis and ordered French soldiers to salute him whenever they passed. Donating costumes to Manneken-Pis became popular in the twentieth century and a random selection of the 800 or so outfits now in his possession is on display in the Manneken-Pis clothes museum section of the Musée de la Ville in the Grand Place. The costumes are tucked away in a corner of the museum, sitting rather incongruously above two floors of seventeenth-century tapestries of people having their heads chopped off and some very drab, but no doubt important, fifteenth-century paintings. At the entrance to the Manneken-Pis section a short, rather dated, film shows tourists' reactions to seeing the statue. The most common being a surprised look on their faces when they realise they have found the statue, followed by a snigger then, turning to their friends, a disappointed, 'Isn't he small?'

The display includes national costumes and themed costumes, celebrities, professions, world events and thinly-disguised advertising. There is a fireman, a beekeeper, an astronaut, Elvis Presley and a whole case of Japanese costumes. The Japanese have donated seventeen costumes in all and have a slightly disturbing above-average interest in the small peeing boy. In the 1930s a Japanese industrialist was so fond of Manneken-Pis that he commissioned a replica for his house in Osaka, complete with costumes for special occasions. There is also a Manneken-Pis, again with costumes, between the tracks at the Hamamatsucho train station and a freaky-looking modern version of Manneken-Pis, presented to the Japanese by the Belgian ambassador, stands on a cliff-side in the wilds of Tokushima.

The costumes in the museum are rather creepy. There is a Sabena pilot's costume with his smart hat, jacket, trousers and briefcase. So far so good, but the last thing I expect to see in a pilot's costume is a hole in the front with a willy sticking out. Strangely, the hole in the costumes is rarely in the trousers but instead sticks out of a specially made slit in his jacket, which is all the more disconcerting.

Behind a throng of Japanese tourists and bored children who have found something in the museum with buttons to press, is an interesting touch screen computer display of

Manneken-Pis costumes where you can search for pictures of the outfits by nationality or date of donation. The collection is maintained by a civil servant, who, together with the Ordre des Amis de Manneken-Pis, filters through hundreds of applications a year by countries and organisations wanting to donate costumes. Civil servant Mr Jacques Stroobants had been handling Manneken-Pis for nearly thirty years before retiring in 2004. He had grown so fond of Manneken-Pis that he asked to come back to work to continue looking after the statue. An official government handler is also referred to in one of my favourite books on Belgium – a Thomas Cook guide to the country published in 1908. The guide only contains a few lines on Manneken-Pis, observing that he 'has a salaried custodian, and on fete days he is dressed out in gay costume.' The curious thing about the description is that it makes no mention of what Manneken-Pis is doing. The guide even omits the '-Pis' part of his name, referring instead to 'Manneken' or 'Manneken Fountain'. In prudish, post-Victorian Britain, the publisher has censored the very thing that has made Manneken-Pis famous, just leaving us with the enigmatic and inaccurate observation: 'Manneken possesses endowed property'.

From the museum it is a few hundred metres walk along the Rue Charles Buls and Rue de l'Étuve to the statue. It's quite easy to find as you only need to follow the parties of Japanese tourists leaving the south-west corner of the Grand Place. The route is lined with tourist tat and chocolate shops, and you know you have reached Manneken-Pis when the strategically placed Chocolaterie Manneken-Pis, Godiva, Leonidas and Neuhaus shops converge at the crossroads with Rue du Chêne.

We followed the same pattern as the people in the video in the museum.

Surprise!

We have found him!

Snigger.

'Isn't he small?'

'Is that it?'

Ruben added a question that I hadn't heard in the video clip in the museum:

'Dad, are all these people here paedophiles?'

'No. Not all of them.' I replied.

We mingled with the Japanese and a few other bemused tourists wondering what all the fuss was about and waited our turn to take our photos with Manneken-Pis peeing behind us. Today he was without costume and thankfully was just peeing water. The Amis de Manneken-Pis have been known to rig him up to pee beer and hand it out to passers-by in paper cups. If you are not keen on drinking warm beer that has just imitated urine, or if you are still feeling rather underwhelmed by the whole Manneken-Pis experience, a visit to the Poechenellekelder, a cafe directly opposite the fountain, is guaranteed to lift your spirits. Thank you to Tim Webb's *Good Beer Guide Belgium* for recommending this. It is a gloriously eclectic mix of old puppetry, weaponry, theatrical props, Manneken-Pis memorabilia and Belgium's finest beers, and it makes the walk down Rue de l'Étuve from the Grand Place thoroughly worthwhile.

It is also the ideal place to sit with a Belgian beer and contemplate the meaning of Manneken-Pis and whether he merits inclusion on the interesting list for Belgium. He has certainly come a long way since his Renaissance beginnings as a fashionable *putto pisciatore* drinking fountain. The multi-layered meanings and his primary function as a clean water dispenser have long since gone, and for the last 300 years or so the Belgians have bestowed him with a different role. He is their rebellious spirit, their symbol of protest, the epitome of their self-mocking sense of humour. It is two fingers in the air to the country's occupiers, the rule-makers, the bureaucrats, the tax man and to those who say you can't pee in public.

While mulling over these thoughts I was distracted by a cartoon on the wall in the Poechenellekelder, a lithograph dating from 1846 titled *The Arrest of Manneken-Pis* which shows the reaction of the Bruxellois to *l'Ordre de Police sur les Pissoirs*, a law forbidding the public from relieving themselves near urinals. Quite a sensible law, one would have thought. In the cartoon, a policeman up a ladder tries to arrest Manneken-Pis while down below a lady has a stand up pee against a lamp post and a man takes a dump on the pavement. That's not really very funny and against my usual, open-minded persuasion, I find myself coming down on the side of the puritanical 1908 Thomas Cook publisher and Mr Teets in Ohio. Manneken-Pis is just a small boy taking a pee and the suit jackets with holes in, the Michael Jackson style white glove, the celebrity status, are all, frankly, rather disturbing. He is an impostor on the A-list of iconic sculptures of the world. Manneken-Pis has not helped me in my quest and instead I must turn in hope to another symbol of Belgium to see if I can find an object that can make it on to the interesting list. An iconic symbol of Belgium that many non-Belgians have never heard of – the Atomium.

CHAPTER 4
THE ATOMIUM

Without a shadow of doubt, the Atomium should be Belgium's national symbol: its Eiffel Tower, Big Ben or Statue of Liberty. The mere mention of Belgium should cause a mental image of the Atomium to flash before your eyes or, conversely, catching sight of a picture of the Atomium should cause BELGIUM to be lit up in your mind with all the positive attributes of this little country welling up inside you. However most people, on seeing a picture of the Atomium, say, 'What's that?' and instead of this modernist masterpiece, Belgium's most famous symbol is Manneken-Pis – the stupid little statue of a boy taking a pee. Proof of this can be seen in every tourist shop in Belgium where you will be lucky to find even one postcard of the Atomium, but there will be at least a dozen of Manneken-Pis and a bewildering assortment of corkscrews, beer glasses, posters, paper weights and key chains, all sporting the little boy holding on to his willy.

For readers still trying to conjure up a picture of the Atomium, it is a fantastic, futuristic structure – a replica of a carbon crystal multiplied 165 billion times. Imagine an invisible cube balanced on one of its corners, standing 100 metres high. Now place a huge shiny metallic sphere at each corner, and one in the centre of the cube, and join them all together with tubes large enough to contain escalators, stairwells and the fastest lift in Europe. The nine shiny spheres, each one nearly 20 m wide, are the carbon atoms and also conveniently represented the nine provinces of Belgium at the time it was built. This sublime structure stands in the Heysel Park in the northern part of Brussels and was the centrepiece of the 1958 Brussels World Expo, the first World's Fair after World War Two. Like the Eiffel Tower of the 1889 World's Fair, the Atomium was only designed as a temporary exhibit, to be dismantled once the last World Expo visitor had closed the gate. Fortunately the demolition orders were never given and the Atomium stands today as a symbol of post-war optimism when modern, scientifically advanced Belgium was going to lead the world in harmony and progress. Other exhibits at the Brussels World Expo were not so lucky. The highly acclaimed Philips Pavilion, a concrete and asbestos tent designed by Le Corbusier containing nothing but a whacky *poème électronique*, did not survive. Although architectural students lament its loss, my traditionalist father-in-law, a life-long employee of Philips in Belgium who had visited the pavilion on a works outing, only had one word for it: '*Belachelijk!*' Having listened to the *poème électronique*, which regrettably survived destruction and lives on for eternity on YouTube, I can see why. It's the crackly sound of an old radio with very poor reception, and a constipated Clanger being strangled somewhere just out of sight. Try it out on YouTube if you can, but don't expect to last the full 8 minutes 27 seconds.

All the mighty nations of the world were in Brussels at World Expo 58 proudly showing off their scientific advances. The Americans had a colour TV behind a glass screen and something called an 'electronic computer', and the Russian pavilion boasted a replica of Sputnik 1, a huge statue of Lenin and the world's largest ball bearing. Perhaps large ball bearings were crowd-pleasers in 1958.

A classic Brussels World Expo exhibit in the shadow of the Atomium, which mercifully did not survive a day longer than the duration of the fair, was the Congolese village. Several hundred natives of the Belgian Congo lived out their daily life for the amusement of the fair's 42 million visitors in what has been described as the last shameful example in the twentieth century of a 'human zoo'. The work of the Belgian missionaries spreading Catholicism to the grateful inhabitants took centre stage and a large bust of King Leopold II stood at the entrance, over the inscription 'I undertook the work of the Congo in the interest of civilisation'. Apparently not everyone agreed with this view, and just two years after Expo 58, Congo had declared its independence from Belgium.

Today there are no signs of where the Congolese village or the funky Philips Pavilion stood, but this is of no consequence because when you arrive beneath the Atomium no thoughts can distract you from the awe-inspiring sight of the shiny metallic spheres suspended in the air above you. An extensive restoration project completed in 2006 replaced the corroded aluminium surface of the spheres with mirror-like stainless steel, and sunlight now bounces in all directions off the giant carbon atoms. Standing under the Atomium you are transported back to the futuristic Belgium of Expo 58, and on the day we visited I kept looking over my shoulder expecting to see scientists in white coats holding clipboards, telling me about washing machines or nuclear fission. However my attention was soon diverted from this thought by seeing the price of the entrance tickets, which is very twenty-first century, and wondering if I could pass both my children off as under twelve. Hannah, aged fifteen at the time, was having none of it.

Once past the ticket desk we waited in the queue for the small lift that travels up the central column of the cube to the top sphere. The lift had a glass top, revealing the structure and chains and pulleys inside the column – presumably the restoration job had included renewing these, but they all looked worryingly old and rusty compared with the shiny new exterior. The ride was made even more nerve-racking when our cheerful lift attendant announced that this had been the fastest lift in Europe in 1958, travelling at a speed of over 5 metres a second. It was a relief to exit safely, after the remarkably short ride, into the comfort of the 360-degree viewing platform inside the top sphere, looking out at the view across Brussels. Not that there's a great deal to see on the Brussels skyline, since being inside the Atomium you are already in the one building of interest. Down below we could see the Heysel Park and practically beneath us, a strange theme park called 'Mini Europe'. As the name suggests, this contains small European things – we could see a mini Big Ben and a mini Venice, and all of a sudden a man in an orange onesie being chased by someone we took to be a police officer. This looked about as much excitement as you could get in Mini Europe, and we decided that having seen it all from above we could forgo the experience of paying for an entrance ticket once we were back on the ground. Please note that if seeing small replicas of large buildings with a European theme is your thing, Mini Europe and its improbable logo of a jolly turtle wearing EU underpants has now moved from its home under the Atomium and is rumoured to be looking for a new location on the Belgian coast.

After running out of things to look at (a car park and a Holiday Inn was all that was left after Mini Europe) we moved to the trendy restaurant in the top half of the highest sphere. It was all exposed steel girders and shuttering, fortunately with no signs of rust. The highest restaurant in the Heysel Park had matching sky-high prices and very surly service. Even the miserable-looking lobsters on death row in the fish tank glared at us as we sipped our fruit beer and fizzy drinks and it wasn't long before we made the descent down long escalators in the connecting tubes, where neon tube lights flashed colours like in a 1970s disco. Despite the surly service, high prices and lack of anything of interest to see when you are up there, I am still a huge fan of the Atomium. It is an iconic Belgian building, a massive 'must-see' and shoots to the top of the list of interesting things about Belgium. CNN are right with their number 1 ranking for the Atomium on their list of Europe's most bizarre buildings.

What is extraordinary is the story of why the Atomium is not better known. Why is it not on the cover of every book on Belgium, on every tourist brochure, postcard, poster, jigsaw puzzle and beer mat? The answer lies in the misguided brilliance of the engineer, André Waterkeyn, who was so proud of his concept that he managed to put a copyright not just on the design but also on the *image* of the Atomium. Anyone wishing to put a photograph or drawing of the Atomium on a postcard, poster, brochure, or random piece of tourist tat needs to apply for permission before doing so, and may have to pay a royalty depending on the use of the image. Unsurprisingly, few businesses can be bothered with the hassle and cost, and the wonderful Atomium remains in obscurity, allowing the statue of the little peeing boy to hold on to the limelight as Belgium's best-known symbol. Copyright, however, will run out on 1 January 2076, so if you are reading this book after that date (presumably in a museum where they have peculiar rectangular things made of paper called 'books') you will be free to publish as many photographs of the Atomium as you like, and the Atomium can at last start to take its rightful place as the national symbol of Belgium.

The Atomium is much more than just a logo, or badge for the country. It is hugely symbolic, gathering up all the emotions, aspirations and hope of post-war Belgium. It captures the spirit of the 1950s – a decade of peace and progress, placing Belgium at the heart of modern Europe. There was a European institution starting up in the 1950s that Belgium wanted to be part of: an organisation aimed at bringing peace to Europe, showing the best of Europe to the world. Belgium was determined to be a leader of this new organisation, and was there from the beginning as a founder member. Yes, you have guessed it – Belgium was a founder member of the European Broadcasting Union, and a proud participant in the first ever Eurovision Song Contest. After the success of the Atomium, could this be Belgium's next score on the interesting list?

CHAPTER 5
EUROVISION

Every year since 1956, on a spring-time Saturday evening, the Belgians have been slogging it out in some salubrious conference centre in a distant European city, with the pride of their linguistic half of the nation at stake. Every year that is, apart from 1994, 1997 and 2001 when they hadn't scored sufficient points in the previous year to be allowed back, but we don't talk about those years because the Eurovision Song Contest is a serious matter if you are Belgian.

The British attitude towards Eurovision has been embodied for many years in the commentaries of the BBC's Terry Wogan and more recently, Graham Norton, who leads us chortling through our Saturday evening at the likes of *'Diggi-Loo Diggi-Ley'* (Sweden's 1984 winner) and 'Celebrate' by Piero and the Music Stars (Switzerland's 2004 entry, voted 'worst Eurovision song ever' by readers of the *Eurovision Times*, which must be saying something). But the Belgians see nothing amusing in *'Ding Dinge Dong'* (the Netherlands, 1975) or the intriguing *'Bra Vibrationer'* (Sweden, 1985) and there is little merriment on the Belgian television channels as the Walloons and Flemish take turns to represent their country and their side of the linguistic divide. This is a matter of both national and regional interest. At the first contest in 1956 Belgium was represented by the French-speaking Walloons, in 1957 it was the turn of the Flemish, in 1958 back to the French-speakers and so on to the present day. The poor German-speakers of Belgium are overlooked in this linguistic tit-for-tat and to add insult to injury, both the French and Flemish-speakers have even entered songs in entirely made-up languages ('*Sanomi*', 2003 and '*Oh Julissi*', 2008) when they might have had the decency to give the German-speakers a go.

Conny always referred excitedly to it being 'our turn' when the Flemish picked up the baton, and no doubt Walloon families eagerly await 'their turn' to show the rest of Europe what they are made of the following year. Depending on whose turn it is to enter, the French or Flemish-speaking television station will have shown many hours of pre-Eurovision coverage to elect their song, and then both Walloon and Flemish channels will cover the competition simultaneously on the night.

The Belgians are even avid followers of Junior Eurovision, a dumbed-down version of the grown-ups' contest with saccharine-sweet participants aged between ten and fifteen. Junior Eurovision has been gracing the same Belgian television stations every November or December since 2003, bringing us such joys as '*Yioupi Yia!*' (Cyprus, 2008) and '*Eooo Eooo*' (Macedonia, 2010). Belgium has hosted the event but has yet to place its name on the leader board.

In many ways, this abnormal degree of fervent national interest in Eurovision is exactly what its creator, the Swiss

Marcel Bezençon, would have wanted. His idea in 1953, as head of the newly formed European Broadcasting Union (EBU), was to unite post-war Europe while simultaneously holding back the tidal wave of American culture that was threatening to engulf this side of the Atlantic. Bezençon first suggested a 'Eurovision cup for amateur entertainers'. He was way ahead of his time with this idea – a sort of Euro-version of *Britain's Got Talent*, fifty years before Simon Cowell first hauled his navel-height trousers on to the judges' platform. The other members of the EBU, including Britain, voted the idea out as ludicrous, saying 'Who on earth would want to watch such nonsense?' and instead went for Bezençon's second idea: a glamorous European singing competition along the lines of the classy San Remo Song Festival.

I have been aided in my research for this chapter by the extraordinary amount of information concerning Eurovision that has been placed on the Internet, whether on official or semi-official websites or by the many Eurovision-addicted bloggers who clog up cyberspace with mindless Eurovision trivia. I now know that the winning Spanish entry from 1968, *'La, la, la'*, contained 138 repetitions of the word 'la' and that prior to Graham Norton and Terry Wogan, the BBC programme has even been hosted by Rolf 'Have you seen my didgeridoo yet?' Harris. I found that Eurovision and Formula One bloggers display many of the same characteristics: a lot of time on their hands, and many late nights sitting alone in front of the computer.

One of the items I stumbled across was the rules of the very first contest in 1956, *Le Grand Prix Eurovision de la Chanson Européene*. The rules are in French only and are typed out. Not using a funky retro font from Apple or Microsoft of course, but a real typeface from a real typewriter. It is a strange sight in our word-processed world. The rules state that the aim of the competition is to encourage the production of *'chansons originals et provoquant'*. Showing off cutting-edge technology, the show would be broadcast *'en direct'* and *'non-stop'*, through national radio stations and the exciting new medium of television.

As you would expect with anything with 'Euro' in the title, Belgium was a founder member of the Eurovision Song Contest. And as you would expect with anything with 'Euro' in the title, the UK wanted to tell everyone else what to do from the outset, but only joined the following year. Continuing with the 'Euro' stereotype theme, the excuse given by the UK for not joining in the first year was 'European red-tape'. The British claimed that they had misread the overly complicated rules (the rules being in French wouldn't have helped) and had indeed intended to join in the first year, but hadn't filled out the correct forms, and subsequently missed the date to submit their entry.

Eurovision wasn't the only grand idea to come out of the EBU. The EBU was also behind that other great European institution that kept families across Europe glued to the television on weekend nights: *Jeux Sans Frontières*. Credit for this idea is given to French president Charles de Gaulle who thought that French and German youths were less likely to want to kill each other if they played ridiculous games dressed up in large animal costumes. Had he lived to see the 1974 penguins in Aix-Les-Bains, or the 1978 ostriches in Tuscany, where giant costumed birds came to blows, he might have changed his mind. If you happen to be sitting by a computer while reading this (perhaps you are sitting alone doing some late night Eurovision or Formula One blogging), I highly recommend a small detour from the book to look up these *Jeux Sans Frontières* classics where grown men in penguin or ostrich suits battle it out to collect buckets of water or large plastic rings for their national pride.

The BBC's *Jeux Sans Frontières* catchphrase 'Here come the Belgians' takes us neatly back to the Eurovision Song Contest and the inaugural competition on Saturday 24 May 1956 in Lugano. Confidently opening for Belgium was the Walloons' answer to Frank Sinatra: Fud Leclerc. Fud kicked off with what we would now see as a strange choice for Eurovision: a bleak *chanson* titled '*Messieurs les noyés de la Seine*'. The dismal lyrics, mechanically delivered by Fud, tell the woeful tale of his friendless, loveless existence and his desire to join the drowned men of the River Seine. By the end of the song, if you can stick with it that long on YouTube, you are thinking of jumping off the Pont Neuf yourself. It's not exactly the pop schmaltz of 'Boom Bang-a-Bang' (Lulu's UK winner, 1969) or Spain's '*La, la, la*' winner of 1968.

Due to the low number of entrants in the first competition, only seven in all, each country was allowed a second go. After Fud's suicide-at-the-Seine fiasco this was just as well for the Belgians. It might have been a nice opportunity for the Walloons to share the stage with the Flemish-speakers, but rather greedily they took both slots for themselves. Mony Marc was the next act on for Belgium. I had assumed that Mony Marc would be a man, so was somewhat surprised when I clicked on the crackling recording to find a lady's shrill voice assaulting me through the headphones, sounding like a high-pitched Edith Piaf having swallowed a vibrator. At least the song about her wedding day, *'Le Plus Beau Jour de ma Vie'*, was far more upbeat than Fud's dirge and was arguably way ahead of the Eurovision curve, with an annoying, often-repeated, 'ding-dong, ding-dong' vibrating chorus line.

The scores from that first competition in Lugano have never been released and apart from knowing that the Belgians didn't win, mystery surrounds the second to seventh placings. I would take a hefty bet that Fud wasn't near the top. As for the winner, cries of 'Fix!' ring around the Internet. Each country had been allowed to award itself points for its own songs. As if being able to award yourself points in a secret ballot wasn't dodgy enough, the Swiss hosts also managed to wangle the rules to allow themselves to hand out the votes on behalf of the Luxembourg jury. And, er, can you guess who won? Yes, by complete coincidence, Switzerland, the host nation and the only country that could vote for itself twice, won the inaugural Eurovision Song Contest. Perhaps there is a reason why the scores have gone missing from the archives in cupboards 37 to 42 in the vaults under the EBU headquarters in Geneva.

In 1957 the Flemish had their first turn, with Bobbejaan Schoepen singing *'Straatdeuntje'* ('Street Tune'), an excruciating combination of whistling and 'tra la las' from Bobbejaan backed by loud oompah-pahs from his live orchestra. Bobbejaan stood nonchalantly on stage, with his hands in his pockets and what looks like a living organism, perhaps a mole, strapped to the top of his head. Now that the scoring was made public, it could be revealed that strange-haired man Bobbejaan came a humiliating, if unsurprising, second from last. This didn't seem to dent Bobbejaan's career in entertainment and literally building on the success of hits such as *"k zie zoe gère m'n duivenkot'* ('I love my pigeonary so much') and *'De jodelende fluiter'* ('The yodelling whistler'), he drained 30 hectares of marshland in the province of Antwerp to build one of Europe's largest theme parks, modestly calling it 'Bobbejaanland'. In 2007 Bobbejaan won a Belgian Lifetime Achievement award for his contribution to Belgian music. When I pointed this out to Conny, I was told that there is nothing amusing in this fact, a reminder that irony does not feature prominently in the Belgian sense of humour.

Fud was back in 1958 for the Walloons. Surely he could do better than Bobbejaan? His performance of *'Ma Petite Chatte'* ('My Little Sweetie') was exemplary, and if you like fifties French-singing crooner-type music I can see that this might be quite pleasant. Eurovision trivia fans will know that Italy's 1958 entry, while only coming third on the night, became one of Eurovision's most successful songs ever, eventually hitting the number 1 spot in the US charts under the name *'Volare'* and winning two Grammies. Fud wasn't so lucky. It turned out that the international juries didn't like fifties French-singing crooners, and Fud again took Belgium to the humiliating second-from-last place.

It was the turn of the Flemish in 1959, with the improbably named Bob Benny giving it all in his tuxedo with a fine rendition of *'Hou toch van mij'* ('Do love me') and scoring a respectable nine points. In the year that the Russians were sending spacecraft around the moon, the Belgians had something to be proud of too on the international stage: sixth place out of eleven entrants, a new personal best. In 1960 Fud was back again and with the smouldering love song *'Mon amour pour toi'* ('My Love for You') pulled off an even greater victory, placing Belgium sixth out of thirteen entrants – the first time Belgium had been in the top half of the field.

To the delight of the EBU, the competition continued to grow in popularity and five more countries joined in 1961, bringing the total number of entrants to sixteen. Bob Benny, the highest-achieving Flemish-speaker to date, was back in his tux, representing Belgium and the Flemish-speakers again. He was hoping to beat his personal best of sixth place and beat the Walloons' position of the previous year. I can't pretend that these 'large orchestra, man in tuxedo singing a ballad' type of performances are my thing, but I do feel the judges were harsh on Bob that night and that he didn't deserve what was to come. *'September Gouden Roos'* ('September Golden Rose') bombed, coming equal last, with just one point. It was the closest to a *nul points* that Eurovision had ever seen.

Next year the French speakers put Fud back into the competition, for his fourth and ultimately last time. They were expecting the Fud factor to blow away the *un point* embarrassment of the Flemish from the previous year. It would be a walkover for the Walloons. If Fud had been backed by an English-speaking football crowd, he would have heard chants of 'Easy! Easy! Easy!' as he took to the stage. His performance of the romantic *'Ton Nom'* ('Your Name') went without a hitch. There was no suicide attempt in the Seine. It was fine. Perhaps not standing-ovation-fine, but again as it's not my bag I find it hard to tell when one of these tuxedo ballads stands out from another one. Evidently *'Ton Nom'* did not stand out for the juries, as Fud entered the history books on 18 March 1962 – not in the way the Belgians were hoping, but as the first performer ever leaving Eurovision with *nul points*. Fud was not alone in defeat that night: Spain, Austria and the Netherlands joined him at the losers' table in the green room, also going home with *nul points*.

It was an ignominious exit from Eurovision for Fud. Unlike Bobbejaan, there was to be no Fudland, although a footnote in a Eurovision blog informs us that he ended his career as a building contractor, so he may well have got to drain a marsh or two after his crooning days were over.

The years 1963 and 64 were only marginally better for the Belgians, with more dull ballads producing two successive tenth places with points scraping along the bottom of the scoreboard. Perhaps the Belgians were simply following Bezençon's cultural ideology by resolutely ignoring the dramatic changes that were taking place in the music industry in the 1960s. The charts of 1965 were topped by the likes of The Beatles, The Kinks and The Hollies, and on the night of the Eurovision Song Contest, The Rolling Stones had the number one spot in the hit parade with 'The Last Time'. The Belgians, apparently oblivious to the 60s swinging around them, had entered yet another boring ballad into Eurovision: *'Als het weer lente is'* ('When it is spring'), sung by Lize Marke. Poor Lize didn't stand a chance against France Gall's sexy rendition of Serge Gainsbourg's *'Poupée de cire, poupée de son'* ('Wax doll, rag doll'), the winner for Luxembourg. Belgium tanked again. *Nul points* for the second time in three years.

The goal of Eurovision victory remained stubbornly elusive for the remainder of the 1960s, throughout the whole decade of the 70s and up to the mid-1980s. If you were living in Jordan in the late 1970s, you may be surprised to learn that Belgium did not have a winning entry during this period. In 1978, one of the most blatant acts of geopolitics in Eurovision's history took place – greater even than the machinations of the Greek–Cyprus love-in and the back-scratching Balkan states combined – when the Jordanian broadcasters, having trouble acknowledging the very existence of the country with the most votes, showed a still photograph of a bunch of daffodils in the closing minutes of the show and announced that Belgium had won. Viewers around the world who were not tuned in to Jordanian TV saw Israel as the winner, and Belgium placed second.

Putting the Jordanian proclamation to one side, the Belgians had to wait until the mid-1980s before winning in front of all nations. Hopes were running high when it was 'our turn' for the Flemish in Gothenburg on 4 May 1985. The Belgian entry followed Turkey's white-suited trio singing *'Oh oh oh oh oh, didai, didai, dai'*, and cries of 'We must be able to beat that!' were hurled at Flemish television sets as Linda Lepomme took to the stage with *'Laat me nu gaan'* ('Let me go now') for the Flemings and the nation of Belgium. It was a faultless performance from Linda, but another Fud-flop of a song which has you fumbling for the off button so you can get this depressive funeral music out of the headphones as quickly as possible. Linda Lepomme came last, saved from *nul points* by a generous geopolitical vote from the Turkish jury.

Undeterred and ever optimistic, the Belgians were back again in 1986 on 3 May at the Grieghallen in Bergen. The preamble to the Belgian song shows little Sandra Kim at the fish market, buying a fresh cod to match her 80s mullet. This time, the Belgians had got it right. Drowning in the Seine, funeral marches and general crooning were out, and inane 80s pop schmaltz was in. Sandra Kim burst on to the stage in her big-shouldered white tux and pink bow tie, singing her heart out to the upbeat, if mildly annoying *'J'aime la vie'* ('I love life'). The British jury, I am happy to say for reasons of marital harmony, helped her on her way to victory with a generous *dix points*. After thirty years of humiliation, the Belgians had finally made it. Regional differences were put aside: the Belgians had won the most important singing contest in Europe, no, the most prestigious competition in the world! The ten million people of this little country could hold their heads up high. 'We have won! We have won! We have won!' echoed around those Belgian sitting rooms.

If you think it sporting to annoy Belgians (not an activity I condone or recommend), you might like to point out to them that Belgium shouldn't actually have won that night. It was a fraud, a con, a violation of clearly-stated Eurovision Song Contest rules. Sandra Kim cheated. She was just thirteen – thirteen and one hundred and sixty-nine days to be precise – which was below the minimum age requirement to enter Eurovision. The Swiss, who came second, lodged a complaint and tried to get little Sandra disqualified for this gross deception, but to no avail. As I say, I don't like to bring this up. It was won fair and square I say. Well, square, anyway.

The spoils of Eurovision victory include the winning nation hosting the following year's competition, and with a win finally in the bag, the Belgians set about showing off their country at the Palais du Centenaire in the shadows of the Atomium in Brussels in May 1987. Watching the show on tape is an amusing reminder of mid-80s fashion: there was no shortage of shoulder pads and big hair. After the mandatory travelogue that Terry Wogan reminds BBC viewers every host nation 'inflicts on the 500-odd million viewers', the Belgian hostess Viktor Lazlo (yes, Viktor is a hostess) came out with a song and introduced the acts. The night is only memorable for one act: not Johnny Logan's repeat win for Ireland or Belgium's average eleventh place, but for the surprise appearance of famous Belgian Plastic Bertrand, popping up for Luxembourg. Although not recognised by the Belgians as one of their 'famous names', any Brit of a certain age, when pushed to name ten famous Belgians, will place Plastic Bertrand firmly near the top after his 'Ça plane pour moi' 1977 hit. (Younger readers might be familiar with the song due to the many indie rock band cover versions, or as the soundtrack to advertisements for a diverse array of products, including processed bread, fizzy drinks and small cars.) Ten years later, and looking just as fresh-faced, Plastic Bertrand bounced around the stage of Palais du Centenaire singing Luxembourg's 'Amour Amour' in a big-shouldered pink tuxedo jacket with the sleeves rolled up and what looks like a pair of black tights. Being awarded just four points and coming second from last, ahead of Turkey's nul-pointer is a travesty of Eurovision justice – for that performance he should definitely have been last.

Unless something miraculous has happened in the intervening period between the writing and the reading of this book, 1986 remains Belgium's only Eurovision victory. I notice that the current odds at the bookmakers are 250–1 for a Belgian win, so I think I am fairly safe making this comment. I know that statistics don't really work this way, but it is tempting to think that if the odds of winning remain at 250–1, it could be the year 2236 before

Belgium has another Sandra Kim. In recent years the Belgians have also started to become disillusioned with Eurovision, none more so than in 2006 when the French-speakers' entry failed to make it past the semi-finals and the Finnish hard rock band Lordi went on to win with 'Hard Rock Hallelujah'. *'Belachelijk!'* my father-in-law called out from the sofa as Mr Lordi and his monster-headed friends shot to the top of the leader board with a record-breaking 292 points. This wasn't the crooning Fud or Europop the Belgians had tuned in to watch.

Only Norway holds the record for having more last places than Belgium, a fact I may have let slip by accident one evening while carrying out my research for this chapter.

'You are not making fun of Belgians are you?' Conny called across to me at the computer.

'No, of course not,' I replied. Despite five wins and sixteen second places under the belt, Britain has been unable to laugh at anyone's Eurovision results since 2003, when the UK joined the infamous *nul points* club with the cringing off-key performance from scouser pop duo Jemini. It was the beginning of the end for the Brits, who have clung pretty much to the bottom of the loser board ever since, notching up even more last places since the Jemini debacle. Britain's Europop supremacy has well and truly gone, butchered and cut into small pieces by angle grinder-wielding Finns and stuffed into black plastic bin liners behind the stage of a former Soviet bloc conference centre.

It could be argued that Eurovision, voted in by Belgium as a founder member of the EBU back in 1953, has given the world much to be thankful for. We are now familiar with the names of hitherto unknown territories in Eastern Europe, we have the 1974 discovery of ABBA and we haven't gone to war with each other (much) since the first contest in 1956. But the overall winner from Eurovision is not a country or an act, but the English language, which would be all the poorer without the phrase: *nul points*.

The Oxford English Dictionary included it for the first time in 2004, defining *nul points* as: 'no points scored in any context... a hypothetical mark awarded for a failure or a dismal performance'. The OED traces the origins of *nul points* to the 1978 Norwegian entry when the spectacular Jahn Teigen was the first act under the revised voting system to achieve *nul points* for his performance of *'Mil etter mil'* ('Mile after mile'). It is worth watching Jahn's video clip once, if only for the excruciating build up to the desperate braces-twanging in the dying seconds of the song, followed by Jahn's grand finale of a red-trousered mid-air splits. Once is enough.

Despite Norway's impressive tally of *nul point*ers – four in all – the *nul points* epithet appears to be coupled in popular culture with Belgium. I can only put this down to the word associations – from *nul points* to Eurovision; to European Union; to Brussels; and on to Belgium. And so by way of a fairly tenuous connection, innocent Belgium is linked to the 'dismal failure' of *nul points*. To add insult to injury, the words *'La Belgique – nul points'*, however easily they roll off the tongue, have never been said by a Eurovision presenter. *Nul points* scores are not announced on the programme, and in any case Belgium has not had a *nul point*er since 1965, well before the phrase entered the English language.

So how does Eurovision fare in the quest to find all that is interesting about Belgium? Firstly, you have to admire the pluck of the Belgians for entering year after year and always thinking – despite their monumental track record of failure – that: 'This is going to be our year, yes, this year. No more Fuds, no more mole-topped yodelling whistle-crooners, no more *nul points*. Nobody will laugh at us. Belgium will be taken seriously!' Secondly, using a song contest to reinforce the linguistic divide between the Flemish and French, while alienating the German-speakers, is quite clever, and thirdly, not seeing anything even vaguely amusing about the largest, kitschiest, campest celebration of musical mediocrity on the planet is in itself quite amusing. But in the end I am going to leave the Belgians' obsession with Eurovision as 'odd' rather than 'interesting', and I will need to continue my quest, delving further into the Belgians' love affair with Europe in the hope that something of interest may lie ahead. Frankly, I think it's unlikely. I have been trying to avoid taking a look at the elephant in the room, but I can't ignore it any longer – I'm going to have to search for something interesting in Belgium's biggest European love-in of all time – the European Union.

CHAPTER 6
THE EUROPEAN UNION

If you play a word association game with the people sitting around you now, the first word likely to be connected with 'Brussels' will, perhaps unsurprisingly, be 'sprouts'. However, as neither the production nor consumption of sprouts has much to do with Brussels these days (Belgium accounting for under 10 per cent of Europe's Brussels sprout production, mainly for the food processing industry rather than the market stall), I am going to omit the doubtless fascinating story of sprout cultivation from my quest. I shall move instead to the next set of words that you are likely to hear in your Brussels word association game... 'The European Union'.

Like Brussels sprouts, the EU polarises opinion, with those fervently in favour and those who would push it to the side of the plate in disgust at its dull appearance, bitter after-taste and fart-rendering properties. The EU isn't officially headquartered in Brussels, as it also generously shares its expense accounts across Luxembourg and as far as Strasbourg in north-eastern France, but it is Brussels that has become synonymous with the European Union and all the wonders that it brings to the world. But what do the Brussels-based institutions of the EU bring to Belgium? Do they make Belgium an exciting political powerhouse, or, like the Brussels sprouts on their way back to the kitchen after Christmas lunch, is the EU boring, unloved, surprisingly costly and ultimately destined for the compost bin?

Several nations try to take the credit for the idea behind the European Union. None more so than the French who point to their Robert Schuman, French Foreign Minister from 1948 to 1953 and author of the 'Schuman Declaration' of 9 May 1950, which the European Commission's official history credits as 'the beginning of the creation of what is now the European Union'. To commemorate Schuman's call for a European Federation, the EU has even declared 9 May to be 'Europe Day' when all Europeans are supposed to get together and wave European flags at one another to celebrate their Europeanness. However, until all Europeans are given a day off work on 9 May (surely not long to come?), this day has little chance of being adopted as a supranational holiday across the whole of Euroland. Coincidentally, in my home of the Channel Islands, 9 May is already celebrated as a public holiday, although this is not to commemorate the coming together of the Europeans, but rather the departure of the Germans from their five-year visit to the islands which ended abruptly on 9 May 1945.

Schuman does not need an annual one-day holiday to be remembered, as together with the likes of Jacques Brel and Eddy Merckx, he lives on forever as the name of a Brussels Metro station. Schuman is also the lucky owner of a Brussels tram stop and his name has been granted the ultimate in immortality: a sizeable roundabout in the centre of the EU quarter. No one visits the EU institutions in Brussels without passing around, under or over the *rond-point* Schuman.

An unlikely contender for the claim to have planted the seed of the EU is Winston Churchill. Four years prior to Schuman's declaration, Churchill called for 'a kind of United States of Europe'. This quote has been used by the UK's Europhiles to demonstrate Britain's early pro-European tendencies, but Churchill wasn't suggesting that Britain should join a European Union. Far from it, he was suggesting that a United States of Europe would be a good idea for Johnny Continental Foreigner as a counterbalance to the USA and USSR, while the British would go it alone with their Commonwealth.

The Germans, Italians and Austrians all make their claims too, highlighting quotes from illustrious ministers, who called for a gathering together of European nations long before Schuman. Even the Americans get in on the act, pointing to a letter written by George Washington to the Marquis de Lafayette, predicting that, 'one day, on the model of the United States of America, a United States of Europe will come into being.'

However, while the larger nations boast about their grand ideas and fancy declarations, research into the embryonic stages of the EU brings us to much humbler origins and our unsung heroes: little unassuming Belgium and even littler, even less assuming Luxembourg. Life is tough if you are a small country. At best, your larger neighbours humiliate you by telling jokes about your nationhood and taking the credit for your culinary inventions, and at worst they attempt to take a short cut through you to fight another large neighbour, obliterating your country in the process.

Fed up with being pushed around by their bullying neighbours, little Belgium and tiny Luxembourg signed the Convention of Brussels on 25 July 1921, creating the Belgium–Luxembourg Economic Union. This treaty took the first tentative steps towards linking together two European nation states by eliminating customs tariffs between the countries and fixing the exchange rate between the Belgian franc and Luxembourg franc at the handy rate of 1:1.

The union seemed to work well, and while the Belgian and Luxembourgish governments were sitting it out in London during World War Two, the Dutch government, also in exile in London, sidled up to them. Would there be room at the Be-Lux party for one more? For another small(ish) European nation which was also currently in the process of being flattened by its larger neighbours? The Belgians and Luxembourgers, generous and welcoming as they are, readily agreed, and on 21 October 1943 entered into an exchange rate agreement with the Netherlands. This was followed by the signing of the London Customs Convention in 1944, in which the three countries agreed to do away with trade barriers in order to create the Be-Ne-Lux Customs Union.

The Benelux experience paved the way for Schuman's grand plan for Europe and on 18 April 1951, the Benelux countries joined France, Germany and Italy in signing the Treaty of Paris, creating the European Coal and Steel Community (ECSC). This may sound pretty dull and readers with a low boredom threshold, if they have managed to get this far into a chapter on the EU, may be tempted to switch off at this point. However, the creation of the ECSC should not be seen as an act of mind-numbing continental bureaucracy, but as a momentous world-changing event. For instead of seeking revenge and retribution on Germany for bringing the world to war, again, Schuman and other European ideologists, including the Belgian Paul-Henri Spaak who had negotiated the Benelux deal in London, did something unthinkable – they invited the Germans and Italians to the post-war party. Their argument was that if the requirements of twentieth century war – coal and steel production – were jointly controlled across Europe, the countries could never go to war with one another again. Schuman deserves his roundabout in the European hall of fame. And Spaak, notching up an impressive tally of no less than nine *boulevards*, *avenues*, *esplanades*, *rues* and *strasses*, also lives on as the name of the vast European Parliament building in Brussels, a Eurocrat's short stroll down the road from Schuman's *rond-point*.

They didn't stop at coal and steel, and just six years later signed the Treaty of Rome, creating the European Atomic Community and the European Economic Community. Other European nations asked if they could come in, but France's President De Gaulle, not exactly acting in the spirit of the founding fathers, used his power of veto to keep the EEC as an exclusive club just for the European six. Acting as club bouncer, De Gaulle looked down his nose, barking *'pas de trainers'* at all who came to the door until finally in 1973, Denmark, Ireland and the UK were allowed in, with the UK delegation muttering under their breath that Europe had been their idea all along.

Further enlargements and mass signing of agreements followed, including the Maastricht Treaty of 1992, which paved the way for the Euro and coined the title 'European Union' and the Lisbon Treaty of 2007, which increased the power of the Parliament and created the post of a long-term President for the European Council (enter Belgian Herman Van Rompuy, stage right).

While most of its inhabitants understand the basic principle behind the EU, the exact workings of this complex, bureaucratic beast remain shrouded in mystery. The Eurocrats are well aware of this and spend a significant amount of their tax payers' money on offices, websites, museums, national curricula, glossy brochures, CD-ROMs and even tours of their facilities in a vain attempt to explain the EU to its citizens. Having availed myself to as much of their published material as I could manage without falling into a coma, I concluded that I would have a better chance of staying awake if I took the opportunity to join one of the advertised visits to the European Parliament in Brussels. The EU website helpfully tells you to 'Come to the visitors' entrance about fifteen minutes before the start of the tour', but doesn't tell you where the visitors' entrance is. It informs you that there are tours every day, at 10.00 a.m. and 3.00 p.m. except for holidays and Friday afternoons. I checked the calendar on the website to see that Parliament would be open and duly took the morning train from the family's base in Hasselt, aiming for the 10.00 a.m. tour in Brussels. It was an early start in Hasselt and I looked into my reflection in a window on the station platform, trying to brush my hair to make it look less like I had spent the night on one of the station benches. Peering closer into the window, it dawned on me that there was something wrong with my reflection. When I ran my hand through my hair, the hair of the person I was looking at in the glass didn't move. A surly middle-aged man stared back at me, with his hand in a very different position to mine. He adjusted his flies and walked off, revealing a row of men behind him in Manneken-Pis poses. With some surprise I realised that I was looking straight through a clear glass window into the *urinoir* section of the gentlemen's toilets. I hurriedly jumped on my train. What is it with Belgians and public displays of urination?

I read my EU papers to pass the time on the train. I learnt that the EU has three main divisions: The European Council, which consists of a minister from each state and manages security; the European Commission, which has commissioners from each state proposing laws for the EU and the European Parliament, home of the elected MEPs. There is a Conference of Presidents, and a group of people known as 'quaestors', whose purpose in life is not clear to me. Parliament has twenty committees, consisting of twenty-four to seventy-six MEPs and each committee has its own bureau (a writing desk?) and a secretariat. Committees can have sub-committees but I didn't find out if sub-committees could have sub-sub-committees, although there is something called a 'special committee', I assume for when an ordinary committee or sub-committee won't do.

The Parliament's secretariat, the Secretariat-General, is somewhat confusingly based in both Luxembourg and Brussels. Meanwhile, Parliament sits in Strasbourg and Brussels. The Secretariat-General has 5,400 staff and each of the seven political groupings has its own secretariat, which accounts for another 700 staff, not including the 1,000 'parliamentary assistants'. And then there are the 'quaestors', wherever or whatever they may be. No wonder the hoteliers rub their hands when the EU comes to town.

Informative as the EU's literature is, none of this was helping to keep me awake. Only one fact stood out from the names and numbers: Herman Van Rompuy is known as 'Haiku Herman' for his love of the short Japanese poems. I looked out at the flat Belgian countryside: flat ploughed fields for flat mile after flat mile. The monotony was only broken when the train track briefly bisected a little village with its individualistic Belgian brick houses and postage stamp front lawns before running across the ploughed fields again. There was still an hour of flatness to go and my eyelids were growing heavy as I struggled to register the difference between the European Council, the Council of Europe and the Council of the European Union. I couldn't get the Judean People's Front out of my mind, or was it the People's Front of Judea? I needed a distraction.

How hard could this haiku business be? Three lines long with seventeen syllables: five in the first line, seven in the second and five in the last line. If Herman could do it relaxing in his apartment after a hard day running the EU, it could be just the thing for a Belgian train journey.

I sit on the train
I wonder what haiku is
And why he does it.

I discovered that it is surprisingly difficult to cram any meaning into a five-seven-five syllable poem. Reading more about Herman's efforts, I learnt that each three-liner also has to include an observation on nature and something to do with the seasons. How would that fit in?

There was a young man
Who didn't like limericks
So he wrote haiku.

It wasn't working for me. How could Herman relax with this?
The only effect it had on me was one of extreme frustration.

Fed up with haiku
Stupid rules and even more
Stupid syllables.

But the frustration was serving a purpose – it was keeping my
mind off the EU papers and the monotony out of the window –
and I had overcome the urge to sleep. So this is why Herman does
it: haiku is not a means to relax, but a stimulant he uses to avoid
nodding off. All those long meetings debating the latest herring
directive, and Herman is not frantically taking notes but scribbling
down haikus on his European Council headed notepaper.

Now wide awake as the train pulled into Brussels Gare
Centrale, I finally came up with my haiku masterpiece. It
follows the five-seven-five rule. It's observational. You've got
nature and there's a season thrown in for good measure:

Carp are in the pond
They taste muddy in summer
So I eat them now.

Rather like achieving level seventy in the 1980s two-player
Atari tank game (Christopher Bong, Lhasa, 1991 will know

what I mean), I was satisfied that there was no higher level that my haiku could reach and I could now kick the haiku habit that I had developed over the last hour.

From the Gare Centrale in Brussels to the European Parliament building is just four Metro stops to the Schuman underground station, a decrepit lift ride to the surface at *rond-point* Schuman and then a frequent map-checking walk in a south-westerly direction into the land of glass and steel inhabited by the Eurocrats. There didn't appear to be many around on the day that I was there, and I was having trouble identifying the Parliament building until I remembered that the Bruxellois refer to it not by its official name of the 'Paul-Henri Spaak Building', but as the 'Caprice des Dieux'. This double-barrelled insult translates literally as the 'whim of the gods' and, helpfully if you are trying to identify it from a distance amidst a sea of EU buildings, it tells you that the structure is shaped like a giant French cheese of the same name.

Paul-Henri Spaak-ville was deserted; the cafes were closed and there were no signs of life as I approached the big cheese. The silence was broken by a lonesome father who appeared from behind a concrete pillar, calling after his son who sped across the otherwise empty Espace Léopold on a tricycle. Security cameras followed their every move. The nation state flags fluttered in the wind. It is not easy locating the side entrance of a building shaped like a giant oval cheese, and it took some time before I found a sign saying 'VISITORS' ENTRANCE' and another beneath it with the words 'CLOSED FOR HOLIDAYS'. So much for the website telling me that it would be open – my first trip to the heart of Europe had come to a dead end. I crossed the road to the Parc Léopold and sat on a bench watching green and red parakeets squabbling over winter berries in the shrubs while reassessing my day. For a brief second I considered getting out my haiku book again but fortunately, while rummaging through my bag, I found my copy of *Good Beer Guide Belgium*. This soon made up for the disappointment of missing a tour of the European Parliament and I salvaged the day by dedicating it to the pursuit of my vow, with the well-intentioned, but ultimately unfulfilled, promise to read the rest of my research papers on the EU.

Having learnt that Eurocrats like long holidays, and that the official EU website cannot be trusted to record all of them, I called in advance of my next trip to check that the building was open. Four months later, on a warm April morning, I was back at the side entrance to the cheese and this time being welcomed in more European languages than I knew existed. The beaming receptionist eventually ran out of ways to say *'Bienvenue'* and instead moved on to enquire my nationality following a robotic multilingual script. 'Ah, British!' she said pleasingly when I interrupted her. 'I think you are the only British today.' She scanned her nationality chart for confirmation, and nodded as she placed a tick in her book, like a happy twitcher with a rare sighting to record.

Groups and individual visitors have separate check-ins, and I made my way to the individuals' waiting area, joining a handful of international students, two elderly Bruxellois ladies, a suited delegation from Andalusia on an official tour and a family of four from Germany: mother, father and two pre-teens who I had noticed exiting the Metro Schuman, street map in hand, fifteen minutes earlier. What a fun holiday announcement that must have been.

'Children, despite the difficult economic situation we are having in Germany and the problems in the Eurozone due to the poor fiscal management by the governments of Cyprus, Greece and Portugal, we will still be going on holiday this Easter!'

'Hooray!' shout the children excitedly. Tension mounts as they wait to go crazy like in the Disney ads. Which palace of fun they will be going to? A beach holiday, a resort, close your eyes and wait for *Mutter* and *Vater* to say 'Majorca', or 'Tenerife' or could it really be 'Disney'? Would it be Paris, or Florida?

'This year we're going to Belgium and on Monday morning at 10.00 a.m. we shall take a special tour of the European Parliament building to see where all the MEPs sit when they are in meetings.'

'Huh?' German pre-teen disappointment follows in very large amounts.

We were each given a bright yellow lapel sticker saying 'Visitor' in French, English and German, to identify us in case we wandered off. I was disappointed not to receive an A4-sized badge with all twenty-three European languages, an improvement that could perhaps be noted for future tours. The Andalusian delegation managed to fit in a snooze while waiting on the benches in the waiting area – presumably following a boozy night on their Euro itinerary, or perhaps just in anticipation of what was to come. So popular was the parliamentary tour today that the small waiting area was soon filled to overflowing and groups of school children and scouts queued up in the sunshine outside. Those waiting in the park missed the welcome speech and security announcement – spoken in French then English (what happened to Belgium's Flemish and German languages?) – that ushered us in through the airport security scanners and up the steps to the main reception area. Here we queued to receive our multilingual iPod-type devices and perused the brochure stands to pick up yet more material: a glossy brochure in each of Europe's twenty-three languages, complete with linguistically matching CD-ROM. Through my headphones I heard the exciting news that MEPs have been elected by member states since 1979 and that the Parliament has moved from a consultative body to a representative one. Our virtual guide ushered us up in the lift and across a landing to look down on the giant Confluence sculpture – a tangled mess of wires 36 m high that looks like a crushed electricity pylon and is supposed to represent the European nations. According to the guide, if you move one piece of wire, the other parts move to show the interdependence of the nations. Hmm. The German family were busy taking pictures while the Andalusians plodded on. After Confluence, the next and final stop before being returned to the inevitable gift shop, was the glorious Hemicycle – the giant debating chamber of the European Parliament. Or more precisely, one of the giant debating chambers of the European Parliament, since they maintain two chambers – one in Strasbourg and one in Brussels. The Parliament building in Strasburg is used for twelve plenary sessions per year, while the MEPs and their entourages leg it back to the Brussels Parliament building to hold committee meetings. It has been estimated that the additional cost of holding a meeting in Strasbourg is €10 million per plenary session, so a mere €120 million of Euroland tax payers' money per year. The only reason that Strasbourg enjoys the expense accounts is a historical one – it was one of the seats of the ECSC in the 1950s. As northern French towns are not currently famous for their prosperity, the French government is understandably reluctant to let the travelling circus stay in Brussels and for Strasbourg to miss out on the spending power of the thousands of MEPs and Eurocrats who empty their pockets in the city's hotels, restaurants and bars for three days each month.

However a new threat to the Strasbourg economy is coming over the horizon – the EU Climate Commissioner – who has announced her intention to allocate 'personal carbon quotas' to EU officials. This would have a major impact on the Eurocrats' travel. A senior EU official has been quoted as saying that the policy may be necessary, but he would still need to travel first class as a 'good selection of wines is indispensable' when taking a journey within Europe. This story appeared in an official EU briefing dated 1 April, so it may just be a wind up – it's sometimes hard to tell with stories coming out of the EU.

The quote from the unnamed 'senior official' is a reminder that it is not always gravy that is being consumed on the train. The Strasbourg-based Council of Europe (not to be confused with the Brussels-based European Council) has been described by Paul Flynn MP as 'a pretext for shameless alcohol-fuelled jaunts'. Flynn tells stories of speed champagne-drinking competitions and British MPs projectile-vomiting at official Council of Europe dinners. Britain leading the way in Europe again.

Fortunately there was no evidence of British MPs projectile-vomiting in the visitors' gallery of the Hemicycle on the day of my tour. I sat next to the German family, looking out on an empty sea of orange and black: wave upon wave of orange desks with their blacked-backed chairs and lonely microphones. The flags of the member states hung from the wall opposite the visitors' gallery, above the podium where the president and his friends sit. The side walls between the visitors' gallery and the plain grey wall above the president's chair were filled with two stories of glass-fronted interpreters' booths, numbered from 1 to 23 for each language of the EU; from *deutsch* to *gaelige*. Each booth contained four chairs and microphones, presumably to seat the principal interpreter and three backups in case he falls asleep. MEPs and visitors can tune in to the language of their choice by selecting the appropriate number on their headsets and receive simultaneous translation of the stimulating debates from the floor.

Swollen by the number of large tour groups that had poured in behind us, several hundred of us now filled the seats in the gallery: scout troops, school parties, political students, elderly Belgian ladies, Andalusians, the German family and me. No one spoke as we fiddled with our multilingual headsets, watching video clips of debates in progress and learning about the different groupings of MEPs. I have to admit that if you like large-scale political organisation, the Paul-Henri Spaak building is very impressive. I learnt from my audio guide that each of the 736 MEPs has a numbered seat in the chamber and that the waves of seats are arranged in a semi-circle in order to avoid the confrontation of a Westminster-style parliament. There are 160 political parties represented here, each of which has been fed through a kind of Hogwarts political sorting machine and allocated to one of seven pan-European political groupings arranged across the chamber from left to right, depending on their political stance. Nationalities are unimportant in the chamber, as MEPs sit in their political groupings. So a French leftie will sit on the left in the same group as a German leftie, and the anti-European nationalists of different nationalities, surely the most unnatural of coalitions, sit together at the right of the rainbow. Beyond the far right hand side of the chamber are seats for a small group of independents – those spat out by the Hogwarts sorting machine as being too awkward to fit into any of the seven parties.

In terms of selecting the MEPs back in the home countries, the UK voters have consistently been at the bottom of the league table when it comes to taking an interest in who is sent to represent them in the European Parliament. In 1979, the first year of European elections, while excited Belgians topped the table with a 91 per cent turn out, followed closely by the Luxembourgers with 89 per cent, the UK could barely scrape enough interest together to manage a 32 per cent turn out. The collective verdict from the UK: 'Europe? Can't be arsed.' At each subsequent European election, the UK has remained in the apathetic 30-something per cent bracket, with the notable exception of 1999 when the UK electorate decided that it was 'stay at home to wash your hair day' resulting in a paltry turn out of just 24 per cent. In keeping with the Brits' enjoyment of irony, when they can be bothered to vote in a European election they tend to vote for anti-European candidates and a surprising number of the British MEPs are from the United Kingdom Independence Party (UKIP), a party whose unambiguous aim is to remove the UK from Europe.

As I looked out across the orange seats of the Hemicycle I recognised the spot to the far right of the semi-circle where UKIP leader Nigel Farage had berated poor Herman Van Rompuy, after Herman's first ever speech to the parliament as the newly elected President of the European Council. Herman may have been hoping for polite applause or, in his wildest imagination as he toyed with a five-seven-five poem on his note pad, he might have been dreaming of a standing ovation. Instead, the unsuspecting Herman was met by a torrent of abuse from Farage who opened with the lie, 'I don't mean to be rude...' and went on to describe the Belgian as having 'all the charisma of a damp rag and the appearance of a low-grade bank clerk'. Farage exposed his ignorance of European affairs by announcing, 'I'd never heard of you' and went on to insult the whole of the Belgian nation by stating that Belgium is 'pretty much a non-country'. Watching it again on YouTube is positively toe-curling. It's like watching Basil Fawlty without the funny bits.

Farage caused me, and no doubt many other Brits in Belgium, a great deal of discomfort after his unprovoked attack on Herman. My Belgian father-in-law in particular was decidedly frosty to me for quite some time after Farage's outburst was given extensive coverage on the Belgian TV channels. Being offensive and ignorant were now seen as core British character traits: a nice addition to our projectile-vomiting skills.

Back on the tour, the visitors' gallery had all but emptied. Only the German family was left, as the father fiddled with his camera to get the best shots of the empty auditorium. That's going to be a great one for the family album. Meanwhile *deutsche* mum sat quietly reading every page of her pack of the EU brochures, while the children dismantled the headphones and multimedia apparatus.

With no other large sculptures or chambers to see, our tour ended with the compulsory stop at the official European Parliament gift shop. This exciting opportunity for some Euro retail therapy proved to be a disappointment; with only a mediocre selection of blue-flag-and-yellow-stars tat on offer and the surprise inclusion of over a dozen Manneken-Pis related items. I was nearly tempted by a 1,000 piece jigsaw of Manneken-Pis cutely dressed in sixty of his hole-in-the-trousers costumes, but then I remembered that I don't have any interest in jigsaws or statues of small urinating boys. As usual, the only reference to Belgium's greatest monument, the Atomium, was a single picture at the back of a postcard rack.

I wondered what the elderly Bruxellois ladies had made of the tour. Did they see the EU as the pride of the Belgian nation or as a curse on their land? Within Belgium, opinion on the effect of the EU is divided. While the retailers, hoteliers, landlords and businesses of Brussels have undoubtedly prospered and it has been estimated that up to 30 per cent of the city's income is derived from the activities of the Eurocrats, others complain that the EU has pushed up prices and consumed large areas of the city. The patriotic Belgians are immensely proud that the EU is principally headquartered in Brussels, interpreting this as Belgium playing a major part on the world stage. They fail to realise however that Belgium's association with the EU does nothing to foster a positive impression of the country, and all the negativity focused on the EU's institutions rubs off directly on the Belgians. Thanks to the EU, it will not be long in your Brussels word association game before someone matches Brussels with 'bureaucracy', and if you are playing the game at a tabloid headline writers' party, or a London cab drivers' convention, a word that will quickly be associated with Brussels, is 'bonkers'.

'Bonkers Brussels' read the headline in the *Yorkshire Evening Post*, regarding an EU directive that restricted the length of journey of certain types of seafaring craft. A reader from Scarborough was quoted as saying, 'It's absolutely crackers' and the *Evening Post*'s columnist added, 'I'd go further, *I'd call it stark raving bonkers.*'

'Bonkers Brussels' headlines and the foaming-at-the-mouth columnists behind them have perpetuated many a Euromyth, some of which are based on fact, some are indeed bonkers, and others are pure works of fiction.

Banning curvy cucumbers

Yes, the EU had something to say about the curvature of your cucumber. Commission Regulation (EEC) No 1677/88, in place from January 1989 until July 2009, told us that Extra Class cucumbers may only bend 10 mm per 10 centimetres of length, whereas Class I cucumbers could bend up to 20 mm. Further curvature was not permitted. It is quite hard to see the benefit of this regulation, other than having created a black market in cucumbers that deviate more than their permitted 20 mm.

Banning bendy bananas

Most people who recall this 'Bonkers Brussels' story remember it as the banning of straight bananas, but as with cucumbers, the culprits were the bendy ones. Commission Regulation (EC) 2257/94 of September 1994 tells us that bananas must be 'free from abnormal curvature'. As there is no definition of 'abnormal curvature' (surely a missed opportunity to add several thousand more words to regulation 2257/94), one man's curvy may be another man's straight. In a rare flash of common sense, the European Commission voted in July 2008 to abandon the regulations dictating the shape of twenty-six fruit and vegetables (granting freedom once more to the curvy cucumber) but forgot to mention the banana. And so we are left none the wiser as to how bendy a banana has to be before it is deemed to have an 'abnormal curvature'.

Banning English 'chocolate'

This is one of the oldest and longest drawn out of the EU's bureaucratic battles, dating from the original Chocolate Directive of 1973 until its eventual repeal by the European Parliament in 2000. The twenty-seven-year-long conflict concerned the word 'chocolate' and the different definitions given to it by various EU members. 'Chocolate' consumed by the continental Europeans tends to have a high cocoa (i.e. 'chocolate') content, whereas the 'chocolate' manufactured for the UK market is typically low in cocoa and high in milk and vegetable fat. Or as Conny put it, the Belgians eat 'real' chocolate while the British eat a sickly sweet fat concoction unfit for human consumption. It was the Belgians who led the assault on the British chocolate manufacturers, attempting to block the sale of the 'inferior' British products and insisting on dramatic changes to the labelling. The Germans tried to calm things down by proposing that British chocolate could be labelled as *Haushaltmilchschokolade* which would translate onto the wrappers of British chocolate bars as 'household milk chocolate'. The British managed to collect a small band of allies in the Chocolate Wars; presumably countries with an equally dismal palate, or perhaps those who were prepared to trade a vote with the UK for something of slightly more significance than the contents of a chocolate bar. The Chocolate Allies, (the UK, Austria, Denmark, Finland, Ireland, Portugal and Sweden) won the day, and since August 2000, the British have been able to sell their chocolate without declaring on the label that the product may be closely related to a household detergent.

Banning British bangers

In a similar vein to the Chocolate Wars and other EU attempts to rename sub-standard British products, some readers may recall the 1980s campaign to re-label the British banger as an 'emulsified high-fat offal tube'. However realistic this may sound, and I am sure it would be possible to find a *Daily Express* reader who will swear that it is true, this wonderful line comes from an episode of the political TV sitcom *Yes Minister*. The EU only went as far as saying that sausage manufacturers had to declare the quantity of MRM (Mechanically Recovered Meat – a grey sludge produced by squeezing animal bones through a mangle) in their products, and banned the use of L&A (Lips & Arse) altogether. I'm not sure that L&A is a recognised industry term, but I would like to see the phrase introduced in a European Directive, which would require confirmation to be printed on the label of Iceland cocktail sausage rolls (a staggering £2 for a pack of 80) that they are indeed 'L&A free'.

There are many more wonderful Euromyths out there, from the banning of 'Bombay Mix' and 'scampi in the basket' to the tabloid feeding frenzy over the banning of barmaids' cleavages (allegedly due to a proposed directive regarding the harmful effects of the sun on workers' skin). No matter how absurd the

EU-bashing becomes, or how bonkers the directives, one thing is certain: the EU has put Brussels, and therefore Belgium, on the map.

But is it interesting? Member states without internal wars for the last seventy years? No more L&A in my sausages? A fancy roundabout in Brussels and Herman's book of haiku? That's a mixed bag from Belgium and Luxembourg's first cosying up together in 1921. It is likely that Belgium would be a duller place without all the EU institutions, and the international commuters, characters and spending power they attract. I might go so far as to say that the EU is necessary in one form or another, but I am sorry Mr Van Rompuy: to describe it as 'interesting' would be a misuse of the English language. Probably necessary. Definitely boring.

As a footnote to this chapter, be warned that if you play the word association game at a Suttons Seeds brassica sales conference, instead of the 'European Union', or 'bonkers' coming up, the first word likely to be shouted out when you say 'Brussels' is 'Brilliant'. Yes, as all Suttons Seeds brassica salesmen know, the 'Brilliant' is a top-selling variety of Brussels sprout, famed for its tolerance to hardy mildew. There's a fact to share at the dinner table next Christmas, although if you are trying to win over a particularly ardent Belgium-basher, you might want to hold back on that one. The Belgians do however have another connection with Christmas which could well be just the boost that my quest needs. After failing to register either Eurovision or the EU on the interesting list, could there be something of interest in the way the Belgians celebrate Christmas, and their story of a man in a pointy hat, a white horse and a black and white minstrel with a hessian sack?

CHAPTER 7
FROM *SINTERKLAAS* TO SANTA CLAUS

If you are a Belgian boy or girl aged below eight or nine (what are you doing reading this book – shouldn't you be playing *CoD: Zombies* or a mindless Nintendo game involving puppies?) you may want to skip this chapter as it could call into question some of your beliefs around the magical happenings in December.

While the majority of British and American children are whipped up into a commercially-induced frenzy of wrapping-paper-ripping excitement on Christmas morning, waking up especially early to see if Santa has brought them all the contents of their Christmas wish-list, their Belgian and Dutch counterparts will be attempting to sleep in, with the only excitement of the day ahead being multiple church services and extended family visits. Father Christmas will not have been down their chimney on Christmas Eve – not because the Belgian children have been excessively naughty, but because

Sinterklaas has already done the present-delivering job for him on the night of 5 December. In this quite clever way, the Belgians keep a distance between the commercial and religious sides to Christmas. It also avoids overloading small children's minds with two physiological mysteries/impossibilities – the Virgin Birth and how *Sinterklaas* got the ping-pong table down the chimney.

Unlike Father Christmas, *Sinterklaas* does not live at the North Pole, making instead the far wiser choice of Spain for his year-long residence and the manufacturing base for all the toys. Accompanied by his helpers, he travels on a steamboat from Spain to Belgium and the Netherlands at the end of November, where he rides around on a white horse to oversee the handing out of presents. His arrival at the various Belgian and Dutch towns is broadcast on the national television stations and thousands come out on the streets to greet him, singing traditional *Sinterklaas* songs. The songs are to encourage *Sinterklaas* to stop by your home and leave presents, as typified by the '*Sinterklaas kapoentje*' song, an annoyingly catchy number that is hard to escape from on the airwaves, in the shops, family sing-a-longs and the free *Sinterklaas* CDs that seem to get stuck on loop in the car from mid-November. A quick YouTube look up, and you can have this stuck on endless play in your brain too:

Sinterklaas kapoentje,
Gooi wat in mijn schoentje,
Gooi wat in mijn laarsje,
Dank je Sinterklaasje.

(Dear *Sinterklaas*,
Throw something in my shoe,
Put something in my boot,
Thank you *Sinterklaas*.)

The Belgian and Dutch expat communities bring their *Sinterklaas* tradition with them wherever they end up in the world – even to my home island of Jersey, where a handful of dedicated expats arrange the magical arrival of *Sinterklaas* to St Helier harbour every year on the Saturday closest to 6 December. Unlike the fake Father Christmasses in garden centre grottoes, Hannah and Ruben were convinced that this was definitely the real *Sinterklaas*, who was stopping off on his way from Spain to the low countries. He would arrive in full *Sinterklaas* kit on a little boat after much singing of *Sinterklaas* songs by the Dutch and Belgian children gathered on the harbour wall. He didn't manage to bring his white horse with him (he would tell us that he had sent the horse on to the Netherlands in advance) but he spoke Dutch, knew Hannah and Ruben's names and while *Sinterklaas* songs blared out of a portable CD player in the harbour arrivals hall, handed out presents to all the Dutch and Belgian boys and girls, much to the consternation of bemused ferry passengers. You can't get more real than that.

Sinterklaas is even bigger in the Netherlands than in Belgium, where in an extra twist of the story, and perhaps as a precursor of today's 'Secret Santa' in the workplace, grown-ups make bizarre surprise presents for each other and read out humorous poems. Names are drawn from a hat to determine who is going to give to whom, and weeks are then spent on planning the gift (which must be of the 'it's the thought that counts' variety), the elaborate packaging (which must be a challenge to remove) and writing the poem (which must be funny, personal, and read out very loud by the recipient).

As with Father Christmas, *Sinterklaas* has white hair and a long white beard but, despite the fun that the Dutch have around their extended *Sinterklaas* traditions, he is a rather sombre, saintly fellow, not the jolly fat chap that Santa has turned into. He wears a white robe with a red cape and a large red pointy hat with a yellow cross on the front, which Conny as a small girl thought he had borrowed from the Pope. You never see his hands, as he always wears white gloves.

So far so good and so innocuous, but now the *Sinterklaas* story takes a decidedly dodgy turn, as his helpers are not elves (or dwarves with pointy ears – perhaps not so politically correct when you come to think of it) but *Zwarte Pieten* (Black Peters). The *Zwarte Pieten* are white people with their faces blacked up wearing fuzzy wigs and colourful stripy clothing. They accompany *Sinterklaas* on the steam boat from Spain carrying the presents for him in large hessian sacks. For several days towards the end of November Belgian children will have been leaving a shoe out by the fireplace (or radiator if there is no fireplace in the house) together with a drink for *Sinterklaas* and a carrot for the white horse. If they have been good boys and girls, *Sinterklaas* directs the *Zwarte Pieten* to put sweets in the shoes in the run up to the night of 5 December when, hopefully, *Sinterklaas* will turn up with presents. The sweets are special *Sinterklaas* ones that only make an appearance at this time of year: *nik-naks* (tiny biscuits with a twirl of rock-hard sugar icing), *speculaas* (ginger biscuits typically in the shape of St Nicholas), chocolate *Sinterklaases* and *guimauve* (sugary marshmallow things in the shape of Our Lady). If they have been naughty, there might be nothing at all in the shoe, or one of the *Zwarte Pieten* may have left a birch twig for their parents to beat them with, or worse still – they could be bundled up in the sack and taken back to Spain. I didn't get to find out what happened to them then – presumably they would be set to work in the *Sinterklaas* toy-making sweatshop, ruled over by whip-cracking *Zwarte Pieten* while sewing [insert famous brand name here] footballs for half a Euro a week. Hannah and Ruben would diligently put out a shoe in front of the fireplace at home in Jersey, and on some nights, close to *Sinterklaas*'s arrival at the harbour, they would even be filled with *pepernoten* and *suikerbeesten* in the morning. When *Sinterklaas* arrived at St Helier harbour, he would always be accompanied by several *Zwarte Pieten,* usually including a naughty one who would climb over things and throw *Sinterklaas* sweets in the air for the children to catch. One year, and I still can't believe that this really happened, the parents had a message that *Sinterklaas* was short of helpers, and Hannah and Ruben didn't notice that just before his arrival at the harbour Conny disappeared, only to return quite some time after *Sinterklaas* and the *Zwarte Pieten* had been waved back on to their boat. They did say afterwards what a kind *Zwarte Piet* there had been this year, who knew exactly what gifts they wanted. I'm still slightly troubled by this.

The *Zwarte Pieten* have divided modern-day Belgium. Some Belgians, desperately trying to hold on to their childhood traditions, insist that the helpers are only black because they have come down the chimney. Others, on the more politically-correct side of the fence, say that this doesn't explain why the

Zwarte Pieten are white people dressed up like black and white minstrels (without the white bits) with curly black wigs, red lips and large gold earrings. Their attire of a brightly coloured satin blouse, velveteen waistcoat and matching stripy breaches is not the usual dress of someone who climbs chimneys for a living. There have been attempts to bring *Zwarte Pieten* into the twenty-first century and the main Dutch TV station broadcasting his arrival in the Netherlands in 2005 reported that *Sinterklaas*'s steamboat had sailed through a rainbow on the way from Spain with the result that the *Zwarte Pieten* had red, blue, green and yellow faces when they turned up. This didn't go down well with the traditionalists, and the following year the steamboat had managed to avoid rainbows and the *Zwarte Pieten* were back to their usual black.

Each of the following multiple-choice answers to the question 'Who is the original *Zwarte Piet*?' can be found in different literary and Internet sources. You can select whichever answer you would like to believe and if you want a lively debate with a Belgian, or Dutch person for that matter, try choosing a different answer to the one that they give. A word of warning: they can become quite agitated on this subject and you may not be invited round for New Year's drinks if you give the wrong answer to this troubling *Sinterklaas* question.

Who is *Zwarte Piet*?

• an orphan from Ethiopia who *Sinterklaas* saved from slavery
• a chimney sweep who *Sinterklaas* employs for his chimney-climbing skills and who loves the job so much that he comes back year after year

- *Sinterklaas*'s best friend who happens to be 'Moorish', as he met him in Spain. Like Batman and Robin, or Frodo with a very Moorish Sam
- a little black devil who wears the costume of the Spanish soldiers who occupied Belgium in the 1500s
- *Sinterklaas*'s black slave who he forces to carry heavy bags and climb down chimneys against his will while *Sinterklaas* sits in comfort on the white horse
- an innocent fairy-tale character bringing harmless fun to millions of children
- an evil butcher who likes pickling small children in brine
- a racist stereotype reinforcing Belgium's inglorious colonial past and/or
- the original model for the now thankfully defunct 'golliwog'.

Despite the Jimmy Savile hair and Michael Jackson gloves, the *Sinterklaas* character is less controversial than *Zwarte Piet* and there is general agreement as to his origins. He is seen as the modern-day embodiment of St Nicholas, the fourth century Bishop of Myra, in what is present-day Turkey. St Nicholas spent his life doing godly deeds, performing miracles and giving to the poor. He is perhaps most famous for helping a man who had fallen on such hard times that he could not afford the dowries to enable his three daughters to marry. The unfortunate man was about to sell his daughters off for prostitution, when St Nicholas intervened by turning up late one night and throwing money into the girls' bedroom. Some of the coins fell into the girls' shoes on the hearth and into their stockings hanging up by the fireplace. With the recent *pedopriester* phenomenon, some might now interpret this story as St Nicholas paying the girls a visit as their first client and stuffing his tips down their stockings by the fireplace on leaving, but fortunately for St Nicholas the story passed down for the last 1,700 years or so is that he was a kindly benefactor whose generous donation saved the girls from following their father's career advice.

St Nicholas' association with children stems from the time that he rescued three small schoolboys who had been abducted by an evil butcher and stored in a pickling tub behind the meat counter. Not only did he save their bodies from whatever unpleasant uses the butcher had in mind for them, but as the butcher had already pickled them, St Nicholas also brought them back from the dead. This rather miraculous event created his reputation for being the 'protector of children' and in combination with the three prostitutes legend we now have the origins of the *Sinterklaas*/Santa Claus/Father Christmas story: gifts left overnight for children in stockings hanging by the fireplace. St Nicholas (presumably just 'Nicholas' at the time) died and ascended into heaven on 6 December AD 346. With a long list of miracles to his name and health-restoring properties attributed to some magical 'manna' liquid that apparently oozed from his remains over the following centuries, it is no surprise that by the Middle Ages the relics became an important stopping-off point on the medieval pilgrimage circuit. However, Myra on the Anatolian coast of Asia Minor was not the easiest place to reach for European pilgrims, and the expansion of the Muslim Seljuk Empire in the eleventh century gave the Italians the excuse they were looking for to 'save' the relics and bring them closer to Europe. By 'save', read 'beat up the monks who were looking after them, use a crowbar (or medieval equivalent) to break open the tomb, steal the remains, scoop up any manna, and leg it back to the harbour to bring them to Italy'. With both glory and considerable commercial gain at stake, sailors from Venice and Bari raced to save the relics. The sailors from Bari were the first to make the smash and grab and brought the remains back home to cash in on the lucrative pilgrimage market, with a celebrity grand opening of the Basilica di San Nicola in 1089 by none other than Pope Urban II. With the relics miraculously producing an endless supply of manna ooze, Bari became one of Europe's greatest, and wealthiest, medieval pilgrimage centres. To this day the place to pay homage to the majority of the real St Nicholas is not Myra but the Basilica di San Nicola in Bari. If travel to Bari is a little too far, you could always try the San Nicolò al Lido in Venice, as the Venetian sailors, despite being second in the race, still managed to scoop up the small fragments that the Bari sailors missed in their haste to be first. And if neither of these Italian churches is in your neighbourhood, you can still visit bits of St Nicholas by popping in to a staggering thirty-five other churches around the world which claim to have a fragment or two; a finger bone here, a leg bone there, or a tube of some holy oozy liquid donated on a papal visit.

Despite the inconvenience of death, St Nicholas still made many return trips to earth to continue his good deeds, in particular giving to the poor. To celebrate these acts of kindness the tradition of giving presents on 6 December – the Catholic Church's feast day for St Nicholas – was born. The practice is said to have been passed by sailors from Catholic Spain to the Catholic and Spanish-owned low countries of Belgium and the

Netherlands. Popular thinking is that Dutch settlers in America brought the tradition of present-giving on St Nicholas Day, 6 December, to their new territories, where *Sinterklaas* (Saint Nicholas) later morphed into Santa Claus, merging with the English character of Father Christmas – a non-present-giving, green-jacketed jolly chap who had been around since Tudor times. But one line of research claims that it was the Belgians who are the unsung and unlikely heroes of the *Sinterklaas* to Santa Claus story. When the Netherlands turned Protestant Calvinist in the late sixteenth century, the veneration of saints was forbidden – both at home in the Netherlands and in the new territories being acquired by the Dutch West India Company. The inhabitants of the low countries in the area that is now Belgium, however, remained Catholic and could venerate their saints whenever and wherever they wanted – including in America. The second generation Belgian Maria van Rensselaer living in New York provides us with the first reference to *Sinterklaas* in America: a receipt for '*Sinterklaas* goods' from Walter's bakery in New York, dated 1675. Mrs van Rensselaer's grandson became the Mayor of New York, and the story goes that this influential family kept the *Sinterklaas* tradition alive, long enough for it to be picked up again by a wider audience after the American Revolution.

Having freed themselves from colonial rule, the newly-independent Americans scoured their short history looking for a suitably non-British tradition to celebrate, and *Sinterklaas* fitted the bill. The author Washington Irving published his first novel on St Nicholas Day in 1809, giving St Nicholas twenty-five mentions including references to 'making presents' and 'hanging the stocking in the chimney'. The following year a piece of artwork commissioned for the New York Historical Society's St Nicholas Day dinner depicted a jolly St Nicholas filling children's stockings at a fireplace. The transformation was completed in 1821 with the publication of a book titled *The Children's Friend* showing a 'Sante Claus' arriving from the north on a sled pulled by a flying reindeer, not on the night of 5 December but on Christmas Eve.

So there we have it: from Nicholas' saintly deeds in Myra, to the traditions of *Sinterklaas*, through to Father Christmas himself. If it wasn't for the link provided by Mrs van Rensselaer and those seventeenth-century Belgian Catholics in America, we wouldn't have the large man in the red coat coming down the chimney on Christmas Eve, some really bad Hollywood movies, Santa's grotto at the local garden centre, but above all, we wouldn't have our own wonderful childhood memories (I am assuming here that the reader has wonderful childhood memories of Father Christmas – of course if you don't, you won't be quite so pleased with the Belgians). Dodgy sidekick apart, we have a lot to thank *Sinterklaas* for. This definitely rates as interesting and my quest is back on track.

While *Sinterklaas* and *Zwarte Piet* sensibly leave Belgium for the warmer climes of Spain shortly after 6 December, there are many odd characters in Belgium who can be seen throughout the year. There is Alfred David, a strange man living in Brussels who likes to walk the streets dressed up as a penguin, but I think he is more clinically insane than interesting and I don't propose writing a chapter on why *Monsieur Pingouin* eats raw fish while flapping his arms and making penguin noises. There are, however, a great many cartoon characters in Belgium, and following the success of *Sinterklaas* on making it to the interesting list, Belgium's star status in the cartoon world might just make it two interesting scores in a row. Belgium is home to one of the greatest cartoon characters of all time and my quest would not be complete without checking out Belgium's comic scene and *The Adventures of Tintin*.

CHAPTER 8
THE 'NINTH ART'

By Belgian standards I had an extremely deprived childhood when it comes to comics. My parents didn't approve of *The Beano* or *The Dandy* (too downmarket), or *Disney* or *Marvel* (too American). I had to make do instead with a weekly hand-me-down from my brother: his thumbed-through copy of the educational but exceptionally dull *Look and Learn*. During short stays in the summer with my French pen friend I was introduced to *Asterix* and *Lucky Luke*, which I spent as much time reading as possible in order to avoid the dreaded object of these trips – speaking French with French people. Although the books were in French, the picture stories were quite easy to follow, especially as the words consisted mainly of *'Bif!'*, *'Poof!'* and *'Paf!'* I didn't know at the time (and certainly wouldn't have cared) that *Lucky Luke* was created by the Belgian artist Maurice De Bevere (aka Morris), and that *Asterix* only came about due to a Belgian publisher bringing illustrators René Goscinny and Albert Uderzo together. I now appreciate that this is no coincidence, as Belgium, as you may or may not know, is the world's comic strip capital, boasting more comic strip authors per square kilometre than any other country. A fact that must be true as it comes from the recognised authority on such matters, none other than the Belgian Comic Strip Center (BCSC) in Brussels.

'Comic strips', it turns out, may not be the right phrase to describe this Belgian publishing phenomenon, as the word 'comic' is a bit of a misnomer. Many of the present day comic strips have nothing comedic about them at all and the French term *bande dessinées* or *BD* (literally 'drawn bands') and the Flemish *stripverhalen* ('story strips') are perhaps better descriptions. However be aware that walking around Brussels, especially around the Gare du Nord, asking for directions to the 'Strip Centrum' (the official Flemish name for the BCSC) may have unintended results. Some writers in English refer to them as 'graphic novels', but if 'comic strips' is good enough for the BCSC, this is the main term I shall use throughout my investigation into whether Belgium's world-leading status in the comic strip industry is an interesting fact, or the equivalent of a 1971 issue of my brother's *Look and Learn*.

The Belgians certainly take their comic strips very seriously, having elevated them to the status of an art form; the 'ninth art' to be precise. This phrase was coined in 1964 by Morris, writing in an edition of *Spirou* magazine in which he tagged *bande dessinées* onto the end of a list of the eight established arts. In case you are having trouble recalling all of the first eight, or, like me, were previously unaware that anyone had even come up with eight categories of art, they are apparently: architecture, sculpture, painting, music, dance, poetry, cinema and television. The ninth art features prominently in Belgian culture, and every major town in Belgium has its own comic strip shop and each regular bookstore will have an entire section or room dedicated to comic strips. Belgium's best-selling authors are not celebrity chefs or thriller writers, but the creators of comic albums. Most of these writers and illustrators are practically unknown outside Belgium, with the exception of the Flemish authors selling into the Dutch market and the Walloon authors having best-selling albums in France. It is estimated that Belgium prints over 40 million comic albums a year – quite something for a country with a population of less than 11 million.

A visit to the BCSC is the starting point for any investigation into the ninth art, and one crisp winter's morning, having taken the train to Bruxelles Central, Ruben and I followed directions to the BCSC, a five-minute walk from the station along Brussels' ice-covered pavements. We only slipped once, Ruben unfortunately landing hand-down onto a frozen dog turd which no amount of highly perfumed and hugely over-priced wet-wipes from the local pharmacy could remove from his hand. It wasn't a good start to the day, but it was more than compensated for by the excitement of arriving outside the BCSC in the Rue des Sables. The building was originally a warehouse designed in 1906 by the art nouveau architect Victor Horta. Tall sandstone pillars led to glass ceilings, exposed girders with rows of rivets and an endless amount of twirly art nouveau ironmongery. It seems hard to imagine that this magnificent building was destined for demolition and was only saved when a coalition of artists and architects came up with the wonderful idea of using the space to house the exhibitions and collections of the BCSC, which opened its doors in the refurbished warehouse in 1989.

A giant red-and-white Tintin rocket pointed the way upstairs to the exhibition rooms where banks of A-frame stands presented a selection of the BCSC's 7,000 original drawings and magazines. I expect this would be interesting if you were familiar with any of the authors, but Ruben and I zigzagged our way through the displays of the likes of *Boule et Bill* and *Blondie en Blinkie*, leaving the peculiar odour of perfumed dog turd behind us, as we made our way to the Tintin room. Apart from the excitement of seeing some original Hergé sketches, the best part of this display was a large wall chart showing when all the characters arrived. Did you know that Captain Haddock first appeared in 1941 in *The Crab with the Golden Claws* and was then in every edition to *Tintin and the Picaros* in 1976? Professor Calculus only turned up for the first time in 1945 and Thomson and Thompson arrived in 1931, but mysteriously skipped 1960 and 1968. Do you care? Probably not, but the chart is an excellent source of information to store up and drop on those annoying Hergé know-it-alls, the self-declared Tintinologists, who pop up out of nowhere once they learn you have an interest in Belgium.

After visiting the BCSC, the next part of the Belgian *BD* experience is to follow the *BD* trail around the streets of Brussels. Thirty-three house-sized murals of various Belgian comic strips appear on random gable ends around the city centre. If you are not familiar with the characters, the walk on a winter's morning can be little more than a dangerous, frozen dog turd-avoiding skate along the icy pavements of Brussels, mundanely ticking off murals one by one. In order to increase the enjoyment level of this trek, some knowledge of the 'ninth art' is required and to this end I have compiled a summary for the reader of the main Belgian comic strips.

This information is also handy in case you find yourself short of conversation with a Belgian person, trapped in a lift with a Tintinologist or unexpectedly stuck between two Belgians at a dinner party. I have listed the comic strips in chronological order, which conveniently lets us start with Hergé – the grand master of Belgian *BD* and a name to hold on to for that inevitable 'ten famous Belgians' question.

Les Aventures de Tintin
Original language: French
Creator: Georges Remi, aka Hergé
Year created: 1929
Tintin's creator, Georges Prosper Remi, was born in the French-speaking sector of Brussels in 1907. For his pen name he inverted the initials of his first and last names, RG, which, when pronounced in French, create the name 'Hergé'. He was just twenty-two years old when he introduced Tintin to the world in the 10 January 1929 edition of *Le Petit Vingtième*, a weekly children's supplement to the Catholic newspaper *Le Vingtième Siècle*. The comic strip was an immediate success and sales of *Le Vingtième Siècle* soared on Thursdays as eager readers picked up the supplement to find out what had happened in the next instalment of Tintin's first adventure: *Tintin in the Land of the Soviets*.

Tintin was cast as a boy reporter on *Le Petit Vingtième*, living an ordinary life that exploded into excitement as he chased baddies across the world. Hergé also introduced a new style of drawing: *la ligne claire* – artwork with strong basic colours, simple graphics and a 'less is more' philosophy, encouraging readers to use their imagination as they followed the characters on their adventures. Despite never having visited the countries he wrote about, Hergé had an exceptional eye for detail and undertook meticulous research using newspaper clippings, photographs and contemporary travelogues to ensure the accuracy of his drawings and storyline. He had a keen interest in modern art, even squeezing the Russian artist Kasimir Malevich's 'Black Square' into *Tintin in the Land of the Soviets*. (In case you are wondering, that's not a painting of a lesser-known relative of Moscow's Red Square, it is literally a black square painted on a white canvas. Some people like this kind of thing.) Hergé was still experimenting at this time and it was only on the eighth page of *Tintin in the Land of the Soviets*, when Tintin drove his captured open-topped Mercedes at high speed, that he gained his trademark hairstyle, leading to his name in Flemish: *Kuifje*, which translates as 'Quiff', or more precisely as 'Little Quiff' or 'Quiffy'. Fortunately the name Tintin was retained for the English translations. I'm not sure that *The Adventures of Quiffy* would have had quite the same appeal, especially as I learn from the Urban Dictionary that 'quiffy' has a wide variety of interesting meanings, none of which I can imagine Hergé was thinking of when he came up with the name. *Tintin in the Land of the Soviets* was written under the influence of Hergé's right-wing Catholic editor, Father Norbert Wallez, and delivers a clunky anti-communist message. His second book, *Tintin in the Land of the Congo* steers way off the course of political correctness, celebrating the worst of Belgian colonialism. Hergé later called these books '*les péchés de jeunesse*' ('the sins of youth'), and once he was free from Father Norbert and right-wing Catholic control he was able to develop his own storylines, fighting racists in *The Blue Lotus* and mocking fascists in *King Ottokar's Sceptre*. Hergé faced stiff competition from the American comics that were flooding Europe, but *Les Adventures de Tintin* struck a chord with his Belgian readers. He offered a realism that was different to the American imports, with their flying superheroes, aliens and Gotham City Batmobiles. The arrival of the Germans in Belgium in World War Two heralded the closure of *Le Vingtième Siècle* and *Le Petit Vingtième*, and Hergé moved to the Nazi-supervised newspaper *Le Soir*, becoming editor of its youth supplement, *Le Soir Jeunesse*, in October 1940. Paper shortages during the war led to a change in style, as Hergé was forced to write in fewer strips, quickening the pace and inserting more jokes. His first story was *The Crab with the Golden Claws* which saw the arrival (as we know from the chart in the BCSC) of a new character: the blistering barnacles-cursing Captain Haddock. World War Two put the American imports on hold, and despite the production difficulties and the close supervision of the occupying forces, the Belgian comics flourished. After the war, the publication of comic strips in France was restricted by the French government, nervous about the possibility of comic strips being used for political means. The Belgians had no such constraints, and with the end of Nazi censorship and before the American competition could regroup, the Belgians secured their place as world-leaders in *BD*. Hergé left *Le Soir* at the end of the war, co-founding a weekly magazine, *Le Journal de Tintin*, publishing both French and Flemish editions for the Franco–Belgian market. At its peak, in part due to a clever marketing hype involving *les chèques Tintin* (something along the lines of

Green Shield stamps), *Le Journal de Tintin* sold a staggering 500,000 copies a week and together with its rival, *Le Journal de Spirou,* became a hotbed of Belgian *BD* talent. As the comic strips flourished, the newly formed Studio Hergé pumped out albums – twenty-three in all, reprints of the early releases and new albums up to *Tintin and the Picaros* in 1976. A twenty-fourth album, the unfinished *Tintin and Alph-Art*, was published posthumously in 1986, neatly rounding off Hergé's life-long love of modern art from his black square homage in his very first album to *Alph-Art* – a story based around an avant-garde Brussels art gallery. After his death, his widow, the admirably named Fanny Remi (née Flamynck) inherited the rights to Hergé's work and set up the Hergé Foundation. In 2009 a Hergé museum was eventually opened in Louvain-La-Neuve on the outskirts of Brussels, where much of his work can be seen, including his lesser-known and unless you are Belgian, not very interesting, Quick & Flupke characters. Tintin's popularity has led to a succession of unauthorised and copyright-infringing spoofs. One of the most outlandish of these is the seriously out of order *Tintin in Thailand*, written by a Bud E. Weyser, in which the deposed dictator, General Alcazar, is running a bar in Chang Mai. Tintin and friends come to visit and the story takes a twist not usually seen in Hergé's books: Haddock and Calculus get off with prostitutes, Tintin comes out of the closet and Alcazar runs off with a ladyboy. I can't think why the Hergé Foundation didn't approve. All that's missing is a Quiffy and a set of ping-pong balls. My former employer also had a run-in with the Hergé Foundation. Working in the Holiday Inn, Lhasa in Tibet in the late 1980s, we turned the failed delicatessen (we had long given up on the hope of finding anything 'delicate' to sell on the Tibetan plateau) into a small bar. We named it the 'Chang Bar', *Chang* being the name of the local barley beer and also rather conveniently, the name of Tintin's Chinese friend who Tintin comes to rescue in my favourite Hergé adventure, the superb *Tintin in Tibet*. Someone (not me, just for the record, in case the Hergé Foundation lawyers are still on the case) had the bright idea of decorating the bar with framed pages from *Tintin in Tibet*, and the hotel's artist made a stunning mural using *la ligne claire* method for the entire back wall of the bar. Who from the Hergé Foundation would ever find out? None other than the redoubtable Fanny, widow of Hergé and creator of the Hergé Foundation, who made an unannounced visit to Tibet in the mid-1990s. Madame Remi, holder of the copyright to Hergé's works, was aghast at this unauthorised use of the Tintin name. The Hergé Foundation is fiercely protective of the Tintin brand, and as we were to learn, has a stipulation that it cannot be associated in any way with alcohol or tobacco. Our chances of receiving permission to name a bar after one of his characters and filling it with knock-off Tintin memorabilia were rather slim. It was the end of the Chang Bar. At least there were no arrests, as there had been in Brussels following a sting operation around the outlawed *Tintin in Thailand*. These spoofs and dodgy bars in obscure parts of the world are all testament to the international success of Tintin. While most of the Belgian comic strips manage to go no further than the Franco–Belgian borders, Tintin has sold an astonishing 200 million albums worldwide, with subsequent TV, computer games, clothing lines, shops and even Steven Spielberg/Peter Jackson films bringing Tintin to an ever-growing audience.

Hergé's last wish, that there could be no new Tintin books after his death, has had the odd effect of immortalising his creation, and we can rest assured that brand Tintin will keep popping up around the world, whether in new animated Hollywood films, Happy Meal tie-ins, or themed shows in Patpong.

Spirou (*Flemish: Robbedoes*)
Original language: French
Creator: Robert Velter aka Rob-Vel
Year created: 1938

In marked contrast to Tintin, Spirou is practically unheard of outside the Franco–Belgian countries. However, within Belgium, saying that you have never heard of Spirou is like telling an IT person that you have never heard of Microsoft. Spirou is massive in Belgium. Massively massive. It is the story of a young reporter (originally a bellhop from the Hotel Moustique) who goes on adventures aided by a friendly squirrel called Spip. During World War Two the publisher bought Spirou from its creator, Robert Velter, leading to the unusual situation of the copyright resting with the publisher, who commissioned different teams of artists and writers to pick up the Spirou baton and run with it for each new generation of readers. This worked well in the early years, with new characters being introduced to liven up the stories: Fantasio, Spirou's best friend, arrived in 1944 and eccentric inventors and new super baddies were added in the 1950s and 60s. The writer André Franquin added South American monkey-like animals called Marsupilami, which went on to feature in their own best-selling comic strips spawning cuddly toys and even a Disney cartoon. Franquin had one of the longest stints writing the *Spirou et Fantasio* albums until he got bored in the 1960s and started writing what look very much like spoofs of his own work. Spirou buffs like to debate when Franquin turned and if you are stuck in the lift with your Belgian, you might want to throw in the question, 'Was it in *QRN sur Bretzelburg* or in *Panade à Champignac* that Franquin first lost the plot?' This should keep them going for a while. Like Tintin, Spirou was the lead comic strip in a weekly magazine, *Le Journal de Spirou*, and together the two magazines dominated the huge Franco–Belgian *BD* market. While their glory days may well be over and the Flemish language version of *Spirou* was discontinued in 2005, French language *Spirou* still sells over 100,000 copies a week – more than many of the Belgian newspapers. Not bad for a kiddie cartoon created before World War Two.

Suske en Wiske (*French: Bob et Bobette*)
Original language: Flemish
Creator: Willy Vandersteen
Year created: 1945
You might think that Belgium would be knee-deep in Tintin and Spirou magazines by now, with no room for any other artists, but the Belgians' insatiable appetite for *BD* seems to know no bounds. *Suske en Wiske*, first appearing as a daily comic strip in *De Nieuwe Standaard* newspaper in 1945, is the original Flemish blockbuster. *Suske en Wiske* are a girl and boy team who go on adventures around Belgium, the Netherlands and fictional countries, having fun and doing the standard chasing of baddies. The drawing is *la ligne claire* style, with Suske, the boy, rather Tintinesque with a small spike in the place of Tintin's quiff, and Wiske, the blonde-haired girl with a red

bow in her hair and her trademark white dress. Success in the English language has been hard to come by for the creator, Willy Vandersteen, with a flop translation in the US under the name *Willy and Wanda* (perhaps attracting the kind of reader who was expecting something different between the covers) and the UK translation *Spike and Suzy* not faring much better. Current hopes for breaking into the major export markets lie with *Susu and Weiwei*, a Chinese translation of ten albums. But, and this is the hard bit to understand, Willy really doesn't need it – his work already sells at the rate of three million albums a year, having sold over 200 million since 1945! Putting this into context, Willy has sold half as many *Suske en Wiske* albums as J.K. Rowling's total Harry Potter sales. The Flemish are naturally very proud of their *stripverhaal* grandmaster (even if no one else has ever heard of him), and a bronze bust of Willy stands outside the Aldi in his home town of Kalmthout. There are even statues of *Suske en Wiske* dotted strategically around Flanders where the Flemish can admire the work of their best-selling author: one on the Belgian coast at Middelkerke; another in Antwerp Zoo; and a third in a shopping gallery in Hasselt. There is something very Belgian about this – while the rest of the world reserves bronzes for forgotten politicians, generals and monarchs, the Belgians are busy churning them out for cartoon characters.

Blake and Mortimer
Original language: French
Creator: Edgar P. Jacobs
Year created: 1946
This is a story of a duo of trench coat-wearing detectives: the improbably long-chinned Captain Francis Blake from MI5

and his friend the ginger-bearded pipe-smoking scientist, Philip Mortimer. The chinny, gingery heroes of this best-selling series are decidedly British, often defeating their nemesis Colonel Olrik in the streets of London, yet there are fewer Brits who have heard of Blake and Mortimer than there are characters in one of their adventures. Another huge Belgian author selling in volume only to the Franco–Belgian audiences.

Lucky Luke
Original language: French
Creator: Maurice de Bevere, aka Morris
Year created: 1946
Lucky Luke is the story of a sharp-shooting cowboy who rides in the Wild West on his trusty steed, the Jolly Jumper, aided by a rather stupid dog called Rantanplan. Together they save goodies and chase baddies. From his start in *Spirou* magazine in December 1946, Lucky Luke grew to become one of Belgium's most successful *BD* heroes, spawning TV shows, films and eighty albums. But unlike Tintin, Lucky Luke has not stood the test of time. The jokes are clichéd, shocking racial stereotypes pop up every now and again, and Lucky Luke's main habits of chain-smoking and gun-toting are both frowned upon today as anti-social.

Nero
Original language: Flemish
Creator: Marc Sleen
Year created: 1947
Nero is an unlikely character to be a comic strip hero. He is a dim, balding, middle-aged, rotund figure. Fortunately he is

assisted by his exceptionally clever five-year-old son Adhemar, and together they go on adventures around the world, often to Africa but always returning to Flanders at the end of the story in time to have a slap-up dinner of Belgian waffles. His creator, Marc Sleen, had none of the assistance of the studios at Tintin and Spirou, where teams would work on story lines and juniors would colour in the pictures. Sleen toiled away alone at *De Nieuwe Standaard* newspaper, creating a daily panel of two rows with a cliff-hanger ending that would eventually be put together into an album. Sleen is recognised by the *Guinness Book of World Records* as being the world's most prolific comic strip artist, having produced nearly 126,000 individual drawings, and even has a museum (and yes, bronze statues) dedicated to his work in the same road as the BCSC. As an indication of the high esteem for the 'ninth art' in Belgium, the Marc Sleen museum was opened by no less than King Albert II, who, as a native French-speaker, admitted to having learnt Flemish by reading *Nero*. If it is anything like my French from Asterix, he will have been very good at saying the Flemish for '*Bif!*', '*Poof!*' and '*Paf!*'; no doubt useful vocabulary for dealing with non-government forming Flemish politicians.

Jommeke
Original language: Flemish
Creator: Jef Nys
Year created: 1955
Jommeke is a young Flemish boy with a pudding bowl mop of straw-blond hair, and a parrot on his shoulder. I am told that the stories are funny. Unlike Tintin, there are no politics or trendy modern art and Jef Nys wrote in his will that the

Jommeke series should be continued after his death, so we can expect straw-hair boy to continue catching baddies and being hilariously funny (if you are Flemish) for some time to come. The stories haven't translated that well into other languages, not even into French. But with nearly 250 albums and sales of over 51 million to date, Jef probably wasn't too concerned about the export market.

Gaston Lagaffe (Flemish: Guust Flater)
Original language: French
Creator: André Franquin
Year created: 1957
Gaston is a rather annoying character: a lazy, irritating, office junior who spends his day taking naps and avoiding work. Apparently this is very funny. He is certainly very popular, having sold more than 30 million albums to date and with more than 300 licensed products to his name. André Franquin created Gaston while writing *Spirou et Fantasio* stories, taking the character with him when he left *Spirou*. An American translation in the 1990s, *Gomer Goof*, failed to take the English-speaking world by storm, and Gaston remains a distinctly Belgian phenomenon. Belgian slapstick. Need I say more?

Les Schtroumpfs (Flemish: the Smurfs)
Original language: French
Creator: Pierre Culliford, aka Peyo
Year created: 1958
Sadly, there can't be many people in the world who are unfamiliar with these smug little blue gnome-like creatures, living in mushrooms in their little Smurf village, speaking their

Smurf language and spending their time being chased by the evil Gargamel and his loathsome cat. What is probably less well known is that the two largest collections of Smurfobilia (that's general Smurf-related memorabilia) are located in Belgium – land of the Smurf's creator: Pierre Culliford. The owner of the largest collection, perhaps understandably, likes to keep her collection and identity secret, but no such shyness holds back Veronique and Michelle Leyseele from discussing their collection of over 12,000 bits of blue plastic. Known collectively as 'The Sisters' they organise the climax of the Smurf collectors' calendar – the annual Blue Paradise Smurf Fair, where 600 people from around the world descend on the town of Evergem to trade, swap and drool over small plastic figures and anything which has had the word 'Smurf' inserted into its name. On 25 June 2011, in a PR hype of gargantuan proportions, a *Guinness Book of World Records* attempt was launched for the snappily titled 'Largest Gathering of People Dressed as Smurfs within a 24-hour Period in Multiple Venues'. A record-breaking total of 4,891 Smurf fans took part, including an enthusiastic blue-painted, Belgian flag-waving crowd under the Atomium in Brussels. The reason for this euphoria? 'Global Smurfs Day'. And the reason for 'Global Smurfs Day'? A creation by the clever marketing people at Sony Pictures in order to garner as much publicity as possible prior to the release of their first 3D Smurf film. What it must be like to have a bottomless marketing budget and a room full of 'creatives':

'Let's invent a Global Smurfs Day!'

'Let's get as many suckers as possible to paint themselves blue – in as many countries as possible – and get a world record!'

'Let's paint an entire town blue!'

'What?'

This is when the meeting should have been disbanded, and the creatives sent back to their cubicles, but the 'painting a town blue' idea stayed on the flip chart and 4,000 litres of Smurf-blue paint later the small *pueblo* of Júzcar, perched high in the Andalusian hills above Marbella, received a life-changing makeover. You may think that having your village turned Smurf-blue for a publicity stunt would not be well-received, but the residents of Júzcar voted in December 2011 to keep their new Smurfiness and not return to their traditional white. The Smurfs, or *Los Pitufos* in Spanish, have been good to Júzcar. Prior to the transformation, a mere 300 visitors a year made their way to the hillside village. In the first six months since becoming Smurf-blue they received 80,000 tourists, and at this rate the Júzcar economy may soon be overtaking Madrid's. Peyo, the Smurfs' creator would no doubt find this very amusing. His Smurfs have come a long way since he first introduced them to the world in a 1958 edition of *Spirou* magazine. Smurf legend has it that the original name for the Smurfs – *les Schtroumpfs* in French – was decided upon during a dinner between Peyo and his Belgian friend and fellow comic strip author, André Franquin (of Spirou and Gaston Lagaffe fame). Peyo forgot the word for salt and asked Franquin to pass him 'le schtroumpf'. Franquin replied, 'Here's your schtroumpf, when you are done schtroumpfing, schtroumpf it back.' And so the word 'Schtroumpf', the Walloon, and original, word for 'Smurf' was created. Smurf legend continues that the pair spent the entire weekend talking in their new language. What a fun-packed two days that must have been.

The Smurfs join Tintin as the only Belgian comic strips to have made major breakthroughs onto the world stage. The turning point for the Smurfs was in 1981 when Hanna-Barbera created a TV cartoon show, pumping new shows mercilessly through our TV screens for the next eight years. I shall leave the last word on the Smurfs to the members of the online Smurf Fan Club who were asked to vote on the question: 'OK, so weird question, but who else had a crush on Smurfette?' I am pleased to report that only 20 per cent voted for 'Hell yeah, she was banging, lol' and a rational majority of 80 per cent voted for 'Hell no, u weirdo,' demonstrating that there may still be hope for mankind.

Epoxy
Original language: French
Creators: Jean Van Hamme and Paul Cuvelier
Year created: 1968
Perhaps bored of writing for the weekly *Tintin* magazine, Paul Cuvelier, who was adept at painting nudes, and Jean Van Hamme, who had some rather alternative story lines in his head, worked together in 1968 to produce *Epoxy* – the first European adult comic and the start of a new genre: Belgian adult comix. It is curious that this should happen in deeply Catholic Belgium, where the mere thought of a minor premarital flirtation in the 1960s would have meant a trip to Lourdes and at least a month of self-flagellation. Even more curious that the choice of their first erotic comic was some romp with Greek gods, large-bottomed nudes and aroused centaurs. The mind boggles. Current Belgian adult comix leave nothing to the imagination, and I never cease to be amazed

that graphic and deeply unpleasant porn sits happily in the same rack in the bookshops as *Suske en Wiske* and the Smurfs.

De Kiekeboes
Original language: Flemish
Creator: Rob Merhottein, aka Merho
Year created: 1977
De Kiekeboes is a real 'comic' with the emphasis on humour (albeit Belgian) rather than adventure. The story follows the trials and tribulations of a 'typical' Flemish family: *de Kiekeboes*. Marcel, the balding middle-aged father, is the main protagonist and the entertainment is provided by the antics of his extended family, neighbours, ex-wife and his busty, mini-skirted daughter, called Fanny. (I didn't make that up.) Merho says on the official *de Kiekeboes* website that the character he most resembles is Fanny. Interesting. Perhaps this is what makes him the best-selling author in Flanders, with 128 albums to his name to date and current sales within Belgium of a staggering 800,000 albums a year.

Thorgal
Original language: French
Creator: Jean Van Hamme
Year created: 1977
Thorgal is at the opposite end of the *BD* spectrum to *de Kiekeboes*. There is no jokey middle-aged Dad with his flirty, buxom daughter; instead think blood-thirsty Vikings meets *Aliens* and *The Lord of the Rings*. There is even a character called 'Gandalph the Mad', father of Thorgal, who spends his spare time, when he is not terrorising innocent villagers, trying

to kill his son. It is all very strange. Perhaps unsurprisingly, Thorgal is not that well known beyond its Franco–Belgian readership, except in the northern Scandinavian countries, where Lordi-loving Finns consume vast quantities of it.

Le Chat
Original language: French
Creator: Philippe Geluck
Year created: 1983
Le Chat is a large cat with a bulbous nose who stands upright and is normally found wearing a suit and tie. It is clever humour, and you need to speak very good French to appreciate the puns and word play. I wish I found it funny. If you mention that you are a fan of *Le Chat* to the Belgians you are stuck between at your dinner party, they will be very impressed, unless of course they are Flemish speakers.

Kabouter Plop
Original language: Flemish
Creator: Studio 100
Year created: 1997
Not all the comic strip albums packing the shelves of the Belgian bookshops have come from the traditional weekly cliff-hanger in the newspaper route. *Urbanus* is a comic strip written by a stand-up comedian of the same name, *FC De Kampioenen* is the comic book series of a popular TV sitcom, and then there is my favourite, the story about a large gnome and his gnome friends: *Kabouter Plop*. (*Kabouter* translates as 'gnome'.) This runs counter to my rampant gnomophobia, and I am at a loss as to why I find Plop so amusing. It certainly

can't be the repetitive Plop music (*'Eeh Oh, Eeh Oh, Sloebi Doebi Dabi Dee'*), which is still ringing in my ears from the CD of the same name that was played for hours in the car when the children were small, or from sitting through the Plop live-shows, or from the visits to Plopsaland – the Plop-related theme parks that attract two million visitors a year in Belgium. I hope that the reason is not due to a subconscious attraction to low-grade toilet humour, but it may lie in the fact that the Belgians see nothing funny in saying the word 'Plop'. *Plopsa Indoor*, the indoor theme park – not funny. *Plopsa Winkel*, the high-street shop selling Plopobilia – not funny. They don't even find anything vaguely humorous in the main character's frequently repeated catch phrase: *'Plopper de plopper de plop!'* Or the audience participation rapping section on track number five on the 'Best of' Plop CD collection, in which Plop calls out his name and the audience (i.e. everyone in my car) shouts it back to him:

Kabouter Plop: *'Plop!'*

All together: *'Plop!'*

Kabouter Plop: *'Plop!'*

All together: *'Plop!'*

All together: *'Plopper de plopper de plop!'*

Kabouter Plop lives in the Plop forest along with his gnome friends Kabouter Lui the postman (who is lazy), Kabouter Klus (who makes things) and Kabouter Kwebbel (a girl gnome who talks and giggles a lot). Plop's red gnome hat has two pointy ends with bells on, which are normally drooping down. When he is surprised, the ends with the bells on (I was careful how to say that) become erect, accompanied by a rising whistling noise and his *'Plopper de plopper de plop!'* catchphrase. This is not amusing to Belgians. Plop and his friends go on adventures, which are captured in the comic strip books, in TV shows and even in feature-length films. The most bizarre of these is *'Plop in de Wolken'* ('Plop in the Clouds'), a feature film in which Plop and the crew fly in a hot air balloon, crash-landing in a forest where they encounter 'Kabouter Snot' (no need for translation) who forces them to eat his speciality: 'snot soup'. My children are still traumatised by this film and Belgian soup has never been seen in the same light again.

With the high population density of comic strip authors in Belgium there are of course many more Belgian comic strips than the best sellers and classics I have listed above. However, this list should provide enough knowledge of the 'ninth art' to keep even the most ardent Tintinologist or Belgian dinner party guest at bay, and hopefully a stroll around the Brussels *BD* trail will be slightly less weary. You might even be inspired to go in search of some Belgian *BD* of your own. For some of the older, more bizarre titles, you could try one of the many flea markets that are held most weekends in the larger towns. Liège and Tongeren have particularly good markets but for a more centrally located spot, try la Place du Jeu de Balle, a few minutes' walk from the Gare du Midi in the Marolles district of Brussels. The daily market here appears to have been created by emptying the contents of several dozen skips across the square. Some of the landfill has fallen on carpets laid out on the pavements and the rest is just sitting in large piles, waiting for prospective hagglers to rummage through before the dustmen clear it up at the end of the market. Ruben managed to find a

1954 Flemish edition of Hergé's *Destination Moon* on our last visit, and you never know what indispensable piece of old tat you will find. Perhaps that missing 1970s Smurfette model you have been looking for is lurking in a cardboard box amongst the Barbie torsos, Nana Mouskouri music cassettes and chipped ashtrays. If you would prefer something that feels less like picking over a rubbish dump, you could venture into one of the full blown comic strip stores, such as Europe's largest *BD* store: Mekanik in Antwerp. Here you can browse through thousands of titles, both new and second hand. They boast of having every European and US comic in stock, including some rare first editions. When Ruben and I flicked through the racks we found a tatty old copy of *King Ottokar's Sceptre* for €500 and a first edition of *The Seven Crystal Balls*; a snip at €1,950. We managed to resist the temptation to buy these but feeling that we ought to leave with something, purchased rubber gloves and a graffiti spray can each. We just need to find a wall now. So, Belgian comic strips, *bande dessinées*, BD, *stripverhalen*, – the 'ninth art' – is it interesting? I would happily describe it as a giant snooze-fest, something of practically no interest to anyone beyond the Franco–Belgian–Benelux borders, apart from some lonely perv with his 'collector's' copy of 1968 Belgian centaur porn. However I can't reach this conclusion because of one man: Georges Prosper Remi. His creation of Tintin and *la ligne claire* propels the 'ninth art' from the depths of boredom to the epicentre of the interesting zone. 'Hergéen realism' inspired a new generation of *BD* artists, and through putting drug barons, despots and diamond thieves behind bars, his stories ignited childhood dreams of exploration and adventure. Hergé's exotic tales lead to another contender for the interesting

146

list. Diamond thieves are tempting – two of the largest diamond heists in history (£58 million and £30 million) took place in Belgium, but it is Tintin's adventure to Congo that might lead to something interesting. What were the Belgians up to? How did tiny little Belgium end up with such a large slice of the African continent, and was the Belgian king really interested in bringing civilisation to the country, as his quote beneath the Atomium at the Brussels World Expo had claimed? Could there be anything of interest here?

CHAPTER 9
KING LEOPOLD'S CONGO

With the exception of some Flemish break-away extremists, who sit locked away in their bedrooms at night longing for an independent Republic of Flanders, the Belgians in general have a great affection for their royal family. As a little girl, Conny dreamt of growing up and marrying a prince (yes, sorry about the disappointment there) and my Belgian mother-in-law had an unnatural degree of knowledge, not just of the Belgian monarchy, but of the comings and goings of all European royals. In a curious Belgian tradition, a small selection of the population even gets to join the royal family in a type of reproductive lottery, as every seventh consecutive son and seventh consecutive daughter in a family has the king or queen as their godparent. I can vouch that this is true, as our wedding party on 7 August 1993 was one person short when Baudouin, who was meant to be taking the video, couldn't attend at the last minute as he had to be at the funeral of his godfather, King Baudouin I in Brussels. The seventh son/daughter having a royal godparent is a bizarre Belgian fact, but not one that's going to get on to the interesting list and I need to go back to the first Belgian royals in order to explore the next area for my quest.

Despite the occasional invasion by the Dutch in the early years of the country's independence, Belgium's first king, Leopold I, ruled over a remarkably peaceful and prosperous land for his thirty-five-year reign. He busied himself with the Industrial Revolution which had taken a foothold in Belgium on its way into mainland Europe, and on 5 May 1835 he opened the Continent's first railway line – a 25 km stretch from Brussels to Mechelen. When he wasn't playing trains he was writing to his favourite niece, Queen Victoria, giving her advice on how to run her country. Having arranged their marriage, he would also write to his nephew, Prince Albert, (the Saxe-Coburgs liked to keep it in the family) and he spent his reign generally governing and administering his beloved new country in a wise, if unadventurous, way. While certain enthusiasts in the European train-spotting fraternity might get excited about the first train line, this is not what has brought me to take a look at the reign of the Leopolds. In fact it is not Leopold I who I am after, but his progeny, the imaginatively named Leopold II, who had altogether greater plans for Belgium, and did something that just might get a flash of recognition on the interesting list.

Leopold I passed away peacefully at the Royal Palace in Laeken on 10 December 1865, and the thirty-year-old Leo II took the throne. Leopold II was not interested in petty administration, arranging family weddings or dressing up as a train driver. He had plans for Belgium. Not small-scale European diplomacy plans but massive, history-making plans to catapult Belgium into the superpower league. It was the time of the great European empires: the British ruled over nearly ten million square miles, the Germans, Dutch, Italians, Spanish and Portuguese all had large swathes of the world map painted in their colours and European flags fluttered from the rooftops of colonial buildings from Abyssinia to Zululand. Poor King Leopold II had nothing. Not a sausage. Imagine his embarrassment at the royal dinner parties when his *confrères* would brag about their exotic lands and the unimaginable riches of empire, and King Leo II didn't even have an uninhabited volcanic rock in the Atlantic with his name on. King Loser Leo II would sit at the end of the table, shuffling about on his chair, looking down at his feet as the others told their enthralling tales. The humiliation for Loser Leo was unbearable. When the party guests had gone he sat alone stroking his not-inconsiderable, practically of ZZ Top-proportions beard and decided that Belgium would no longer be the laughing stock of Europe. King Leo II had a dream: Belgium would be a mighty nation, with empire, wealth and power. No one would ignore him at parties, no one would ever say that Belgium was boring again – Leo needed an empire, and fast.

After a failed and frankly ridiculous attempt at persuading the Queen of Spain to give him the Philippines, he was forced to look elsewhere for an easier target. The most obvious choice for quick empire-building was Africa: a rich continent with large tracts of unexplored territory and land grabs by the Europeans happening on an almost daily basis. He had to act quickly, but sitting in the Palais Royal in Brussels, without the infrastructure of empire or the military might of the other European nations, how could he quickly misappropriate a sizeable chunk for himself? His cunning plan was to employ the services of explorer-for-hire, Henry Morton Stanley, of 'Dr Livingstone I presume?' fame, to travel to Africa, find a large piece of land which no one else had claimed yet, and stick a Belgian flag in it quick before anyone else turned up. With apologies to readers without Internet access for my frequent YouTube references, if you are able to log on now take a quick look at Eddie Izzard's superb 'Do you have a flag?' (Lego version) for a short explanation of how empire was won.

Deciding that following in Stanley's footsteps around Central Africa for six months would have been a bit beyond my research budget, I settled for the next best thing – a trip to the Congo Museum on the outskirts of Brussels to see how Leopold's empire-building dream had turned out. It took me nearly as long to reach the museum as it would have done to fly from Brussels to Kinshasa, starting with the monotonous train journey to Bruxelles Central followed by a few stops on the Metro to Montgomery station, then a tram ride along the grandiose Avenue de Tervuren and through a strange no man's land of graffiti-covered trees until stopping abruptly at the tram terminus in Tervuren. There was no sign to the museum, but the friendly tram driver waved me up the road, where several hundred metres later I stood outside Leopold's Congo Museum, now officially titled the Royal Museum for Central Africa. It was a most un-African setting: Leo had built a replica of an eighteenth-century European palace in the style of Versailles, with sweeping terraced gardens, lakes and standard roses. The song of blackbirds filled the air and water gushed from the fountains. The palatial splendour theme continued inside with copious amounts of inlaid marble lining the massive domed entrance hall and a circle of gilt statues looking down serenely on the visitors.

After the expectation built up from the lengthy train, Metro, tram and hike to reach the museum, the contents were, to say the least, an anti-climax. The first glass cabinets encountered had titles such as 'Axes and Clay Pots' and contained, no surprise here, axes and clay pots. A glass cabinet labelled *la cèramique* contained: ceramic pots. No history, no context, no explanation, just a ceramic pot with a label in French which translated as 'ceramic pot'. It's not difficult to walk quickly past these static displays of inanimate objects, and I soon found myself at the end of the first hall and the start of the section devoted to African animals – great, small, slimy and creepy. A huge stuffed elephant took centre stage. It would be hard to find a sadder-looking object. When I looked into its dusty glass eyes, all I could think of was the journey this poor beast had undertaken, from the magnificent creature it had been while minding its own business in central Africa, to being shot, emptied, preserved, transported, stuffed and mounted – all for the pleasure of gawping turn-of-the-century Belgians. I tried to imagine the scene when the stuffed elephant was unveiled to the public for the first time, no doubt with whoops and gasps and possibly with some fainting of the long-dressed, bonnet-hatted ladies. Today a few one Euro cent coins lay at his feet where visitors had tossed them at him – perhaps thrown there in the hope that Dusty the Elephant may convey some kind of wishing-well powers, or perhaps just thrown at him out of pity.

The next hall was devoted to smaller dead animals. Six dead crabs on some sand. Glass jam jars filled with formaldehyde, pickled earthworms and tape worms. Glass cases of mosquitoes, some barely a millimetre long, painstakingly pinned out and labelled with the name, location, date and collector's name. A Dr J. Schweiz seems to have been particularly prolific and there can hardly have been a Congolese invertebrate that he didn't pin, mount or pickle. Flies, beetles, ticks, ants, wasps, butterflies and termites were all laid out flat, spread-eagled and speared in the name of early twentieth-century science. As if the lengthy tape worms and bilharzia-carrying snails (is it true that they infect you by crawling inside your bottom while swimming?) hadn't been enough to discourage the thought of ever visiting the Congo in person, the next hall put an end to the idea once and for all. Two giant crocodiles stared straight at me – jaws wide open with long mouthfuls of razor-sharp teeth ready to snap closed. Fortunately the Congo Museum pair is 1910 vintage, and very stuffed, so unlikely to do any harm, but they did set the mind racing as to what a stroll along the banks of the Congo River might lead to. They reminded me of a news clipping I had seen of an expert kayaker who had been happily paddling down the Lukuga River in December 2010, raising awareness for the clean water crisis in Africa, when a giant croc leapt out of the water and dragged him below. He was never seen again.

To set my mind straight I mused over the fine collection of pickled frogs and toads in the display cabinets around the edge of the room, just out of reach of the crocs. Presumably someone finds exhibits of bottled amphibians interesting, but I'm afraid their grey elongated bodies with extended legs and flippers floating around in specimen jars didn't quite do it for me and I hurried into and through the next hall, which contained hundreds of stuffed birds of various shapes and sizes. Just when I thought that there couldn't possibly be any more dead animals, the last hall presented itself, with rows of wall-mounted rhino and zebra heads. At the time of my visit, the rhinos, while missing bodies, still had complete heads; however due to a spate of rhino horn robberies, the heads have now had their horns removed and may now be in competition with Dusty for the Saddest Exhibit on Display award.

Thankfully the museum has changed its focus from the pickling, stuffing and mounting of every living creature in the Congo, to becoming a centre for research and home to 80 scientists and 175 trainees who have been bestowed with the highly commendable aim of contributing to Africa's sustainable development. I have also learnt that the museum is undergoing a several-years-long period of renovation, so hopefully by the time you read this, the tape worms and pickled nematodes will be back in the research labs where they belong.

Once through the dead zones, I found myself at the most interesting part of the museum: a display of Stanley memorabilia and the story of King Leopold II's empire. Leo's journey from sitting alone at the royal dinner table with no empire to acquiring an African land mass of nearly a million square miles had not been easy. For a start, the Belgian government had been singularly unsupportive, having seen through Leo's hare-brained schemes and wanting nothing to do with them. Leo was left to set up the Association Internationale du Congo (AIC) on his own, in his capacity as a private individual. The AIC was ostensibly a study and research organisation bringing Christianity and 'civilisation' to the natives, but in reality it was merely a front for Leo's land-grabbing plans. He secretly dispatched Stanley to Africa in 1879, with instructions to plant flags and acquire as much territory as possible for the AIC. Stanley offered trinkets and cloth to the tribal chiefs in return for their land. If they didn't acquiesce he simply shot them and negotiated with the chief's newly appointed, and understandably compliant, successor. The chiefs were presented with lengthy Belgian legal documents, written in French, which in summary said 'I hereby hand over all my land to King Leopold II. Signed ....' For the most part, the tribal chiefs did not even have their own written languages, relying instead on an oral heritage, and the chance of understanding the significance of scratching an 'X' on the dotted line of Stanley's royal decrees was rather slim. Some of these grand documents were on display in the Congo Museum and for the second time in the day (the first was looking at the pickled tape worm collection) I felt rather ill. The shaky 'X' was plain to see, scrawled on the spot where a tribal chief had been hoodwinked or forced into handing over his people's lands, for ever.

Stanley was a prolific flag-planter and collected sufficient 'signed agreements' to amass an area of Central Africa a staggering eighty times larger than Belgium. This was a promising start, but Leo still had the threat of other Europeans coming along and removing his flags. As was often the case, luck was on his side when the colonial carve up of Africa came to a head at the Berlin Conference of 1884. The German Chancellor Otto van Bismarck had invited ambassadors and dignitaries from fourteen European nations to decide the fate of Africa. King Leo attended in person and declared to the fellow conference attendees that Africa was 'a magnificent cake' waiting to be sliced up by the 'civilising' Europeans. In the absence of any African delegates, who might have known a thing or two about their own continent, the Europeans spent three months drawing up the irrational geometric divisions that have led to many of the tribal tensions in present-day Africa. While the other delegates squabbled over longitude and latitude references, Leo managed to sneak out of the conference with a giant slice of the cake – nearly a million square miles in all – with the new name of the 'Congo Free State'. Astonishingly, this 'free' state was privately owned, 100 per cent, by a Mr Leopold II, King of Belgium. Leo could finally hold his head up high in the courts of Europe. He was no longer just a big beard and moustache, and he swung it about court to let everyone know. Leo had land to brag about and rubber and ivory, copper and minerals, exotic animals, grandiose monuments, a capital city bearing his name (Léopoldville), plans for museums, elephants to stuff and the promise of untold riches to come.

Nobody was laughing now, least of all the people of the Congo Free State, who were starting to learn the significance of putting a wobbly X on Stanley's bit of paper. Joseph Conrad wrote the brilliant, if fiercely depressing, *Heart of Darkness* in 1899, based on his experiences as the captain of a steamboat on the Congo River, exposing the greed, incompetence and brutality of Leopold's men. Leo was not too happy either. The promised riches were not coming fast enough and his mounting debts – the loans taken out to fund the Congo expeditions, policing a million square miles and the celebratory buildings back home of the Parc Cinquantenaire and the Congo Museum – needed paying off. Again, Leo struck lucky with his timing, as the rubber boom – the black gold of the late nineteenth century – began in earnest and the prospect of earning serious amounts of cash from the Congo became tantalisingly close. Leo needed a fast return and set his Congolese subjects ever higher quotas for rubber production. If the quotas were not met, the women and children would be kidnapped, the men mutilated or shot and entire villages raised to the ground. As news of the atrocities slowly came out of the country from a handful of disillusioned missionaries, journalists and civil servants, international pressure grew on the Belgian government to take control of the Congo. Leopold was unhappy with the government's interference and took solace in another of his pleasures, when at the age of sixty-five he caused a public outcry by shacking up with a sixteen-year-old French prostitute – so much for Catholic, conservative, boring Belgium.

As I left the Congo Museum I looked closer at the gilded statues in the entrance hall. The figures of tall, beautiful Belgians looked down benevolently on small African figurines. The inscription above one of them read, *La Belgique apportant le bien-être au Congo*: 'Belgium brings comfort to the Congo'. That's not exactly true now is it? Estimates for the death toll during Leo's reign of terror varies, with the average number being somewhere around ten million. That puts Leo on par with Hitler or Stalin in the league of genocide-happy super tyrants. Even Pol Pot only managed to exterminate two million of his people, yet in a pub quiz question 'Name the top ten mass murderers of all time', no one would ever think of scribbling the name of a long-forgotten Belgian king on the answer sheet. Not a fact that you find being trumpeted in the 'Welcome to Belgium' literature.

Leo tried desperately to hang on to his privately-owned Congo Free State, but in 1908 the Belgian government finally wrestled it away from him, renaming it the 'Belgian Congo' and putting an end to the brutality of the king's regime. They didn't put a stop to the forced labour quite so promptly, as money now poured into Belgian state coffers, and in return for the rubber, copper and diamonds coming out of the Congo, the Belgians sent in Catholic missionaries. Quite a swap. In 1930 Hergé sent his character Tintin to the Belgian Congo for his second expedition after *Tintin in the Land of the Soviets*. Still under the influence of Father Norbert, Hergé's right wing newspaper editor, it was not Tintin's finest hour. The text and drawings were so politically incorrect that *Tintin au Congo* was only translated into English in 1991 and now comes with a warning wrapper that has to be removed before opening the book, much like the health warning on cigarette packets, advising the reader that the contents may cause offence. No one seems to have taken more offence to the book than Congolese campaigner Bienvenu Mbutu Mondondo, who took out legal proceedings in Belgium in 2007 to get the book banned due to its alleged racist content. Bienvenu had to wait five years for the court's decision, which ultimately did not go his way, with the final conclusion that Hergé was not being deliberately racist but was just reflecting the colonial attitudes of the time. Bienvenu was not alone in being upset by *Tintin in the Congo*; anyone with the slightest care for animals would also be traumatised by the veritable bloodbath of big game hunting that Tintin conducts while in the Congo. He shoots, skins, kicks and clubs the various exotic animals he encounters, with the *pièce de résistance* being the young reporter inserting explosives into a live rhinoceros, by way of drilling a hole in its back, followed by the rhinoceros being blown to smithereens.

This page was dropped from later editions as Hergé tried to tone it down a bit.

I happen to agree that *Tintin in the Congo* should not be banned and that it serves as a useful reminder of the dreadful colonial attitude of the 1930s. I can't imagine that anyone in their right mind reading the book today would think that drawing 'golliwog' images and inserting explosives into live rhinoceroses would be morally acceptable.

Throughout the 1940s and 50s the Belgians continued to extract minerals in ever-increasing amounts, and a claim to fame that the Belgians don't make much fuss over is that the atomic bombs dropped on Hiroshima and Nagasaki were manufactured from finest-grade Belgian Congo uranium. After World War Two, the independence movements sweeping south from the Mediterranean meant that the Belgian Congo's days were numbered. Five African countries declared independence in the 1950s, most having fought their way out of French ownership, and in 1960 alone a whopping eighteen African states broke free of their colonial masters, including the Belgian Congo, which became the 'Republic of the Congo' on 30 June. It wasn't a good day for the Belgians. King Baudouin I, who is generally remembered as a benevolent and wise leader of the Belgians, arrived in Léopoldville for the ceremonial handover of power. His day didn't quite go according to plan when a Congolese man grabbed his ceremonial sword and danced off down the road with it. The independence celebrations didn't go much better as Baudouin temporarily suspended his usual good judgement by referring in the handover speech to the 'genius' and 'courage' of his grandfather King Leo II. Is this the same King Leo II, mass-murderer of the Congo with the blood of ten million Congolese on his hands? Needless to say it did not go down well, and the king received a hostile reception from Patrice Lumumba, the newly elected Prime Minister of the Republic of the Congo. The handover was a disaster and within days the Belgian government had sent 6,000 troops to the capital, without invitation, to oversee the rapid evacuation of Belgian nationals. The United Nations had to follow up with 20,000 troops and the 'Congo Crisis' developed as the former colony fell apart, becoming consumed by internal power struggles fuelled by the Cold War games of the USA and the USSR. In another dark day in Belgium's history, Belgian officers were complicit in the assassination of Prime Minister Lumumba who had made the mistake of taking sides with the Soviets. After a very shaky first five years of independence from the Belgians, the delightful Joseph Mobutu came to power with the backing of the CIA. In addition to becoming one of the most corrupt dictators in Africa's history, siphoning off an estimated $5 billion of the country's wealth into his own bank accounts, Mobutu was a serial name changer. He changed the country's name, somewhat ironically, to the 'Democratic Republic of the Congo' or DRC (not to be confused with the 'Peoples Republic of the Congo' – the former French colony across the river), and when he was bored with the DRC he changed the name to 'Zaire'. 'Léopoldville' became 'Kinshassa' and best of all, in true African dictator style, he changed his own name to Mobutu Sese Seko Kuku Ngbendu wa Za Banga which translates modestly as: 'the All-Conquering Warrior, Leaving Nothing but Fire in his Wake.' In 1997, with the Cold War over and nobody around to protect him, Mobutu the All-Conquering Warrior was finally ousted in the First Congo

War. 'Zaire' returned to being known as the 'Democratic Republic of the Congo'. In an uncanny parallel with Belgium's reputation as the cockpit of Europe, the DRC became Africa's favourite battleground in the late 1990s as armies from Rwanda, Uganda, Angola, Namibia and Zimbabwe fought in the five-year-long Second Congo War. This war became the world's deadliest conflict since World War Two, claiming the lives of over five million Africans. Today the country clings on to a fragile democracy, and there is at least some hope that the troubles are over. The Belgians, being morally obliged to help out their former colony, could share their own experiences of stabilising Europe after World War Two and at the very least could get the headquarters of the African Union moved to Kinshassa and fill the city with Afrocrats, or they could set up an Afrovision Song Contest or *Jeux Sans Frontiers* with Hutus and Tutsis dressed up as penguins with buckets of water. It's worth a try.

At the start of this chapter I had hoped to find some glimmer of interest in Belgium's empire and King Leo's Congo. The further my research took me, the further away from 'interesting' the idea of Belgian Empire and its legacy became. Apart from millions of deaths, what else did Leopold's Congo achieve? Conrad's *Heart of Darkness*, which led to Coppola's *Apocalypse Now*. Hergé's most dodgy Tintin adventure with the exploding rhinoceros. The atomic bombs of Hiroshima and Nagasaki. That's not a great list. I have to conclude that Leopold's Congo is a giant blood-soaked stain on Belgium's moral history.

Coming back from the Congo Museum in a very depressed state, I paid a visit to the gents' toilets at Bruxelles Centrale station, in the full knowledge that this would depress me even further. No doubt I would have to pay for the privilege of peeing in a dark subterranean urinal, rather than doing what every other visitor to the Congo Museum had done – pee against a tree by the tram terminus in Tervuren. Little did I know that the gents at Bruxelles Centrale was going to be party central. As I opened the door I was hit by the deep boom of Congolese music coming from a giant ghetto blaster being held high by a glorious Congolese Madame Pipi. In full national dress, Madame Pipi and her two friends swayed and laughed and sang to the fast-paced rumba. It was Congolese party time at the Bruxelles Centrale gents and the best €0.50 cents I have ever spent. I came out with my spirits lifted and reminded of the power of music to enrich the soul – even in an underground toilet. If I could be so moved by a short blast of Congolese rumba, what about the music of the Belgian people? Having failed to be inspired by Leopold's Congo, I need to look somewhere more uplifting, more hopeful in order to continue with my quest. What treasures will the Belgian music scene reveal?

CHAPTER 10
THE BELGIAN MUSIC SCENE

I once encountered a strangely coiffed showbiz-type person wearing an over-sized white suit in the gents' toilet of the Crowne Plaza hotel in Antwerp. I thought he was a has-been Belgian Elvis impersonator, perhaps in the hotel bathroom to take the Elvis impersonation to its final conclusion, but with no evidence of burgers or drugs in sight, I was glad to see that he followed me out alive and we went our separate ways. As he crossed the lobby, Conny whispered loudly to me:

'Look! That's Eddy Wally!'

'Eddy who?' I replied.

'You know. Eddy Wally!'

I didn't know. The fame of Eddy Wally, Belgium's twenty-second-highest selling artist of all time, had passed me by. I was blissfully unaware of his big hit, *'Ik spring uit een Vliegmachien'* ('I jump out of an Airplane'– please don't look it up) or that the tax-payers of Hasselt have invested a considerable sum in buying 115 of his outlandish suits for the city's fashion museum. Subsequent research has revealed that in addition to occupying the fringes of Belgian celebrity life, Eddy Wally is even famous in outer space, having an asteroid belt between Mars and Jupiter bearing his name. And to think Schuman only got a roundabout.

However, few Belgians would hold out Eddy Wally as the torchbearer of their nation's musical heritage. This epithet is granted instead to Jacques Brel, the mainstream crooner whose career spanned a quarter of a century from his first recording contract with Phillips in 1953. It wasn't always easy for Jacques, and his career started in a similar vein to that of our friend Fud Leclerc of Eurovision fame. There is a touch of the Fud about Jacques, with the same droning *chansons* and embarrassing early song contest defeats (Fud in the first Eurovisions, and Jacques managing to come twenty-seventh out of twenty-eight at the 1954 *Grand Prix de la Chanson* on the Belgian coast at Knokke). Fortunately for Jacques, their career paths soon parted, as Fud nose-dived into obscurity and Jacques shot to the stars (further even than Eddy's asteroid belt), selling over 25 million records and having his songs covered by artists ranging from David Bowie to Frank Sinatra, and Marlene Dietrich to Nirvana. I would have to describe Jacques as a bit of a Marmite chap. When you have the chance, take a look at 'Ne Me Quitte Pas' ('Don't Leave Me') on YouTube (the three minutes sixteen seconds, black-and-white 1959 version with the man in the corner) as a prime example of his work. How would you describe this? 'Beautiful and heart-rending' or 'dismal and depressive, verging on the suicidal'? A YouTube poster called Sarah seems to have enjoyed it, posting the comment: 'I just keep crying... I am 17 and just discovered the biggest belgian singer... So proud to be belgian!! [*sic*]' On the other hand, I find myself in agreement with the man in the background of the video clip who spends the three minutes and sixteen seconds of the song either staring blankly into space, chatting to his mate off camera, or closing his eyes and falling asleep.

Being only seventeen and Belgian, Sarah will be unaware that Belgium's most famous singer is of course the 1970s pseudo-punk sensation, Plastic Bertrand. Conny found my insistence that Plastic Bertrand was the most famous Belgian musician ever rather amusing at first, and then decidedly annoying. She was torn between wanting to be proud that I could instantly name a famous Belgian singer, and being appalled that the 'singer' I could name was Plastic Bertrand. Unfortunately for any culturally-sensitive Belgians, it is hard to find many people outside Belgium or the French-speaking countries who can hum a Jacques Brel tune unprompted, but ask anyone who was conscious during the 1970s about Belgian music and you are sure to have Plastic Bertrand's '*Ça Plane Pour Moi*' shouted back at you.

This should really be the end of the Plastic Bertrand one hit wonder story, but controversy erupted thirty years after the single's release in a royalty dispute when the hit's producer, a Mr Lou Deprijck, announced that it was he who had sung the lyrics and not Plastic. According to the mustachioed Mr Deprijck, who now lives in Thailand, Plastic's only contribution was to jump up and down a lot and wave his arms about while lip-syncing to Deprijck's vocals, not only on '*Ça Plane Pour Moi*' but also on four other tracks attributed to Plastic Bertrand. Incidentally, the 'j' is silent in 'Deprijck', which must liven up the tannoy announcements at Brussels airport when they call, 'Deprijck going to Thailand to proceed immediately to the gate. This is the last call for Deprijck to Thailand.'

The case has been to the Belgian courts twice, first in 2006 when the ruling came down that Plastic Bertrand was 'the legal performer', and then again in 2010 when a linguistic expert found in favour of Deprijck, having identified his southern Belgian accent in the lyrics. You have to feel sorry for Plastic Bertrand – there is a certain irony about not having good enough vocals to sing a punk song.

After Belgium's fifteen minutes of fame on the international stage with '*Ça Plane Pour Moi*', the Belgian music scene slid back into obscurity. If you disregard Belgium's Eurovision success of 1986 (not a difficult task), it wasn't until the 1990s when the extraordinarily large-trousered Benny B emerged from the Belgian hip hop scene, scratching his way to the top of the charts. It is well worth a quick YouTube look up of Benny B's completely inane '*Vous Êtes Fous*' ('You Are Mad'), which curiously I find myself watching more frequently than I can justify for research purposes. Think Vanilla Ice meets MC Hammer. Add Jedward hair, and just when you thought it couldn't get any worse, the rapping starts in French. And who would have thought that Ya Kid K (that's a person in case you were wondering – the rapper song-writer of Technotronic. 'Pump up the Jam'? Anyone remember them? Anyone at all?) is also largely Belgian, if you discount her first eleven years growing up in the Congo. Coincidentally, Ya Kid K also had a lip-syncing fight on her hands, with a blue-lipped model named Kelly F who was put on stage to mime to her vocals. Is this a Belgian trait? It does make one question the other great names. Perhaps the bored-looking man in the background of the Jacques Brel video is a ventriloquist. It would explain the look on Jacques' face.

More recently, bands such as Clouseau and the excellent Noordkap have enjoyed local fame, but nothing much beyond the Belgian or Benelux borders. The same can be said of K3, Belgium's answer to the Spice Girls; a clever, manufactured girl band managed by Studio 100 (the makers of Plop and a host of other children's TV programmes, comic strips and the Plop-related theme parks). The group's name, pronounced in Flemish as a Geordie would say 'car-dree', is derived from the first letters of the band members' names: Karen, Kristel and Kathleen. The tightly-focused target group for the band is pre-teen Belgian girls and their long-suffering parents. I expect that some musically-inclined Belgians may take exception to the inclusion of K3 in a chapter on the Belgian music scene, but I would hazard a guess that any Belgian with a daughter, niece, sister or granddaughter aged between two and twelve will have listened to considerably more K3 than any other Belgian music. I have certainly spent long hours in the car being subjected to the likes of 'Ya Ya Yippee' and 'Dat Ding Dat Je Dou'. To be honest, moving up to pre-teen music was quite a relief after the endless repetition of 'The Wheels on the Bus' and the Postman Pat theme tune, and I suspect that many a dad secretly enjoyed the transition to K3, trying not to be caught listening to the CD in the car when he was on his own. I never did that.

As with Fud and Jacques Brel, K3 didn't have an easy start to their career and in 1999 they crashed out of a selection contest for Belgium's Eurovision entry, with a judge describing them as 'an assortment of meat products'. That was rather cruel. 'Wholesome meat products' would have been a better description, and I am sure that ten years later when Kathleen, the blonde one, announced that she was leaving the group, many dads, I mean little girls, were broken-hearted. Smart and business-savvy as ever, Studio 100 did not let this be the demise of their money-spinning venture, but instead increased K3 coverage even further by hosting a prime-time reality TV show to find a replacement K: *'K2 zoekt K3'* ('K2 seeks K3'). This resulted in Dutch girl Josje Huisman replacing Kathleen. Surely there is an obvious error with this choice? I am not doubting Josje's singing, her ability to wear matching clothes to Karen and Kristel, and her dancing about skills, but did the judges not notice something wrong with her name? It's more K2J than K3.

However much I admire the clever marketing, and may or may not have enjoyed singing along to 'Ya Ya Yippee' when alone in the bathroom, I do recognise that the K3 phenomenon is not much more than manufactured pop schmaltz for little girls. Today's real Belgian music scene revolves around the *zommerfestivals* – the many superb music festivals that now fill the summer months. The largest of these is Rock Werchter, held by the small village of the same name just to the north of Leuven where 80,000 music fans congregate every July. St Bono, no less, has described Werchter as 'the best music festival in the world' and it regularly wins 'best festival' awards, beating Glastonbury time and again. Better than Glastonbury? Belgium's not looking so boring now!

Second in size and stature to Werchter is Pukkelpop, where 65,000 party-goers gather near the small village of Kiewit every August. 'Pukkelpop' translates literally as 'pimple-pop' or 'zit-pop' and as you may have guessed from the name, is aimed exclusively at the teenage or 'yoof' market. Realising that the massive infrastructure could be put to use for more than just one weekend, the local municipality decided in 2001 to open up the festival scene to an entirely different target market and came up with the idea of 'Rimpelrock' (literal translation: 'wrinkle-rock') – a rock festival for Belgian OAPs. As the site is only a few kilometres from the family's Belgian home in Hasselt, this presented me with two excellent opportunities for research: taking Hannah and Ruben (then aged fifteen and thirteen) to Pukkelpop – home of the pimples – and father-in-law (aged eighty-three) to Rimpelrock – land of the wrinkles.

Rimpelrock has a very reasonable €25 entrance fee but being over eighty, my father-in-law received a free VIP ticket, and a free pass for someone to accompany him. That would be me – thank you the City of Hasselt. On the Saturday before Pukkelpop, Conny's sister Betty drove us across the canal bridge and along the Kempische Steenweg, the long straight road that heads north towards Kiewit. We were dropped off near the church, and made our way to a Portakabin where we presented our letter with the promise of free tickets. It wasn't so much the blind leading the blind, but with our corresponding hearing and Flemish language abilities, it was more the deaf leading the dumb. Fortunately we made ourselves understood at the window of the Portakabin and the nice lady fitted us a paper wristband, like the ones given to toddlers at a Belgian theme park. We walked under the high scaffolding structure of the entrance gates, flashed our wristbands to the security guards and friskers, and we were in. Vast fields of short grass stood before us, separated by tracks lined with tall poplar trees standing over the tents which would each be holding several thousand teenagers on the following weekend. Meanwhile Rimpelrock's 30,000 festival-goers were sitting comfortably in their foldaway chairs in front of giant TV screens by the Marquee tent and in an area several football pitches wide leading up to the Main Stage.

There was a carnival atmosphere at Rimpelrock, with little pockets of fancy dress dotted throughout the crowd. One group of elderly friends had come as dinner ladies, another wore matching pink cowboy hats and a scary-looking lady, coming dangerously close to us, wore a sash with the instructions 'Sixty and Sexy – Kiss Me'. We kept our distance as we negotiated our way through the masses to the 'Eighty-plus platform', where our wristbands allowed us entry to a VIP area: wooden floor, plastic stackable chairs, rows of neatly-parked wheelchairs on a raised stand, and many residents enjoying a supervised day out from the home. In the distance, in the aircraft hangar of a Main Stage, the very youthful-looking Jan Smit was giving it his all. Thousands upon thousands of wrinklies tapped their feet to the sound of the Flemish hit sensation and couples waltzed in the grass aisles. Previous years had seen Eddy Wally entertaining the elderlies and last year the headline act, Engelbert Humperdinck, had caused controversy (even making it to the front page of the local newspaper) by kissing the city's lady mayor on the lips. This could have been a publicity stunt, or it could be that Engelbert always kisses lady mayors on the lips, but I put this down to a simple error due to the complexities of Belgian kissing/greeting etiquette. When a man meets a woman, or a woman meets a woman in Belgium, the two kiss each other three times on the cheeks. In Britain it's a handshake or an optional double kiss for close friends, in France two or four kisses depending on the region. But three? Nobody does three kisses. Following Conny around a room when we arrived at a party would cause me no end of social embarrassment. I would start to panic, 'Is it left-right-left, or right-left-right?' Should I announce halfway through, 'By the way, I'm British, we don't normally do this kind of thing. Shall we stop after one or two?' Sometimes I would follow Conny and go for the full three, only to find that the other person had stopped on two and I would be left hovering in mid-air with expectantly pursed lips. That's not a good look. Or I would pull out on two and embarrass the hostess who was going for three, causing me even greater embarrassment. When in Belgium, I would try and concentrate on the rule of three, and I am still haunted by the memory of our wedding line-up when I kissed at least two of Conny's uncles three times; left-right-left. Oddly, they meekly accepted the three kisses, presumably under the impression that male triple-kissing between new husbands and the bride's uncles was a British custom.

With a name like Engelbert Humperdinck you might think that Engelbert would know a thing or two about Continental kissing etiquette, but Engelbert is in fact an Englishman – real name: Arnold Dorsey. My theory is that Arnold, when faced with greeting the Belgian lady mayor at Rimpelrock, was also fumbling through the left-right-left manoeuvre, and as has happened to me several times, got caught mid-air with the most humiliating of all greeting *faux pas*: an unintentional full smack on the lips.

Back at this year's Rimpelrock, Jan Smit seemed to be pleasing the masses although my father-in-law soon became restless, and we left the security of the over-eighties arena to go in pursuit of the ultimate goal of all his excursions out of the house: the search for coffee and a piece of cake. The stands around the perimeter fence did not disappoint and we traced our way around the edge of the field passing stalls selling waffles, Belgian *frites*, soup and decent Belgian coffee. The Rimpelrock brochure had advertised 'free toilets' as one of the benefits of the €25 entrance fee, a point not lost on my father-in-law, and with no Madame Pipi in sight we came around a corner face-to-face with a man making full use of an open-air trough hanging on the fence. I had seen these in the distance and had assumed they were basins to wash your hands in after eating sticky waffles. My father-in-law was impressed with the facilities and we returned, coffee and waffle in hand, to our blue plastic seats in time to see George Baker come on stage. I expected 'George Baker' to be American or perhaps British, and was somewhat surprised to hear him speak to the audience in fluent Dutch and to learn subsequently that he is in fact one Johannes Bouwens from the Netherlands. George, or Johannes, was certainly a hit with the crowd and after joking that he had more wrinkles than the 30,000 Belgian OAPs in the audience, he filled the aisles with a boom-shawaddy-waddy number, only to empty them again when he played the opening tune from *Reservoir Dogs* – not a film a great many of the audience would be familiar with. My father-in-law reached for his hearing aid, having the distinct advantage of being able to turn the sound on and off at will. Some in the over-eighties area managed to catch a quick nap while others went in search of soup.

But George wasn't going to be defeated by this crowd and for his last number he gave them what they had been waiting for. Hearing apparatus was turned back on, neighbours were woken up, soup was dropped to the floor and the aisles were heaving again as George and his crew blasted out his 1975 super-hit, *'Una Paloma Blanca'*. Conga lines formed in all directions and anyone capable of standing unaided was on their feet with hands waving in the air. Even the over-eighties area was up for a dance, and a run-away wheelchair had to be rescued from the edge of the ramp. 'When the sun shines... on the mountain...' The lyrics and catchy tune are as insidious as any computer virus, but instead of taking control of your PC they invade your brain where they stay lodged as an earworm for days or even weeks, urging you to hum them so they can spread their infection to neighbouring brains. Warning: do NOT look up this song on YouTube. Struggling to clear my mind of *'Una Paloma Blanca'* I told myself that I could at least look forward to The Pussycat Dolls who I had heard were coming on next.

'The Pussycat Dolls' I said loudly to my father in law. *'Zeer goed,'* ('Very good') I continued, making a double thumbs-up sign to emphasise the point.

'Ja! Ja!' he replied, smiling and nodding in agreement.

This reaction was normally a sign that my Flemish had been unintelligible and that he had not understood a word I had said, or that his hearing aid was still turned off. I only realised that something may be wrong when I thought I understood the announcer introduce one third of a trio of Dutch sisters who had topped the charts in Belgium thirty-five years ago with their hit *Mississippi*. That didn't sound like The Pussycat

Dolls – surely they weren't Dutch, or sisters, there weren't just three of them, and they weren't even born thirty-five years ago, let alone having hits in Belgium at this time? A cheer went up from the crowd, except from me, when the remaining third of the 1970s pop trio Pussycat came on stage. I wasn't impressed. My father-in-law, with his hearing aid blissfully turned off since *'Una Paloma Blanca'*, tapped me on the shoulder and looking up at the giant TV screen as the long blonde-haired Pussycat launched into her 1976 hit song, asked me if it was a man or a woman. I think Pussycat might have been hoping for a higher degree of recognition than that.

Next on was *Band Zonder Naam* (Band Without Name, or BZN), a leftover from the 1960s who bounced on to the stage with an aisle-filling number with the repeat line: *'Going to Ibiza for fun, fun, fun, sun, sun, sun.'* I doubted that many of the audience were regular Ibiza ravers, but there was a moment of excitement in the over-eighties section when two first-aiders pushed through a conga-line with a stretcher. My father-in-law was on his feet – this was far more interesting than the stupid Ibiza song – but the stretcher was unnecessary as the octogenarian was helped out of the arena on her feet while *'fun, fun, fun, sun, sun, sun'* reverberated around the arena. BZN stayed on for an encore and produced a foot-stomping, hanky-waving number – something to do with the Lac du Connemara. This had apparently been a big hit somewhere, perhaps in a small part of Belgium, in the 1970s. The song produced a different reaction to the previous performances: 30,000 festival-goers reached into their pockets and brought out neatly folded cotton handkerchiefs to wave in the air. Not a place to be in a flu pandemic. The compère came on stage at the end of the song and announced, 'That's the first time I've seen so many hankies, bras and pants in the air at the same time!' It was bad enough when I thought they were just waving hankies around.

As we waited for the next act to come on stage, my father-in-law met someone he knew in the over-eighties section and they had a competition to guess how old they each were. Curiously, the winner of this competition was the one who declared he was the oldest and my father-in-law had to concede defeat to his acquaintance, who was eighty-five. He nodded in appreciation, telling me under his breath that he thought the eighty-five-year-old had died years ago. Between bands, advertisements came up on the giant TV screen – 'Englebert Humperdink and Elvis Presley will be in Antwerp in December'. I thought I heard someone in the crowd say that Pol Pot was up next. I wasn't sure what to expect – with Elvis playing in Antwerp this December, it could be possible that the 1970s Cambodian dictator was alive and kicking, living out his old age playing to sell-out crowds of elderly Flemish.

A large Welshman in a dinner jacket came on stage – if this was the former Cambodian dictator it was a very good disguise. The compère announced that it was in fact Paul Potts, the mobile-phone-stacker-come-Britain's-Got-Talent-winner of 2007. After starting with a well-received 'Dank u well' (the Flemish for 'thank you'), Paul then droned on at length in English about his love of film scores or something else unintelligible to the audience. When the opera singing started, my father-in-law reckoned we had heard enough of Rimpelrock for one year, and having already accomplished our mission of finding coffee and waffles, we texted Betty to collect us on the Kempische Steenweg, unfortunately leaving before the headline act, Shakin' Stevens in his 'exclusive thirty-year come-back tour', had set foot on stage. It had been my father-in-law's first time to Rimplerock and although he appeared to enjoy it, having switched his hearing aid on for at least two songs, I don't think the experience was enough to turn him into a hardcore festival goer. Once back home, he was back in his comfort zone, sitting in his sofa on a Sunday afternoon, flicking through the television channels to find a cycle race to fall asleep to.

Four days later, an aerial photograph on the front page of the local paper *Het Belang van Limburg* showed a multi-coloured tapestry of 40,000 little tents, tightly-packed flysheet to flysheet in the fields across the road from the music arena. It was the sign that Pukkelpop was about to start. Having the good fortune to live nearby, we were spared the genuine *zommerfestival* experience of sleeping in the smelly tented city and Conny's cousin Hilde kindly acted as chauffeur, delivering me, Hannah, Ruben and their Belgian friend Joost to the Pukkelpop entrance on the Kempische Steenweg. Hilde didn't stop for long as unattended cars were being towed away, and the three teenagers and I jumped out at the traffic lights by the church at Kiewit and joined the queues to swap our tickets for Pukkelpop wristbands. Unlike the paper variety handed out at Rimpelrock, these wristbands were serious cloth affairs and I noticed that many of the teenagers in our queue sported whole wristfulls of these grimy bands being worn as trophies from this summer season and previous years. Clearly the more of these you had, the cooler you were. I didn't have any, and I started to feel self-consciously uncool. This sense of unease was made worse as I looked around at those queuing at the gates while we had our bags frisked and our wristbands tightened, and it dawned on me that this crowd consisted almost exclusively of late teens and very early twenty-somethings. There was no one else sporting the 'boring middle-aged dad' look and rather depressingly I calculated that statistically I was closer to the Rimpelrock crowd than these care-free *pukkel*-faced adolescents.

Once inside, we made our way to an area with lockers to drop off the bag with raincoats that, as boring Dad, I had insisted on taking due to the weather forecast in *Het Belang van Limburg* telling us that there would be 'sun, warm and a chance of thunder'. We headed for the main stage as Belgian rock group The Sore Losers belted out some disturbingly loud noise, presumably Belgian rock, where just a few days earlier George Baker had the oldies in the aisles waltzing to '*Una Paloma Blanca*'. My father-in-law's over-eighties seating arena with the wheelchair podium was gone and 60,000-plus teenagers were now staking out their territory on the open grass fields and in the shade beneath the poplar trees. The sound from the Main Stage was deafening and I could see why the Flemish environment minister, the curiously named Joke Schauvliege, has been keen to introduce legislation to limit the noise level at *zommerfestivals*. Schauvliege is making no friends on the festival circuit and some have even suggested that her proposed limit of 100 decibels is lower than the noise level in the dining rooms of retirement homes. I would be pretty surprised if there was a retirement home dining room with more noise than The Sore Losers were producing. Wary of the Formula One sting of excessively-priced ear plugs at

Spa-Francorchamps, I had purchased ear plugs in advance of our trip to Pukkelpop and I reached into my pocket to hand them around to the children. I had only been able to find swimming ear plugs at the travel shop at Heathrow and had wrongly assumed that these would be equally suitable for noise reduction at festivals as for avoiding your ears filling up with water. No one seemed to be impressed with the Strepsil-sized blobs of soft silicone putty that I peeled out of the pack. I tried rolling mine into suppository shapes and stuck these in my ears for a while until they fell out on to the ground. Fortunately the kind gentleman at the Proximus stand was handing out free pairs of festival-friendly foam ear plugs and my earthy suppositories could be left behind.

With our ears suitably plugged, we carried on with our tour of the stands that line the perimeter of the compound, and after swapping cash for food coupons we made the discovery of *poffertjes* – a heavenly half-pancake, half-donut concoction, freshly scooped from the griddle pan and sprinkled with powdered sugar. A large portion of our coupons was blown at this stand and we carried away a plateful of *poffertjes* to the Marquee tent where we took up our positions, waiting for Eliza Doolittle to come on stage. The tent soon filled with thousands of excited teenage girls accompanied by a handful of disorientated boyfriends. I kept our spot in the centre of the tent by a roped-off area occupied by the sound people, where I had a good view over the teenage heads to the stage.

Looking up from my plate as I finished off the last of the *poffertjes*, I found that the tallest and widest man in the whole of Pukkelpop had taken up a position right in front of me. He stood with folded arms bulging out of a tightly fitted tank-top to show off pulsating, steroid-pumped muscles and a tattoo of a native American which covered nearly every part of exposed flesh – of which there was a great deal. His chin, cheeks and head all sported the same length of stubble, with top hair and beard merging into one somewhere near the bottom of his ears. For a fleeting moment I considered tapping him on the shoulder and pointing out that by standing right in front of me he was what we would describe in English as 'an inconsiderate arse'. I judged that his English might not be too hot and I might have been able to get away with it, but on balance, for health and safety reasons (my health and my safety) I decided that I would just stare at the stubble on the back of his neck instead. In any case, there was nowhere to move now as the tent was packed, with every square metre of grass occupied by at least four people.

Ruben had gone on a mission to 'get as much free stuff as possible' and every now and again I spotted him darting through the crowd in order to collect discarded plastic bottles and drinks containers, which he was cashing in for prizes at the recycling stand. The band took their places to huge girly cheers and Eliza finally bounced on to the stage and started her set. I kept to my patch of grass, unable to see a great deal behind Brick Shithouse Man, who I noticed tapped his feet and sang along to all the songs. Perhaps he was really quite a softy? Or perhaps a pervy stalker? What was he doing, the only thirty-plus male in this tent, stalking Eliza Doolittle and her thousands of teenage girl fans? Then again, he wasn't the only man over thirty in the Marquee, as standing behind him was the only man over forty in the tent, with camera and notebook in hand. I started to feel very self-conscious again and looked down at my notes. When I looked up, Brick Shithouse Man had gone. Just vanished. I wasn't complaining. His place was taken by a Velma from *Scooby Doo* look-a-like. This was much more like it – I now had a clear view of the stage. Velma and her line of five friends liked to make up moves for the songs, and after a bit of practice, dance them in unison. The song with the lyric 'I'd catch a grenade for you (yeah, yeah, yeah)' produced a masterful World War Two re-enactment as the six of them made synchronised dives to catch exploding armaments. 'Thank you Belgium. Pukkelpop best crowd yet,' Eliza said as she launched into her final number, and everyone was happy. When she finished her set, the teenage girls drifted away and a slightly older, mainly shirtless male crowd started to gather for Noah and the Whale. This was also a taller crowd and with Velma and her short dancing friends gone, I lost my view of the stage. Ruben had received a free naff T-shirt for collecting fifty plastic bottles from the floor, and spent the time between sets like a bag lady, scouring the arena for more bits of plastic in order to trade them in for yet more free junk from the recycling stand. I was left to guard his collection while he moved into the crowd, under instructions not to let anyone touch his bags of rubbish. 'That's mine,' I sneered to a rival rubbish collector who started sniffing around one of Ruben's bags of sticky plastic beer glasses.

The males in the crowd displayed the curious fashion concept of wearing their trousers or shorts so low around the knees as to give the impression that the wearer had shat himself. I remember looking ridiculous at a similar age, with a centre-parting and flares, followed by an even more embarrassing, never-to-be-repeated crew cut, but I don't ever remember thinking that it was cool to walk around looking as though I was carrying a number two in my pants.

A *pukkel*-faced teenager with a significant proportion of his sweaty pants on display took up position in front of me where Velma had been standing, and started to glue his face to his spotty girlfriend. It was really very off-putting. Even tattooed Brick Shithouse Man had been easier on the eye than this. If I could have moved I would have done, but I had sworn to stay put and guard Ruben's bags of rubbish. The snogging and slobbering continued, somewhat marring both my festival-going experience and the excellent Noah and the Whale session. Fortunately, sweaty pants moved on when the band finished, presumably to get a tent.

I hoped that his girlfriend had not earned herself the title of *'tentsletje'* ('tent slut') – a new, sexist term that has officially entered the Dutch language as a result of the Belgian *zommerfestivals*. Readers of the leading Dutch language dictionary, the interestingly titled *'Dikke van Dale'*, enjoyed the new word so much that they voted *'tentsletje'* as 'Flemish Word of the Year 2010', beating the newly coined *'pedopriester'* into second place.

Ruben returned briefly to our guarded position in the middle of the tent, having cashed in more rubbish for enough tokens to give us all a ride on the Ferris wheel located in a small fairground area near the Dance Hall. He handed me the plastic tokens for safe-keeping – we could use them later in the evening when we would have some time before the Foo Fighters came on stage.

Meanwhile, there was one more band the children wanted to see in the Marquee, which showing my total lack of coolness, I had never heard of – The Wombats. This was a band with even more appeal to the cack-in-the-pants brigade than Noah and the Whale, and the tent filled to capacity with 8,000 T-shirtless, pant-displaying teenage boys who bounced, waved arms and generally sweated to the beat which was now so loud that it shook internal organs and the ground we were standing on. I don't expect that happens in many retirement home dining rooms. The Wombats, I discovered, get very excitable on stage, with a lot of running around and thrashing of guitars, and were in constant need of new instruments and microphones.

It was quite a relief when The Wombats concluded their set after a particularly frenzied guitar-whacking number, and we left the Marquee along with the crowd of sweaty cack-pants in search of food. It was hot and muggy, with the air so thick that it felt as though you could cut it with a knife. We strolled around the food stalls again, getting past the temptations of the *poffertjes* stall with some difficulty and then with considerable ease passed various fried things, *moules frites* and an oyster bar, before settling for the 'Fresh Market' where we found some mollusc-free food that had not seen the inside of a deep-fat fryer. We sat in the shade at a picnic table under the large awning of the restaurant tent, flicking away the occasional sleepy wasp that ventured too close to our food. The heat was becoming unbearable and Hannah was cursing me for insisting that she had worn her jeans, because boring Dad had pointed out that the weather forecast had mentioned 'a chance of thunder'. The forecasters had certainly been right about 'sun' and 'warm' and we left the shade of the restaurant tent in the sticky heat of the late August afternoon in order to find a place near the Main Stage where we could watch the next act to come on – Skunk

Anansie. Although I am of the right age to know of Skunk Anansie, being uncool Dad, it was another act that I had never heard of. By coincidence, we stood in more or less the same place as I had sat with my father-in-law at Rimpelrock, in the area where the over-eighties had competed with one another to see who was oldest, and where the wheelchairs had been parked up in neat rows. Skunk Anansie's lead singer burst on to the stage – this wasn't going to be *'Una Paloma Blanca'*. The singer, aptly named Skin, had made an interesting choice of attire for her performance: a figure-hugging black leotard stretching up to a metre-wide black feather contraption that sat across her shoulders like an almighty ruff. Fairly difficult to describe, but if I say that it looked like she had stuck her head up an ostrich's arse, you will get the picture. Skin seemed to be enjoying herself and was clearly very keen on the f-word which she ground out with enthusiasm while crawling around the stage performing very passable ostrich impressions.

I could have listened to the fascinating Skunk Anansie all night (well, perhaps another ten minutes) but Hannah, Ruben and Joost dragged me away to the Dance Hall tent, where they were keen to see an artist called Wiz Khalifa sing his hit 'Black and Yellow'. We left the Main Stage area, passing beneath the giant PUKKELPOP letters dangling high in the air on scaffolding poles, and crossed a large field where three tents stood next to each other in close proximity: the Dance Hall, the Shelter and the Boiler Room. I would not normally give such precise details as to the location and names of the various tents, but as will become clear in the narrative that follows, these last three tents became of critical importance to us. While most tents were fully open on three sides, the Shelter was open on all four sides as it served as an overflow dance area for the Boiler Room, whose music pumped out through giant speakers into the Shelter. I noticed that the blue sky had given over to grey clouds and on the way to the Dance Hall I picked up our rain jackets from our locker, on the off-chance that the weather forecasters could have been correct about a thunderstorm. It was still very hot and I was self-consciously uncool Dad again, carrying a large bag of raincoats across the terrain as bare-chested cack-in-the-pants boys ran around us laughing in the heat.

The first few drops of rain fell as we reached the Dance Hall. Wiz was well into his set and we could hear the repetitive lyrics, 'Black and yellow, black and yellow, black and yellow' blaring out of the tent. There was a capacity crowd of 8,000 teenagers inside, waving their hands in the air to Wiz's command. As the Dance Hall was full we could only manage to get one foot under cover of the tent, while the other remained outside, and we stood awkwardly half in the Dance Hall and half in the open space by the Shelter tent, where music from The Black Pacific was blasting out from the speaker towers. We found ourselves at the convergence of two competing sets of sound waves and as my notebook entry says: 'It is stereo but from two different groups. Not very comfortable.' The time was 6.15 p.m.

That was the last entry in my notebook for 18 August 2011. I have difficulty in describing what happened next, not because the events are not clear to me – the following fifteen minutes will be etched on my mind forever – but because my writing is typically of light-hearted travelogues. *Time Magazine*, rather unflatteringly, has even gone so far as to describe my writing style as 'flippant'. I am not used to writing the scripts of disaster movies.

The rain that had started as a few drops became more persistent and Hannah, Ruben and I pressed ourselves into the Dance Hall in order to stay dry. Joost chose to stay outside. I beckoned for him to come inside but he shook his head, preferring to be in the open air, even if this meant getting wet, rather than being crammed in at the edge of the tent with us. He had probably made the right choice as a strong wind had started up, blowing the water that trickled off the roof of the tent onto those of us standing along the edge. We huddled together, wrapping one of the raincoats around us, in a vain attempt to keep dry. Suddenly the sky darkened and the rain strengthened to the intensity of a bathroom shower, sending hundreds of soaked teenagers crashing into the tent to take cover. We were pushed several metres inside and keeping my head up so I didn't lose eye contact with Joost, I beckoned again for him to come undercover. Again he shook his head and despite the pouring rain, he waved for us to come outside. He saw that I wasn't understanding him, and as we couldn't call out to each other over the noise of the bands still playing and the wind and rain, he pointed above my head to the roof of the tent. I looked up. The tent roof was billowing in and the rigging holding the lights and disco balls was swaying wildly above the crowd, in imminent danger of crashing down on top of us. I grabbed Hannah and Ruben by the hand and as hundreds of others pushed their way in, we ran outside to join Joost. We stood together for a moment to work out what to do next. Confusion reigned – it was dark as night and lightning bolts shot from the sky as thousands of teenagers ran screaming in every direction around us. We had given up all hope of staying dry – all that mattered now was safety from the storm. We ran across to the Shelter tent and squeezed in at the edge of the crowd where a further 8,000 teenagers were packed inside. Having been alerted by Joost to the danger of tents collapsing, I looked up to check the roof of the Shelter. To my horror I saw that we were standing directly beneath a long beam of triangular tubes of steel, perhaps 20 metres in length. The beam was shaking violently, bouncing a metre up and down at its centre point. I shouted for Hannah, Ruben and Joost to run outside but my voice was drowned by the roar of the wind and rain and the screams of terrified teenagers all around us. I jumped out and they followed, only to find that the torrential rain had been replaced by hail. Not the ordinary hail of a winter shower, but sharp pieces of ice, the size of large lumps of gravel being hurled at us from on high. We held our hands over our heads for cover, and ran. Visibility was almost nil and I could only just make out Hannah's pink rain coat before me as she ran to the edge of the Boiler Room tent. I turned to my side, grabbed Ruben's hand and pushed him after Hannah. I expected Joost to be next to Ruben. But he was gone.

Joining the 5,000 other teenagers in the Boiler Room, Hannah and Ruben huddled together at the edge of the tent, screaming at the top of their voices with rain and tears falling down their cheeks and the rock-like hail pelting them from the side. Having checked that there was no metal structure above where they were standing, I returned to the no-man's land between the Dance Hall, the Shelter and the Boiler Room to look for Joost. It was difficult to see, as I had to cover my eyes with my hands to protect them from the hail and the storm gusts made it hard to stay upright. I retraced our steps back to where we had been standing at the Shelter tent, to find that the steel-tubed beam had crashed to the ground. A body lay motionless on the floor. Two people were standing next to it, protecting it from the hail. I approached nervously, dreading that it would be Joost. It was a girl.

Het Belang van Limburg later reported that these highly-localised, freak weather conditions were caused by a narrow tube of hot air rising high into the atmosphere, allowing a downburst of cold air and hail from an altitude of 14 km to rush towards the earth accompanied by winds of up to 240 km per hour. *240 km per hour!*

I ran back to check on Hannah and Ruben, where I had left them at the edge of the Boiler Room tent. By the time I reached them the roof of the tent was starting to come down with the weight of water and hail and they were clinging to each other, screaming hysterically. I couldn't stay. I checked again above Hannah and Ruben – it was only canvas, water and ice – and calculating that this was relatively safe, I went out again in search of Joost. The hail was still coming down hard, joined now with other flying debris – leaves and branches from the poplar trees and pieces of flags and stands. Teenagers were running between the tents, stooped low with their hands over their heads to shield themselves from the vicious hail, desperately looking for somewhere safe. I heard screams in Flemish that something was about to collapse, but I didn't understand what it was and I couldn't lift my eyes up from the ground to see where whatever it was might fall. I kept running, calling out Joost's name, until I came across a second body on the wooden dance floor by the edge of the Shelter tent. There was no movement and I could see the person's right arm lay in tatters. Two first-aiders from the *Vlaamse Kruis* (the Flemish equivalent of St John's Ambulance) were giving oxygen. Again I approached gingerly, hoping not to find Joost. I couldn't see the person's face but the body was that of a twenty-something man; taller and older than Joost.

My mind was numb to the emotions that tried to take it over. Should I feel guilty for being glad that the man on the ground was not Joost? Could I have saved anyone if I had told others to leave the tent? – but where was safer, inside where the tent might collapse or outside where trees and debris were crashing down? Should I be leaving my children alone and scared? What if the next body I came across was Joost? I tried to lock these thoughts away for later, but one lodged in my mind: the ever-growing recollection from news stories that most deaths at stadium disasters are not from stage collapses, but from stampedes as thousands of people try to make their escape – news clips from Hillsborough 1989 and the Love Parade 2010 rushed through my mind. I had left Hannah and Ruben on the edge of a shaky tent containing 5,000 terrified teenagers. I ran back to the Boiler Room tent to find them.

They were still holding each other, still screaming. The roof where they were standing was now so low with the weight of water and ice that the taller teenagers were holding it off their heads with their hands. We had to find new cover, and ran out into the hail again looking for something, anything, that could resist the might of the storm. We noticed a lorry at the back of the Dance Hall – the space beneath it, between the wheel arches and the ground, would have been perfect but it was already taken by thirty or so teenagers, crouching in the mud. We kept running until we found a collection of Portakabins and we headed for the nearest one marked 'Crew Only'. As we ran to the door, Joost appeared from the Portakabin next to it! He was safe and sound and my worries were over. I understood that he had been pushed out for continually opening the door to look for us, but none of this was important now – we were together again, and safe. It did cross my mind that there may have been a poplar tree or part of the staging structure above us, in which case the roof of the container may not have been strong enough to withstand a fall, but I weighed up that it was better to be under a metal roof than taking our chances in the open air or in a tent. A handful of nervous-looking crew members and perhaps twenty teenagers stood in silence as the storm raged above us. Hail hammered the container roof – so hard that a policeman later described seeing the metal sheeting dented from the impact as if a shotgun had been fired at it. After two or three minutes in the container, the noise of the hammering came to an abrupt end. A crew member shouted, 'Out! Out! Everybody who is not crew, out!' and we were evicted – pushed out, blinking and disbelieving into the open air. The time was 6.30 p.m., just fifteen minutes since I had written in my notebook about being stuck between the competing sounds of the Dance Hall and Shelter tents.

It was eerily quiet now. The music had stopped. The screaming was over. The wind, rain and hail had gone. There was no panic, no one running, just silence. All heads were bowed, as 60,000 teenagers looked down at their mobile phones, thumbing-in texts to one another, their family and friends. The networks were overwhelmed with the volume of calls and the lines went dead. Joost was trying to get hold of his brother, who was out there somewhere with a group of friends and Conny's cousin Kristel and her nephew Rafael were out there too, but we had no means of getting in touch and it would not be until late in the evening that we knew they were safe.

Bewildered groups of teenagers wandered aimlessly around the site in a daze, squelching through mud and pools of ankle-deep water, which fifteen minutes previously had been dry grass and dust. Some decided to stay on and wait for news, while others made their way slowly towards the exit. Soaked to the skin and very shaken, we decided to cut our losses and we followed the exodus to the gates on the Kempische Steenweg. We had not been able to text Hilde, but we headed for our agreed pick-up point between the Pukkelpop site and the camping, hoping that we might get a message through. We waded through the pools of water, frequently losing our shoes to the mud. Joost decided to go barefoot. Ruben was doubly upset; not only were we going to miss the Foo Fighters but the official Pukkelpop T-shirt that I had promised him now lay out of reach – upstream from a river of teenagers who poured out from the Main Stage area, clambering over the collapsed scaffolding poles and the metre-high letters spelling out PUKKELPOP which all now lay in a twisted heap on the ground.

We carried on to the Kempische Steenweg, passing the circular Château tent which had been flattened by a fallen poplar tree. Press reports later showed photographs of lines of uprooted trees, but this poplar had simply been snapped off, and a 2-metre-high stump projected from the ground, with the rest of the tree lying across the remains of the tent. It is hard to imagine the force of a storm that could wreak such devastation or how any of this could have been foreseen. The Pukkelpop organisers had even checked the trees in May for their ability to withstand high winds – but no one had anticipated a wind speed of 240 km per hour.

Water was still dripping out of our mobile phones when just before 7.00 p.m. the networks partially opened up and a few texts came through. Joost received a one word message from his brother: 'Alive', and a text came through from Hilde saying that as the roads were closed due to fallen trees and police barriers she would try to meet us at the traffic lights by the far end of the Kempische Steenweg, outside the church. Failing that, we were to walk back along the road towards Hasselt. A few minutes later the lines were dead again – the Pukkelpop disaster had been the main item on the national news, and at 7.01 p.m. a significant proportion of Belgium's 11 million population had picked up their phones to text or call relatives, friends, or anyone they knew who may have been near the north-east corner of Belgium.

We reached the traffic lights to find them lying in the middle of the road, blown clean off in the storm. The Kempische Steenweg was closed to all vehicles except for ambulances and police cars which sped past with flashing lights and sirens howling. Joost started counting the ambulances, but stopped after he reached twenty. Some teenagers were crossing the road to look for the remains of their tents in the campsite, while others wrapped in tinfoil blankets started to make their way to the train station in Hasselt, a 5 km walk along the Kempische Steenweg. We waited until nightfall, but there were no signs of Hilde being able to get to us and we decided to join the steady flow of campers walking along the car-less dual carriageway towards Hasselt, only stepping back on the pavement to let the occasional ambulance or police car scream past. A Skoda dealership on the way had had its signs ripped off by the wind, and they now lay on top of cars in the parking lot with smashed windscreens and dented roofs. We carried on walking, Joost still in bare feet, until we had crossed the canal bridge and reached an area where traffic could circulate. Joining a group of teenagers crowding around a car with the door open and the radio on, we heard the Pukkelpop organiser Chokri Mahassine and the lady mayor, Hilde Claes, giving a press conference. The mayor announced in a shaking voice that two people had died and many more had serious injuries. A few cars further on we came across Hilde and Joost's parents – we were safely back with the family nearly three hours after leaving the Pukkelpop grounds.

The full tragedy of the devastation caused by the storm was only revealed over the next twenty-four hours, with the death toll appearing to rise with every news bulletin. A total of five people died that day: two where we had been standing under the metal beam at the edge of the Shelter tent, one in the Château tent where the poplar tree had fallen, another in the restaurant area when the roof came down and one in the camping area when a light stand was blown over.

While it will be little compensation to those who have lost loved ones or to those whose lives were changed forever on that day, the death toll from a 240 km per hour storm, wreaking havoc across an area packed with 60,000 teenagers, could have been far higher. The large grounds with tents spread out across the site meant that there was no stampede in a particular direction. In fact, my clear recollection is of everyone running in different directions as they made their individual decisions as to which tent or patch of grass offered the best chance of survival. The majority of the tents withstood the onslaught of the storm and none of the stages collapsed, as was erroneously reported in the international press the following day.

After deliberating most of Thursday night, Chokri and his team took the decision at 4.00 a.m. to cancel the rest of the three-day event. The message came across on the early morning radio broadcasts and the thousands of teenagers who had been put up for the night in houses, school halls and in the meeting rooms of the Holiday Inn Hasselt made their way to the train station.

We returned to the site on the Sunday to the church in Kiewit where a service was held in memory of the victims. Chokri was applauded as he left the church and he joined the throng gathering along Pukkelpop's perimeter fence to see the tributes that had been laid. Candles, photographs and hand-written messages of love lay on the ground with flowers and Pukkkelpop wrist-bands tied on the wire fence above. The Kempische Steenweg was open now and we crossed between the traffic to the campsite where 40,000 ripped and flattened tents lay abandoned. At the entrance to the site a half-eaten burger sat on a table, while shoes poked out of the drying mud under our feet and a frying pan accompanied by an unopened pack of crêpes lay on a patch of grass.

It is difficult to conclude my investigation into the Belgian music scene on a light-hearted or 'flippant' note. What had started out at the beginning of this chapter with the likes of the frivolous and highly forgettable Eddy Wally, Benny B and Plastic Bertrand ended with tragedy at Pukkelpop. The *zommerfestivals* undoubtedly help to lift the interest level of the Belgian music scene, and compared with what the British call entertainment for their elderly – parish hall coffee mornings and bingo nights – the Belgian idea of an underwear-waving festival for its wrinklies, Rimpelrock, is a truly wild concept. But I'm not yet able to think of Belgian music without an overwhelming feeling of sadness due to those fifteen minutes of darkness on the first day of Pukkelpop 2011, and so the Belgian music scene receives a score of tragic rather than interesting.

My quest is faltering – only four chapters so far have resulted in interesting scores, and it is in need of a serious boost if I am to turn this around and conclude that Belgium is indeed interesting. I need a sure winner for the next chapter. Something that is indisputably interesting. Something that will need a great deal of first-hand research. It is time to take a closer look at Belgian beer.

CHAPTER 11
THE BEER CAPITAL
OF THE WORLD

The Belgians have the same respect for their beer as the French have for wine. It is something to be savoured, enjoyed, studied and talked about, with favourite bottles stored in the cellar and brought out on special occasions. It is not purchased in a six-pack from the supermarket on a Friday night in order to get 'lagered up' at home, and no self-respecting Belgian goes out on a Saturday night to down as many pints as possible before closing time with the sole objective of 'getting pissed'. The binge-drinking Brits could learn a thing or two about the appreciation and enjoyment of beer from the Belgian youth culture. A walk through a Belgian town centre at 1 a.m. for example, is generally a pleasant experience, without the threat of violence hanging in the air that pervades British town centres at this time of night or the necessity to side-step piles of vomit.

With my vow in place for some time now: *No beer shall be consumed for a second time, until all other Belgian beers available have been tried*, I can say from experience that the Belgians take their beer very seriously, producing an astounding array of different types, flavours and strengths. There is certainly life after Stella. In fact Belgium has more types of beer than any other country in the world, brewed in over 100 breweries, ranging from the industrial giants of InBev (the brewers of Stella) to microbreweries serving a few local cafes. The Belgians are more adventurous than any others when it comes to experimenting with yeast and hop varieties, adding fruit, herbs and spices or using top, bottom or second and third fermentations. The apparently limitless combinations of methods and ingredients lead to the vast spectrum of beer, from painfully sour lambics at one end of the scale to sickly sweet, and frankly rather disgusting, banana beers at the other.

According to Michael Jackson (that's Michael Jackson the late, great writer on Belgian beer, not the late, great – if you like that kind of thing – 'King of Pop'), the *Belgae* were brewing beer even before the Romans arrived. And with Belgium sitting bang in the middle of the European grain belt (a swathe of agriculturally ideal grain-producing land stretching west to Britain and Ireland and east to Germany and the Czech Republic), a grain-based alcohol was always going to be the Belgians' alcoholic beverage of choice. By the Middle Ages the descendants of the *Belgae* discovered that grain could also be distilled, and by adding a few Black-Death-curing juniper berries into the mix, created a lethal spirit they called *jenever*. This unpleasant drink, not dissimilar to industrial solvent and the forerunner to English gin, is still going strong in Flanders where locals appear to enjoy it by the small frosted glassful, consuming it at the cafe counter by bending over and taking the first sip hands-free. Unsuspecting visitors on the other hand, having mistakenly thought they were going to be on the receiving end of a decent gin and tonic, tend to pick up the glass, wonder why it doesn't have any ice, lemon or tonic in it, take a sip, wince and spit. Perhaps that was just me. However, I should not be too disparaging of Belgian *jenever*, as it is claimed that this drink had a significant influence on the development of Belgian beer. It is hard to imagine now, with the present day sensible drinking habits of the Belgians, but after World War One the general level of permanent inebriation of the Belgian population was so high that the government brought out a law in 1919 prohibiting the sale of spirits in public places. *Jenever* was off the menu, and to fill the gap in the market, Belgian brewers ramped up the alcohol content of their beers, leading to the eight, nine, ten and above percentages that are commonplace today.

Belgian beers can be grouped together in the general categories of lambics, lagers, ales of various types, white beers, holy beers and speciality 'anything goes' beers. The lambics are the most exciting of the beer types, being produced by what is known as 'spontaneous fermentation'. *Spontaneous*, in that no yeast is purposefully added to the mix of water, grain and hops – the fermentation happens from wild yeast found naturally in the air of the lambic breweries centred around Brussels. This results in some pretty rough beers – sharp, acidic, nearly wine-like – often stored in small tough bottles fitted with champagne corks. Just to make things more complicated, lambics of different vintages can be blended together and further fermented to create the even stronger and rougher *gueuze*. This beer is notoriously difficult to get right, and Belgian brewer Frank Boon who rescued *gueuze* from the brink of extinction in the mid-1970s, writes in the *Good Beer Guide Belgium* that one of the quality issues he faced was that the beer 'contained floaters'. I don't profess to be an expert on beer, but even I can see that having popped the champagne cork off your bottle of *gueuze* and carefully filled up your glass with its contents, the last thing you would want to find looking up at you once the bubbles have died down is a floater.

Lambics are also used as the base of the huge variety of fruit beers. Belgians have a curious affinity with fruit/beer combinations, and no drinks list in a restaurant or row of bottles on a supermarket shelf is complete without at least one cherry beer (known as *kriek*) and possibly a few raspberry, blueberry or blackcurrant beers thrown in for good measure. The traditional method of making *kriek* is to add the dried fruit of the locally grown Morello cherry trees to casks of lambic beer, where a further fermentation takes place before the beer matures in the bottle. However, modern industrial scale manufacture of fruit beer seems to consist of adding a squirt of a sickly fruit flavour somewhere towards the end of the bottling process, which is akin to adding a shot of Ribena to a pint of bitter.

The Belgians are not averse to adulterating their beer in this way, and while in the UK watering down an already watery supermarket lager with sugary lemonade to produce shandy is generally the preserve of nervous, first-time drinking teenagers (again, perhaps that was just me), in Belgium you can find grown men in a cafe ordering a *kivela* (beer and lemonade), a *mazout* (beer and cola), or a *tango* (beer with grenadine). Fortunately these perversities are not that common, and when drinking for pleasure rather than just to quench the thirst, most Belgians will have a favourite beer or beer type to fit the occasion, mood or setting. I soon discovered after Stella that my favourite beer category is the *witbier* (white beers). These are typified by the now ubiquitous Hoegaarden – made accessible worldwide through the massive distribution network of its present owner, InBev. The white beers are a family of light, easy to drink, flavour-filled beers made from a combination of wheat and barley with the strangely acceptable addition of crushed coriander seeds and Curaçao orange peel. In the 1800s there were as many as thirty breweries at any one time in the town of Hoegaarden making *witbier*, but with drinking trends shifting to the newer Pilsner-style beers, and two world wars resulting in most of the copper brewing kettles being carted off to munitions factories, the last *witbier* brewery in Hoegaarden closed its doors in 1957. Hoegaarden beer became extinct and would be nothing more than a footnote in the *Good Beer Guide Belgium*, if it were not for the actions of the local milkman, the late Pierre Celis. Drinking beers with friends one evening, lamenting the loss of their local *witbier*, Pierre decided to take matters into his own hands. He borrowed money from his father, bought up what equipment he could find from the closed breweries and with the advice of a veteran *witbier* brewer, set up a backyard brewery producing white beer again in Hoegaarden for the first time in nearly ten years. It hasn't been an easy journey for Hoegaarden since its 1960s rebirth – a fire destroyed most of the brewery in 1985, and the subsequent 'rescue package' and sell out to InBev led to controversy in 2005 when InBev announced their decision to move the brewing of Hoegaarden from its birth place, the small Flemish town of the same name, to InBev's massive production plant across the language divide at Jupille, in French-speaking Wallonia. Not a very culturally sensitive move, and after a two-year-long 'Save our beer' campaign, InBev made the magnanimous decision to keep Hoegaarden production in Hoegaarden, and the town and the beer have lived more or less happily ever after. While my friends at the *Good Beer Guide Belgium* are not that impressed, describing Hoegaarden as 'a fallen angel, a grey and watery wheat beer lacking flair, passion or authority', InBev's marketing drive has been so successful that forty Olympic-sized swimming pool quantities of the beer are brewed and exported every year. As for our local hero, milkman Pierre Celis, having sold his brewery to InBev he left Belgium for Texas, and at the age of sixty-seven started all over again with a new *witbier* brewery, which his daughter now runs to carry on the family legacy.

While InBev can be credited for bringing Hoegaarden to the world, it is another from their stable that is Belgium's most famous international, and biggest-selling, export beer – my erstwhile favourite – Stella Artois. The international success of Stella Artois always surprises Belgians, as back home its sales figures are remarkably underwhelming, capturing only a few per cent of the local market, chiefly around its production town of Leuven. The Artois brewery can trace its routes here back to the Middle Ages to a brewpub called *Den Horn*, which explains the picture of a horn on the label of every bottle of Stella. Observant, Latin-speaking drinkers of Stella Artois (oh come on, I am sure there are some) will also have noticed the small star on the label and will appreciate that *stella*, being the Latin for star, is a reference to the Christmas star which was embossed on each green bottle when Stella was first brewed as a one-off Christmas beer in 1926. While I am very pleased to see Stella's success from its humble, temporary routes in Leuven to the international best-seller that it is today, Stella Artois is not everyone's favourite beer. The *Good Beer Guide Belgium* gives it just two stars, and users of an American beer rating website keep referring to it as 'a little skunky'. I wouldn't have thought that you would want there to be any similarity between the beer you are drinking and the scent glands on a skunk's bottom, but one rater from Minnesota comments: 'The smell is kind of like a skunk... but in a good way.' Excuse me? He continues: 'The taste is similar to the smell... and kind of like a skunk (again, in a good way).' What? Further research reveals that 'skunky' is an American term to describe what is otherwise known as 'lightstruck' beer – a beer that has gone off in the bottle due to being exposed to UV light and is something that beers in green or clear bottles are particularly prone to. You might want to use this knowledge to impress your friends the next time you are out at a barbecue and the Stella is opened. Try sniffing the bottle and saying, 'Hmm, a little skunky' – at least you'll be spared the small talk on Belgium.

While Stella and its more popular local rival, Jupiler, are sold as Belgium's mass-market thirst-quenchers, the generally skunk-free beers for sipping and savouring are those brewed in the Belgian monasteries. I still find it somewhat of a paradox that Christian brothers in a monastery spend their time between prayer and contemplative silence, running breweries that produce some of the best and strongest beers in the world. Many religious groups demonise drink and with over one million alcohol-related hospital admissions per year in England alone, the misuse of alcohol certainly creates more than its fair share of misery. But in Belgium the monks are simply following the instructions of St Benedict, the founder of modern monasticism, who decreed in the sixth century that monks should 'live from the work of their hands'. Michael Jackson tells us in *The Great Beers of Belgium* that there have been as many as 600 abbey breweries operating in Europe; however reformations, revolutions and world wars have all taken their toll and only a dozen or so remain, with six of them operating in Belgium. These are the Trappist breweries of Achel, Chimay, Orval, Rochefort, Westmalle and Westvleteren. There are also Belgian beers labelled as 'abbey beers' which are produced under licence from monasteries to commercial breweries, but it is only the Trappist beers that are brewed within the monastery's grounds under the supervision of the monastic order.

Chimay is the biggest-selling of the Trappist beers and the most likely to be found outside Belgium, but the Trappist beer that has received most attention is the Westvleteren 12, brewed at St Sixtus abbey near Ypres. The Trappist monks of St Sixtus had been brewing for over 150 years when in 2005 the international and Belgian press, short of a good summer story, noticed that Westvleteren 12 was consistently being ranked as the 'best beer in the world' by two popular American beer rating websites. The media went into overdrive and the legend of Westvleteren 12, Belgium's very own *unobtanium*, was born. With all the press attention, demand for Westvleteren went through the roof and while in the fast buck-making commercial world this would have led to a sharp rise in price, massively increased production and a corresponding decrease in quality, the monks of St Sixtus stuck to their principles, stating on their website: *We are no brewers. We are monks. We brew beer to be able to afford being monks. This must be strange for business people.* The production methods, quantities and price have all remained the same, adding to the hype, its cult status and leading to ever-increasing demand. The St Sixtus abbey monks only have two sales outlets – one at the abbey gates and the other at their cafe across the road. Before the monks came up with ingenious sales limitation methods, this lack of supply led to 3 km tailbacks from the abbey as anxious Belgians descended upon St Sixtus to stock up on the national treasure. To further limit availability, the monks decided only to allow one case to be bought per car, and only with a pre-order booked by telephone on the Westvleteren hotline number given on their website. They take details of the car registration and will not sell to the occupants of the car for a further sixty days.

As I was planning a trip to nearby Ypres with Ruben to see the World War One memorials, I called the Westvleteren hotline well in advance, thinking that while in Ypres we could pop by the St Sixtus abbey and pick up a case of the Westvleteren 12. This simple plan was not to be – it seems that the monks have found a further sales limitation technique: not answering the telephone. Bearing in mind that the Trappist monks are a silent order, I can imagine that answering the hotline could be tricky.

There was no other option than to turn up on spec at the abbey's cafe across the road, to see if they had any bottles available on the day.

Having given the coordinates of the abbey to satnav lady, and in serious need of cheering up after a morning spent in the Flanders Fields museum and the mind-numbing Tyne Cot cemetery at Passchendaele, we were directed through fields of cows and barley and past small groups of brick houses, towards the village of Westvleteren. Every now and again a little war cemetery would appear, 200 or so tombstones here, 100 there, all in neat white rows. Around the town of Poperinge, the barley fields and lines of poplar trees gave way to row upon row of what looked like washing lines suspended between high wooden posts, with a green-leaved plant climbing up wires suspended from the lines. We had entered the hops capital of Belgium, the small area of West Flanders where 80 per cent of Belgian hops are grown. The local brews such as Poperings Hommelbier make a feature of stuffing as much hops as possible into the brewing process and are intensely hoppy – I'm not sure if that's a correct term to describe a beer packed with hops, but if you try a Hommelbier, or a Hopus (made with five varieties of hops) you will see what I mean.

The roads narrowed after Poperinge and a few sharp corners later, past some remote farmsteads and a tractor shop, we found ourselves outside a smart looking cafe complete with coach park, wide paved terraces, box hedging and pollarded lime trees. We pulled to a halt in the shade of a high brick wall surrounding St Sixtus Abbey, and with no signs of activity at the firmly closed gates we went to the cafe next door. Apart from pre-orders at the Abbey gates, this is the only other purchase point for Westvleteren 12 and I eagerly enquired at the small shop inside the cafe if I could purchase a crate. No. They were sold out. 'Just one bottle perhaps?' 'No,' the polite lady replied, they only sold them in boxes of six. Seeing my disappointment, she glanced over her shoulder, checked behind the counter and whispered to me that she could arrange some nice blondes if I was interested. I looked around at the clientele – small groups of elderly Belgians sitting at the wooden tables, as if at a parish hall over-sixties function. I was thinking that it was an odd place to be offered blondes, and run by Trappist monks too, when she plonked a pack of six Westvleteren *blond* beers on the counter, saving me from an embarrassing conversation. While the Westvleteren 12 is the one that all the fuss is made about, the St Sixtus monks also brew a less alcoholic *blond* (5.6 per cent) and a *bruin* (8 per cent). I gratefully accepted the box of *blonds* and took my place in the cafe where I was allowed to purchase a Westvleteren 12, for consumption on the premises. I am not qualified to say whether this is the best beer in the world, but I can say that it was extremely good.

In November 2011 the St Sixtus Abbey monks made an unprecedented foray into the commercial world by releasing a limited number of six packs of Westvleteren 12 in order to raise funds for an extension to the abbey and a new roof. As can be expected with any purchase of Westvleteren, the promotion was a complicated affair of *Da Vinci Code* proportions, involving collecting vouchers from specific Belgian newspapers on one day and finding a Colruyt supermarket with the special packs on the next. The promotion caused chaos on the Belgian roads, as supermarket car parks overflowed and lanes became gridlocked around the Colruyt stores. Thankfully, Pa (my brother-in-law's father of *hanenzang* fame) managed to crack the code, break the car park gridlock, and purchase a box for me for which, as the proud owner of six bottles of Westvleteren 12 and two WXII glasses, I am eternally grateful. In some countries, the offer of a glass in a pack of beer is a novelty sales gimmick, but with Belgian beers use of the correct glass is an essential part of the beer drinking experience and it is practically a criminal offence to serve a beer in a cafe in the wrong glass. There are delicate flutes for some of the fruit beers, goblet shaped glasses for the Trappist beers, straight sided *'pintje'* glasses for lagers, bulb shapes for abbey beers and ales and even stoneware for some of the speciality beers. If you find yourself around the very fruity end of the beer menu in a cafe, and your beer arrives in half a plastic coconut shell, you are in for a treat. You might ask for a bucket to go with it.

The Westvleteren glasses were small goblets with a gold rim and the inscription *ad aedificandam abbatiam adiuvi* ('I helped to build an abbey'), allowing you to feel virtuous whenever you use them. Following the success of the fundraising in Belgium the monks repeated the exercise in the US in 2012, where boxes of 'Westy 12' were released in specialist beer shops under tight control on the auspicious date of 12/12/12. Against the ethics of the St Sixtus monks, unscrupulous purchasers were soon selling boxes for US $600 on eBay. Checking today on the Internet to see if any are still on offer, I see that there are many *empty* Westvleteren beer bottles for sale on eBay.com, with one seller asking a staggering $69.95 for an empty bottle and cap!

I am not so caught up in the hype that I have to spend $69.95 on an empty beer bottle, even if it comes with a cap, but since taking my vow I have become totally enamoured with Belgian beers. In no other 30,540 square kilometres could you find so much variety, quality, quantity, passion and quirkiness. There is nothing remotely boring here, and Belgian beer is going straight to the top of the interesting list. There are so many Belgian beers to discover that I can see my vow is going to last a lifetime, with every trip to Belgium producing more finds: some good, some bad and some arriving in plastic coconut shells. For those taking the vow, I have included a list of beers at the end of the book so that you can keep track of which you have had to date: those you are going to return to, and the mistakes, never to try again.

Some Belgian beer aficionados go so far as to pair different beers with courses of a meal, just as a sommelier will suggest different wines in a fancy French restaurant. A Trappist beer with Belgian beef stew for example, a *kriek* with the chocolate mousse. This does lead to the question of Belgian food. If their beer can be so good, what about Belgian cuisine? This is going to be another area requiring a great deal of first-hand research.

CHAPTER 12
CHOCOLATE, CHIPS AND HORSE

Hercule Poirot tells us two facts about the Belgians. Firstly, they hate being referred to as French, and secondly, they have a love of good food. Nowhere is this more apparent than in a scene from the 1995 TV adaptation of Agatha Christie's *Hickory Dickory Dock*, in the kitchen of Poirot's friend, the very English police Chief Inspector Japp. This is my favourite Hercule Poirot scene, with masterful acting from David Suchet and Philip Jackson, and Anthony Horowitz's screenplay showing that he could have had a career in comedy writing for television if the schoolboy spy thrillers hadn't worked out. Having suffered 'continental cuisine' while lodging with Poirot for a week, the chief inspector invites Poirot to his house to show the Belgian some 'proper English cooking'. The Englishman slops out a plate of watery mashed potato, mushy peas and burnt faggots, proudly identifying each component of the dish to a horrified Poirot. After some quick thinking, Poirot declares that tragically he has 'an allergy of the faggot' or what in Belgium is known as, *'la phobie de faggot'*, and regrettably is unable to eat any of the food. It is a tense moment and with spotted dick still on the menu for dessert, the clearly disappointed Chief Inspector leans in very closely and asks Poirot if he has a *'phobie de dick'*. Poirot diplomatically opts for the cheeseboard only to find it consists of a lump of mouldy Cheddar. It is well worth a quick YouTube look up. Just be careful how you phrase Poirot's phobias when you type them into the search engine, or you may have problems with the pop-up blocker on your PC. Mine is still in overdrive from the time I googled the Brussels Metro station Kunst-Wet.

While being too modest to boast about the virtues of Belgian cuisine, Poirot would not be at all surprised to learn that Belgium has more Michelin stars per head of population than any other country in the world. In fact, a third as many Michelin stars as the French who would have you believe that they are the sole arbiters of fine cuisine, and a whopping five times as many as the Brits, with our over-cooked faggots and manky cheese.

Despite the high density of Michelin stars the Belgians, in line with their modest nature, claim a very humble recipe as their national dish: *moules frites* (French), *mosselen friet* (Flemish) – mussels and chips. On offer at practically every restaurant in Belgium and a firm favourite of my father-in-law, on whose diet I must admit I am basing most of my knowledge of Belgian food. The fancy Michelin stars are not for him – soup, more soup, *mosselen friet*, meat and potatoes, more soup, herrings, waffles, chocolate, cake, coffee and more cake. These are the staples of the Belgian diet.

With the early church's rules forbidding the eating of meat on Fridays, and even for a while on Wednesdays, having decided that one day of penance a week wasn't enough, the Belgian population had to look for meat substitutes. While the well-off could afford turbot, brill or sole from the Belgian coast, the city working class would gather at the ports to purchase mussels brought by small boats along the rivers and canals from the southern Netherlands. The most favoured mussels are still from Zeeland (old Zeeland, not New Zealand) on the Dutch coast just over the Belgian border. Here the shallow waters of the Eastern Scheldt provide ideal growing conditions for huge, tasty mussels. Sixty thousand tonnes are produced in the Dutch waters each year, the majority of which are exported across the border to the expectant Belgians. Size matters if you are a Belgian mussel-eater and the Zeeland mussels are especially sought after, reaching up to 8 cm in length and reputedly being some of the plumpest in Europe.

The mussels are typically served at the table in their cooking pot, either steamed in white wine together with shallots, parsley and butter *(marinière)* or steamed in a stock thickened with cream *(à la crème)*. The Belgians only eat mussels during the months containing the letter 'r' and anxiously await the new mussel season each September. While the tourist restaurants serve mussels from further afield all year long, the Belgians look upon these with disdain, and will disapprove if you think you are 'going local' by ordering *moules frites* when the local mussels are not in season. Staggering amounts of *moules* are eaten in Belgium, with restaurants such as *Chez Leon* in La Rue du Bouchers in Brussels serving nearly a tonne of the molluscs every day.

The accompaniment to the steaming pot of mussels is always a side bowl of *frites* (French), *frietjes* (Flemish) – chips, or 'French fries' as they are mistakenly called in American English. I shall generally refer to them as *frites* in this chapter to avoid writing out all the translations and repeating the insulting description of 'French fries'. The Belgians point out that this phrase dates from World War One when American troops sampled Belgian *frites* for the first time and on hearing French being spoken around them (and probably not being too hot on the geography of continental Europe) declared them to be 'French fries'! And so began a great culinary injustice, with France being given the credit for Belgium's *frites*. This idea is so ingrained in the American psyche that during a boycott of French products in the US due to France's lack of support for the 2003 invasion of Iraq, some Americans gave up eating 'French fries'. Not for too long though – thankfully a Republican politician came up with the idea of renaming them 'Freedom fries' and all was well; they could be consumed by the supersized-bucket load again.

The Belgians claim to have invented *frites* during a harsh winter in the 1680s when villagers along the frozen Meuse River could no longer catch fish and instead took to deep frying small fish-sized sticks of potato. The French counter claim that *frites* were invented by Parisian traders on the Pont Neuf around the time of the French Revolution. No one can really be sure. The fish-substitute story of the Belgians sounds a bit improbable, but as they are particularly hard done by in the whole 'French fries' arena I think we should give them the benefit of the doubt on this one. The Belgians also claim to have brought *frites* to Scotland, with the first chips being sold by the Belgian immigrant Edward de Gernier at a market stall in Dundee in 1874. Thank you, Belgium, for bringing the

Scottish culinary classic of the 'Glasgow salad' to the world. De Gernier is even credited with the idea of serving chips on his Dundee market stall with vinegar and mushy peas – alien concepts to the Belgians back home who consume their *frites* with either the traditional blob of mayonnaise or, since the 1950s, with a bewildering array of exotic and generally rather disgusting sauces, from aioli and andalouse to curry ketchup and Samurai. It has to be said that the Belgians love their *frites*, with recent surveys showing that Belgians would choose a cone of *frites* to be their national symbol, ahead of the Atomium or Manneken-Pis, and that *frites* are what Belgian expatriates miss most about living abroad (well ahead of 'family and friends', who only come in eighth position).

When Belgium broke the world record for not having a government (249 days on 17 February 2011, having pushed the previous record holders, Cambodia and Iraq, into silver and bronze medal positions), Belgian street demonstrators marked the occasion by launching the *frites revolution*. It was Belgium's own little Arab Spring, and thousands of packets of *frites* were handed out free of charge across the country as demonstrators used chips to send a message of Belgian unity to the arguing politicians. The *frites revolution* wasn't entirely successful, as the politicians of Flemish, Walloon, Germanic, right, left, Green, Catholic and liberal persuasion took nearly 300 more days before finally putting together a shaky coalition government. *Frites* may not have worked as a political force, but there is no doubt that they occupy a central position in Belgian culture.

The place to find out more about the Belgians' love affair with the chip is Bruges: not only is Bruges a UNESCO World

Heritage site, but it is also home to the *Friet Museum* – yes, an entire museum dedicated to the humble chip. Museum entrance halls normally smell of cleaning products, gift shop soaps or, in the case of the Congo Museum, dusty dead animals, but the overpowering smell on entering the *Friet Museum* was of a deep fat fryer on full burn. It wasn't clear to me if this odour came from the *friterie* set up in the basement or whether they had a clever mechanism to spray heated cooking oil at you as you opened the door. Once accustomed to the fat-laden air, I concentrated on the exhibits and soon discovered that some Belgians take their *frites* very seriously indeed. There is a national organisation of *frites* fryers known as NAVEFRI (I picture this to be a grand organisation along the lines of NATO, coincidentally also headquartered in Belgium), which hands out knighthoods and medals to the great and the good of the *frites* frying world. They have four tiers of medals: Silver Cross, Knight, Officer and Grand Officer, awarded for varying lengths of service in *frites* frying: at least twenty-five years to become a Knight and a demonstration of 'exceptional commitment to the sector and an invaluable contribution to the defence of the potato frying' for a Grand Officer. What a night the annual NAVEFRI awards ceremony must be, with elated *friterists* walking off stage with their lifetime achievement awards in deep fat frying. I peered through the glass cabinets at examples of these fine medals, with their black, yellow and red ribbons supporting elaborate five-pronged golden crosses with a centrepiece of a little golden cone of *frites*. Further display boards gave the reason why Belgian *frites* are so good – apparently it is down to the double-dip frying and the quality of the fat, preferably unrefined beef tallow mixed with a hint of horse. Yum.

The best part of the museum was a decommissioned *frites* van on the first floor, which unlike most museums' contents in their roped-off sections or behind glass, positively asked to be walked through and played with. I picked up the wire baskets, aluminium *frites* scoops, salt shakers and generally pretended to be frying in the three empty steel drums resembling 1950s open-top washing machines. A sign on the wall read: *Kip in Curry warm 75 francs*. However, there is only a certain amount of time a grown man can play in an empty chip van without it becoming cause for concern and as soon as the next visitors entered the room, I headed off downstairs to the basement in search of the source of the all-pervading *frites* odour, where the museum entrance ticket gave a miniscule discount off a small bag of *frites*. The *Friet Museum friterie* also offered a number of additional deep-fried items for sale – typical of the fare that can be found in every *friterie* across the country. And here lies one of the greatest mysteries of Belgian cuisine – the Belgians, as epitomised by Poirot, are gourmets and gourmands, have more Michelin stars per head than any other nation, the best beer and finest chocolate in the world, invented *frites*, and yet they also consume vast quantities of what can only be described as deep-fried shite. These items (I hesitate to call them 'food' items) are generally animal derivatives: *frikandellen*, *bitterballen*, *kroketten*, suspicious-looking sausages and battered or bread-crumbed shapes with unidentifiable contents. Many are Guantanamo-orange in colour; others, in the form of short sections of tyre track, have a dull, grey hue. *Frikandellen* are amongst the most popular: skinless sausage-shaped products typically made of mechanically recovered meat (MRM) extruded from the remains of chicken and pig carcasses, often including a squirt of knackered old horse extract.

The Belgians see nothing untoward about the consumption of horse meat, fat and burgers, and were generally unphased by the 'horsemeat in the beef lasagne' scandal of 2012 that shocked the delicate UK consumer to the core. Every Belgian town has at least one butcher's shop bearing the sign of a horse's head, selling a variety of cuts of bright red *paardenvlees* (Flemish) or *chevaline* (French). My mother-in-law brought over a suitcase full of Belgian horse steaks for our deep freeze when Conny was pregnant, in the belief that horsemeat is an essential part of a haemoglobin-filled pregnancy diet. A bit of phenylbutazone probably helped for the birth too. While horse is available in every town, Vilvoorde, on the outskirts of Brussels, is seen as the horsemeat centre of Belgium. Restaurants here, such as the subtly named *Horse House*, serve up juicy 500 g steaks, with the only potential for complaints coming from consumers who may suspect that a bit of beef has been passed off as horse.

The Belgians have had far worse things happen to their food, such as the dioxin scandal of 1999, when farmers discovered that adding coolant fluid to chicken feed wasn't a good idea, leading to the resignation of government ministers and the slaughtering of 50,000 pigs and seven million chickens. A bit of horse in your burger – call that a scandal?

Back in the family's home village of Godsheide, standing in the queue at the excellent local *friterie* while waiting for *frites* one Friday night, I couldn't help notice a six-inch long, almost fluorescent pink, shiny sausage amongst the orange and grey nasties in the fridge. The brightly illuminated names of these products displayed on the board above the frying vats didn't make them sound any more appetising than they looked. There was the *bockworst*, the *shaslick* and an all-time favourite: the *grizzly*. Thankfully, the highly suspicious-looking shaft of yellow breaded something with a bulbous orange head turned out not to be the *zigeunerstick* ('gypsy stick') that was listed on the illuminated board, but a *lucifer* ('match'). The proprietor informed me that the shiny pink sausage I had noticed protruding from the orange and grey items was the *Playboy special*, and a fist sized lump of mystery meat that I had been eyeing up was the *Spoetnik*. This last item bursts open when deep fried, presumably in the shape of something which is better suited to a life in outer space. I asked him what was inside it, 'You don't want to know,' he replied with a smile. Even the chief inspector's faggots are more appealing than this.

Having started this chapter with the Belgians' love of good food, Michelin stars and *moules frites*, it seems to have taken an unexpected turn for the worse, with *Spoetniks*, *Playboy specials*, coolant fluid and horse. I now desperately need to bring us back to an area where the Belgians excel and where they have a chance of powering to the top of the interesting list. There is only one food item that can do this, arguably Belgium's most famous product – chocolate.

Just as every Belgian town has its *friteries* and horse butchers, so too will it have a disproportionately high number of chocolate shops: over 300 chocolate companies operate in Belgium, with a staggering 2,000 shops across the country. The main Belgian brands are all present in large numbers: Leonidas, Godiva and Neuhaus, and small ateliers run by fanatical chocolatiers exist in every major town. There is nothing Belgian of course about the origin of chocolate, which is thought to have been discovered by the Mayans of the faulty 'end of the world' calendar fame, on the Yucatan peninsula around 2,000 BC. Cocoa only made it across to Europe some 3,500 years later when the Conquistadors brought it back to Spain. The Spaniards largely kept the secret of cocoa to themselves for a hundred years or so, but fortunately some of the magic beans made their way to Belgium (under Spanish rule at the time) where the first record of cocoa appears in a purchase made by the Abbot of Bandeloo in Ghent in 1635. What the Abbot intended to do with his cocoa is unclear – chocolate bars had not been invented yet, and cocoa powder was either used for medicinal purposes or mixed as a hot drink for the aristocracy. I like to think that the Abbot sat in his cloisters at the end of a long day of prayer, putting his feet up with Belgium's first cup of cocoa. The popularity of the hot chocolate drink soon spread across Belgium and when Henri Escher, the Mayor of Zurich, visited Brussels in 1697, he enjoyed a hot chocolate so much that he took the idea back to Switzerland – perhaps marking the start of the great chocolate rivalry that exists between the two nations today. Joseph Fry made the first commercial chocolate bars in the UK in 1847, and with the industrial revolution underway in Belgium in the nineteenth century, the Belgians bought in chocolate-making machinery from Fry and Cadbury in the UK and from Lindt in Switzerland, making chocolate accessible to the Belgian middle classes for the first time. Jean Neuhaus senior moved from Switzerland to Belgium in 1857, setting up a pharmacy in Brussels serving chocolate-covered medicine. His grandson, Jean Neuhaus junior, replaced the medicine with a variety of soft creamy centres and made chocolate history in 1912 with the invention of the Belgian praline. Mr Neuhaus sold his pralines in paper cones (presumably bought from the *friterie* suppliers) until in 1920, Mrs Neuhaus had the idea of presenting them in a small rectangular box, called a *ballotin*, which has remained the standard packaging for Belgian chocolates ever since.

Belgium was forging its name as the chocolate capital of the world, and a string of chocolatiers set up in the country after Neuhaus senior's arrival in 1857: Charles Neuhaus founded Côte d'Or in Brussels 1883; Antoine Jacques opened a chocolate factory in Verviers in 1896; the Greek–American, Leonidas Kestekides, moved to Belgium when he married a girl from Ghent and started chocolate production in the town in 1913; Joseph Draps opened a chocolate shop in Brussels in 1926, named for some inexplicable reason after Lady Godiva, the naked twelfth-century tax protester from Coventry; and in 1958 Guy and Liliane Foubert joined parts of their first names to come up with Guylian chocolates in Sint-Niklaas from where they manufactured the first hazelnutty seashells and anatomically incorrect chocolate seahorses. While these firms all became household names, the largest chocolate producing company in the world, which can trace its chocolate making history in Belgium back to 1911, is not so well known to the general public. Barry Callebaut (yes, that's really the company name – you would have thought a company with a US $5 billion turnover could come up with something a bit more exotic than 'Barry') produces premium Belgian chocolate for the world's chocolate-making industry. If you are eating something labelled 'made with real Belgian chocolate', chances are that the source of the chocolate is Barry Callebaut. The Belgian company set up production in Africa in the 1950s and has been credited with making the name of Belgium synonymous with chocolate as it exported its 'Belgian' product to chocolatiers around the globe. The 1958 World Expo in Brussels further cemented Belgium's domination of the chocolate market, with four giant chocolate-filled pavilions showing off Belgium's finest creations to the exhibition's 42 million visitors. Côte d'Or even made a special praline bar named the '58' to commemorate the Expo and, like the Atomium, the 58 is still going strong today. The fanciest chocolate shops in Belgium are now found in the Grand Sablon district of Brussels. There are the usual Belgian names and also the beautiful creations of Wittamer, chocolatier to the king, and of Pierre Marcolini, the most upmarket of upmarket Belgian brands. Marcolini is the self-styled 'dream-maker' of the Belgian chocolate world. While consumers of Yorkie bars might see him as something of a knob, his designed-to-impress creations from cocoa beans sourced on his annual Latin American expeditions are pretty much without equal. Just bear in mind that to impress that special someone by sending them, say, a *Suggestion no.3* Marcolini gift box, will set you back a very special €100.

For my foray into the chocolate-making world, and to discover what makes Belgian chocolate so special, I decided to forgo the many chocolate factory tours that are on offer around Brussels and chose instead to go local, visiting the workshop of Limburg chocolatier, Patrick Mertens. In his black trousers and buttoned-up white chef's jacket, Patrick looks like a Belgian Heston Blumenthal – but without the glasses and with a small Belgian flag proudly embroidered on his buttoned-up chef's collar. He has been working with chocolate for over twenty-five years and has a small shop, Boon, in a former Chinese restaurant occupying a 250-year-old building in the Paardsdemerstraat in Hasselt. A short flight of steps from the street took me straight into the chocolate shop, where the heavenly aroma of rich chocolate filled the air and a small queue of shoppers waited patiently in front of the glass cabinets stacked high with the most exquisite chocolate creations – neat rows of pralines, spiced chocolate lollipops for dipping in hot milk and delicate chocolate sculptures of flowers and high-heeled shoes. The cafe was through the back of the shop, in a high-ceilinged room with a dozen or so low sofas and chairs. All signs of the Chinese kitchen have long since gone and Patrick has restored the townhouse to its former glory with its original oak panelling and plaster ceiling. Trendy lightshades hung down into the room, with giant black-and-white photos of Patrick's three-year-old daughter eating chocolate. In contrast to the cosiness of the coffee shop, the atelier across the hallway was stark white tiles and stainless steel, separated from the public by floor-to-ceiling glass, behind which his white-clad team toiled away with molten chocolate.

As we sat with a cup of coffee, Patrick told me of the changes brewing in the Belgian chocolate making world. 'There is a new wind blowing through – the new generation of chocolatiers have their own style; they are more adventurous, not constrained by ways of the past.' He talked passionately about his work, about 'fusion', the search for flavours and his spring and winter 'collections' as though he was talking about haute couture. He showed me his latest creation – a gold-leaf-coated chocolate ball the size of a large hazelnut that fizzes and bobs up and down in a champagne glass. We talked chocolate for a while, about trends and flavours, his collections and about these 'new winds' blowing in the chocolate-making world. And then I asked him my killer questions: 'So what is so special about Belgian chocolate? Why is it so good? Why is it unique?' There was a pause while he contemplated his answer. I sat with pen in hand, ready to take notes from the master chocolatier. I took a sip of coffee and ate a praline while waiting for his words of wisdom. I had read on websites that it could be due to the fine grinding of the cocoa, or the quality ingredients, expert processing, the use of 100 per cent cocoa butter or the dry conching or tempering (I don't know what those terms mean either). Patrick would be able to explain and tell me why Belgian chocolate is so special.

He shrugged his shoulders. 'I don't know,' he said. 'It's just normal. All chocolate should be like this.' So there we have it, from a man who makes the finest chocolates I have ever tasted, whose collections are sold in Harrods, who makes golden balls of Belgian chocolate which fizz in your champagne – Belgian chocolate is 'just normal'. This was a eureka moment for me in my understanding of the Belgians. If I had spoken to a chocolatier from one of Belgium's neighbouring countries, I would no doubt have heard how they make the finest chocolate in the world, how they invented chocolate, how no one else's chocolate is a patch on their own, but for the Belgians producing the best chocolate in the world is nothing to shout about. It's just normal.

It was not the first time I had met Patrick. Hannah and Ruben always insist that we visit his coffee shop whenever we are in Hasselt, but fortunately he did not remember me from our previous meeting. It was two summers ago when a particular coffee had caught my eye on the menu. The Belgians are big coffee drinkers, although thankfully do not yet have the habit of walking down the street with a paper cup of froth from an American coffee chain, preferring instead to sit in a real cáfe for a cup of filtered coffee, typically one of the excellent Belgian roasts of Rombouts or Miko. The coffee is always good quality and is served with a small cake, biscuit or square of chocolate. In Boon, Patrick's coffee chop, the coffee comes with two pralines, a chocolate mousse and a glass of water. The coffee on the menu that had made me look twice was not one of the local brews but had the name *Kopi Luwak of Koffie van de Civetkat*. It was accompanied by a little write-up as to the source of the beans, the advice that it had 'a notable taste' and a staggering price tag of €20 a cup. Civet cat coffee, I learnt, is made from coffee beans that have passed through the digestive tract of a civet cat. Why would anyone want to eat something that has been made from cat poo? Actually, the civet cat is more of a mongoose or weasel creature than a cat, so it's closer to weasel poo than the contents of your cat litter tray. That's still not an attractive proposition. The theory goes that the civet cat sniffs out only the ripest, tastiest berries from the coffee plant, and as the outer part of the fruit is digested, the hard beans in the centre of the fruit make the complete journey from mouth to other end of the animal while being subjected to a cocktail of enzymes and acids that leaves the beans part-roasted when they are pooped out on to the forest floor. The taste for these beans was first brought to Europe by Dutch plantation owners from Indonesia, and from the Netherlands the taste for some fancy poo coffee spread to Belgium. My curiosity got the better of me and I knew I had made the right decision when the waitress's eyes lit up as I ordered a *Kopi Luwak* and she rushed off saying, 'I'll get the chef'. Clearly here was a coffee connoisseur asking for the most expensive coffee in the house. Patrick appeared in his white chef's jacket and showed us a vacuum-packed bag of civet cat poo. It might have been better to see this after the drink, and a dreadful TV image (too readily accessible on YouTube) of Bear Grylls scooping up a bear turd and popping the semi-digested fruity bits in his mouth became fixed in my mind. Patrick told us that he buys the civet cat poo in 100 g bags and that it is the caviar of coffee. I didn't tell him that I don't like caviar. He left and a short while later the waitress arrived with the coffee, proudly placing it in front of me with two hands and murmuring something to me as if she was delivering Holy Communion. It was a small espresso cup with a tiny drop of dark brown liquid wetting the bottom. It had the taste of a very strong espresso. An extremely strong espresso. Quite acidic. Ruben had a sip, instantly regretted it, and asked me if it still counted as one of his five a day if it had come from an animal. I glared at him. It does beg the question – like who first ate mouldy cheese, or first thought it would be a good idea to drink tequila with a dead caterpillar floating in the glass – who first decided to make coffee from poo? Patrick returned while I was pondering this question with Bear Grylls again stuck in my mind with a face full of bear poo, and asked how I was enjoying it. I had just paid €20 for a tiny cup of coffee that had been through the inside of a weasel, but the fear of appearing ignorant in front of the master chocolatier prevented me from telling the truth. I desperately wanted to say, 'It's crap. Literally crap.' It was the emperor's new clothes, but letting my pride get the better of me, I nodded at Patrick with a pathetic, 'Hmm, interesting!' reply.

Patrick advised me to save a sip to last, i.e. until after the two delicious pralines and the small glass of chocolate mousse that accompanied the coffee, as 'it has a long aftertaste'. Unfortunately Patrick was right about the aftertaste – it did have one, and the acrid infusion fought its way back to the top end of my digestive system every so often for the next few hours, as if it was telling me that it had already made one of these journeys and it wasn't keen on making another one.

Civet cat poo coffee is of course an imposter in the Belgian food chapter, as there is nothing Belgian about it apart from its appearance on the menu of some of the fanciest Belgian cafes. In order to get back to the Belgian diet, I shall return to the story of the Catholic Church's influence on Belgian cuisine. We have already seen how the consumption of mussels was a by-product of Church doctrine, but *moules frites* is not the only Belgian classic to have ecclesiastical routes – in an indirect way, we also have the Church to thank for the Belgian waffle.

The humble wafer, according to *Larousse Gastronomique*, has been around in its simplest form of pressed flour and water since the time of ancient Greece and was adopted by the Christian Church in the Middle Ages where it handily transubstantiated or consubstantiated, or did neither, depending on your point of view, into the body of Christ during the Eucharist. During the thirteenth century French holy wafer-makers branched out to make an early form of waffle, the *oublie* – a large circular wafer embossed with religious scenes, made by pressing together two hot irons. Over the next 200 years the *oublie* recipe was enhanced with the addition of yeast and eggs and the circular shape with its biblical scenes was replaced by the plain rectangular grid of the Belgian waffles that we know today. Waffles were especially popular in the lowlands – in the area that is now Belgium – and are clearly depicted in a 1559 painting by Pieter Bruegel the Elder in which a jolly peasant plays a game of dice with three Brussels waffles strapped to his head. An odd place to keep your waffles, but this was sixteenth-century Belgium. In France, the creation of fancier patisserie left the waffle in an evolutionary cul-de-sac, while in Belgium the waffle evolved along two distinct branches. There is the Brussels waffle: a crisp rectangle dusted with icing sugar, so light that Conny used to call it 'baked air', and the Liège waffle; a heavier, doughy, irregular-shaped waffle containing chunks of sugar. Belgian restaurateur Maurice Vermersch took the Brussels waffle to New York's 1964 World's Fair, changing its name for any geographically-challenged Americans to the 'Bel-Gem' waffle. Vermersch's waffle flourished in the US, further evolving over time to become known as the 'Belgian waffle' – a heavy rectangular slab of dough available today in every diner across the States.

While Belgium being the home of the waffle may just slightly nudge Belgian food up the interesting scale, waffles are only a tiny fraction of the pastries and confectionary the country has to offer. As both Conny and my father-in-law used to say, no day is complete without at least one slice of cake or some other Belgian confectionary. The family's home province of Limburg is famous for its *Limburgse vlaai* – giant fruit-filled pies of cherry, apricot or apple on a layer of confectioner's custard. Despite its curious name, the crowning glory of the local fare, and one that must be sampled when anywhere near the north-eastern Flemish province of Limburg, is the *smurfenvlaai* – the glorious coming together of an airy pie crust base, cooked apricot, crème fraîche and Belgian white chocolate shavings. Other regions have their own specialities and in a beautiful Brussels waffle-shaped book titled *Sweet Belgium*, food writers Liesbeth and Robert Inghelram describe nearly 300 further types of pastry, confectionary and 'sugary products' that are enjoyed throughout the country. There are fascinating regional products such as *cuberdons*, nose-shaped cones of raspberry and Arabic gum (which admittedly taste like you have swallowed a small bar of soap); *speculaas*, nutmeg-spiced biscuits (ideal for dunking in your Belgian filter coffee) and a range of curious religious-inspired items such as *guimauve*, squishy marshmallow Mother Marys, *barrette de cardinal* (cardinal's hats) and *nonnenbillen* (nun's buttocks).

If nun's buttocks are unfamiliar outside of Belgium, there is another sweet with Belgian religious routes that is very well known in the UK. In fact, as reported in the *Daily Mail*, it is 'Britain's most popular sweet of all time'. The confectionary was invented in Antwerp in the 1950s by the communion wafer manufacturing business, Belgica. The company was faced with declining church congregations, leading to a fall in demand for their product, and short of coming up with evangelising ideas to fill the churches, they looked for an alternative use for the communion wafer. They had already experimented with sticking two wafers together with medicine in between for the pharmaceutical industry, but now came up with an altogether better invention: the flying saucer. Two communion wafers, a small spoonful of sherbet – and the flying saucer was born.

All in all, Belgian cuisine has turned out to be a mixed bag. There are some obvious lows: the 1990s coolant fluid, the culinary rather than equestrian fondness of horse, the *Playboy special* and its MRM cousins, taking the Glasgow salad to Scotland. But the highs: Michelin stars, *moules frites*, French fries, waffles, cakes, confectionary and above all, Belgian chocolate, far outweigh the lows. Belgian cuisine is definitely going on the interesting list.

The last two chapters have been relatively easy wins: beer was always going to get on the list, and it was likely that Belgian chocolate would triumph over whatever gastronomic nasties the country could throw up. My next research may not be so easy, or enjoyable, as I need to take a look back in time at an activity that has frequently taken place in the country, leading to a fame, of a sort, for modern day Belgium – fighting. It was Julius Caesar who kicked off the popular habit of invading the land that is now Belgium, and for much of the next 2,000 years the small area of land inhabited by the *Belgae* became Europe's most-favoured battlefield, attracting armies from around the globe to kill, maim and gas each other on what is now Belgian soil. While not necessarily an attractive claim to fame, this rather grisly achievement has given rise to Belgium's epithet as 'the Cockpit of Europe' – a far cry from today's populist view of Belgium being the most boring place on earth. There can have been nothing boring about standing in line at Waterloo while the Prussians advanced towards you, hunched in a trench at Passchendaele waiting for the whistle to blow or having a German panzer division camped in your back garden. But is being 'the Cockpit of Europe' interesting, and how could the placid Belgium we know today, with its fine beer, chips, chocolate and no one famous, have been the killing fields of the continent for the best part of two millennia?

CHAPTER 13
THE COCKPIT OF EUROPE

It was Napoleon who said that 'an army marches on its stomach', which may in part explain his keen interest in occupying Belgium, and I like to picture him standing in a queue at a *friterie* in Brussels, waiting to get his cone of *frites* with a dollop of mayonnaise on top. The French had been in and out of what is now Belgium throughout the seventeenth and eighteenth centuries, finally just annexing the whole of Belgium on to France in the late 1700s. They made few friends in the new *départements*, having brought with them religious persecution, compulsory French-speaking, high taxes and mass conscription to feed Napoleon's growing army. According to family legend, one of the men conscripted to join Napoleon's *Grande Armée* was a Mr Houben, Conny's great-great-great-great-great-grandfather. He was enlisted to Napoleon's Russian campaign, setting out in 1812 along with half a million men en route to Moscow, and having the rare and fortunate distinction of being one of the 5 per cent who returned home alive. The family story continues that shortly after arriving home, having survived hand to hand combat with Cossacks, the extremes of the Russian winter, near starvation from the Russian's scorched earth tactics, not to mention having covered the entire 5,000 km on foot, he was promptly kicked in the head by a horse and died. Had Mr Houben lived another year, he would no doubt have been pleased to see the back of Napoleon who was packed off to exile in Elba in 1814, and that, thought the Allies, was that. However, the celebrations would have been short-lived, as in the closing scenes of any good bunny-boiler, just when everyone thought it was safe to come out and play, Napoleon was suddenly back in Belgium with 70,000 French troops at his side. Belgium was an easy target for Napoleon: close by, mainly flat, good food, statue of small boy having a pee. It was the low-hanging fruit of Napoleon's world-domination comeback tour. He stopped off at Waterloo, a day's march from the capital, on 15 June 1815.

Moving forward 200 years or so, even if you are not planning your own world-domination campaign or have little interest in European map-changing history, Waterloo makes a fine stopping-off point on the way to Brussels when approaching from the south. The ideal way to appreciate Waterloo is to sit in the shade of a poplar tree at the edge of the 200-year-old battlefield on a hot summer's afternoon, Belgian beer in one hand and a book on Waterloo in the other. There are of course many books on Waterloo to choose from – 5,087 if Amazon is to be believed – but for me there can be none better than my £8 and £5 eBay purchases of the 1908 and 1921 editions of *Cook's Traveller's Handbook Belgium and Ardennes*. These marvellous little books start with the encouraging opening sentence: 'Few countries within easy access of England offer more attractions to the Tourist than Belgium, and the number of visitors to this interesting kingdom is constantly increasing.' Note the adjective *interesting* being associated with Belgium in the early twentieth century. The books devote thirteen whole pages to the battle of Waterloo, including a chapter reprinted in tiny font from Victor Hugo's *Les Misérables* and the complete set of Wellington's post-battle dispatches, to provide a fully rounded account of the battle.

However, being accompanied by two teenagers meant that an afternoon sitting in the shade contemplating the great European battle of 1815 with a Belgian beer and a chapter from *Les Misérables* was not going to happen. Perhaps unsurprisingly, it is very difficult to generate any interest in old battlefields amongst teenagers. On one hand, encouraging them to conjure up the mental image of a nineteenth-century battle – the sheer terror of the imminent prospect of being hacked to death by a sabre-wielding cavalryman while literally shitting oneself – is not really something you want to instil in a young teenager's mind, and on the other hand, a look at the present day battlefield – a vista of undulating fields of maize, beat and potato – is unquestionably, exceptionally dull. Looking for some middle ground here between these extremes, I opted to splash out on a family 'Battlefield Pass' which promised the excitement of an hour-long battlefield tour, a hike up the Butte du Lion and entry to the Panorama.

Already feeling aggrieved that I had shelled out the best part of €30 on battlefield entertainment, I was none too impressed when the Waterloo Visitor Centre's Madame Pipi informed me that the privilege of peeing at Waterloo would set me back a further €0.40 per person. My very well-argued case that we should have a family discount for three number 1s, which would surely produce less battlefield detritus than any lower combination of number 2s, was not met with a favourable response. No wonder the car park had a whiff of urine about it. We mooched around the gift shop while waiting for the tour to start. Our search for the most outrageous item was won by Ruben, who found small jars of dirt aka 'ground from the battlefield of Waterloo' for €8 a scoop. When the Battlefield Bus finally arrived, it was not quite the air-conditioned coach I had in mind – more of a string of open-air trailers covered in dust, towed behind a lorry. We climbed on board an empty trailer and sat patiently through the French, posh English and Dutch commentaries that welcomed us aboard through loudspeakers hidden somewhere in the trailer upholstery. We should have realised that the several Euros' thickness of dust on the benches was a sign of what was to come, but ignoring this omen we innocently trundled off from the Visitor Centre along the tarmac road in the direction of the potato fields. We learnt along the way from Mr English Posh Voice that the Allies had assembled 168,000 troops under Wellington, set against Napoleon's 78,000 men who were stationed to our left, or it might have been right. I missed the ending as I was sent airborne on hitting the first pothole of a 3 km dirt track that followed a ridge across the potato fields commanded by the Allies. Music between the translations helped set the mood and fill in time as we bumped and juddered our way through choking clouds of dust. We stopped briefly in front of Hougoumont Farm and had a short and welcome respite on a tarmac road before diving back into the dirt bowl between fields of beet and waving sweetcorn. The Frenchman, Mr Posh

Voice and the Dutch-speaking lady were still telling us about cavalry charges and cannon batteries, but the Battlefield Bus occupants were more concerned with hanging on to the trailer and minimising dirt inhalation than the precise whereabouts of the various battalions. Hannah's only comment during the entire tour was to note that we should have brought swimming goggles. We paused at a spot in the beet fields, with dust engulfing the trailers, for the Dutch lady to catch up with us as von Blücher and the Prussians had already arrived in French and posh English. A combine harvester rolled by and we were off again, this time feeling the new and unwelcome sensation of a cobbled road beneath us, when a sudden burst of heavy-duty classical music accompanied the announcement of the end of battle. The statistics didn't make happy listening in any language: 12,000 dead, 35,000 wounded, a large number of amputations without anaesthetic and 12,000 slaughtered horses. We didn't feel very good. There were no more complaints about the bumps or eating dirt, and a few minutes later we crossed the N45 where much to everyone's relief we were on smooth and dust-free tarmac again, with jolly victorious music now blaring through the speakers and a trilingual reminder to visit the gift shop.

While the children were all for cutting our losses and heading for the car, we still had the climb to the top of the Butte du Lion and the Panorama included in our ticket price, and after some parental 'value for money' guidance we passed the sign warning that the 226 steps should only be attempted by 'fit' persons and climbed to the top of the Butte. Built originally by the King of Holland (William I) to mark the spot where his son (William II) was wounded in battle, the 300,000 cubic metres mound of earth, topped with a 28-tonne bronze lion, now stands as a memorial to all those who lost their lives at Waterloo. It's quite impressive if you like large mounds of earth with views of potato and maize fields and squeezing past out-of-breath, overweight American tour groups. Amusing as this is, by far the best attraction in the Battlefield Pass is the wonderful Panorama – a circular building housing a 110 metre-circumference, 12 metre-high depiction of the battle. Opened in 1912, the Panorama was the IMAX cinema of its day, using all the 3D, CGI and digitally-enhanced special effects of the time. Surprisingly, the authors of my 1921 *Cook's Traveller's Handbook* do not appear to share my enthusiasm for the Panorama and having waxed lyrical about the battlefield, Butte du Lion and even given warnings about 'loquacious guides' for thirteen pages, all they could muster to say about the new attraction was: 'at the bottom of the steps [of the Butte] is a panorama of the battle. Admission 1 fr. 25c.'

A waft of musty old museum smell hit us as we entered the building and climbed the rickety wooden staircase to the viewing platform. From here we looked out in semi-darkness around the full 360 degrees of the battle scene, with an assortment of rubble, cannon craters, mutated manikins and stuffed dead horses beneath us. The mural behind the taxidermist's leftovers portrayed the battle scene as it had been imagined by the artist Louis Dumoulin in 1912. French cavalry charges crashed upon the British squares and the various generals looked on from high ground from different points around the circumference. It was like being in a museum of a museum – with faded costumes, stuffing protruding where it was not meant to, odd stains and copious amounts of the famous Waterloo dust. The more recent addition of a looped soundtrack of explosions, screams and neighing horses rendered communication difficult while inside the Panorama and when we stumbled out into the bright sunlight of the summer afternoon a few minutes later, we all agreed that we had experienced enough battle for one day and could drive on to Brussels.

Moving on to Brussels was not an option for Napoleon, who surrendered after a long day of battle on 18 June 1815. Meanwhile, at the Congress of Vienna, European ambassadors had been redrawing the map of Europe since the previous September, and at the start of June turned their attention as to who should be given the Cockpit of Europe. It hadn't always been this way for the Belgians – they had once been in charge of their own destiny, in the time of the Frankish king, Charlemagne, who was born in a small Walloon village near Liège in 742. Charlemagne founded the Holy Roman Empire and went on to rule much of central Europe, giving himself the title of 'Charles the Great' along the way. His not-so-great successors, 'Charles the Bald' and 'Charles the Fat', ruled half of the empire each, and everything went downhill from then on. The superpowers of Europe spent the next thousand years playing pass the parcel with the low countries and using the land as a test site for their latest weapons of slaughter. In 1337, King Edward III of England kicked off the first battle of the Hundred Years War by experimenting with his new weapon, the English longbow, on unsuspecting Flemish fishing villagers on the island of Cadzand. It was the fourteenth-century equivalent of dropping an A-bomb on a small Pacific island to see what would happen, and the Flemish force, led by Sir Guy, the Bastard of Flanders, was annihilated. Sir Guy's title incidentally derives from the dubious marital status of his parents, rather than being an indication of his character. Otherwise it would have been Sir Guy, the Bastard Bastard of Flanders. Edward III had a lot of apologising to do when the English and Flemish became allies a few years later, joining together against their common enemy in the Hundred Years War – the French.

Just when you might have thought it was safe for the Belgians to come out after a hundred years of fighting, the Dutch and Spanish kicked off the Eighty Years War, again running back and forth over what is now Belgium. Once they were done and ownership of Belgium passed from the Hapsburgs to the Spanish, Louis XIV had a go, testing out the impact of 4,000 French cannon balls and 5,000 explosives on a largely undefended Brussels in the bombardment of 1695. A third of the city was flattened before the French army returned home, with no military gain other than the knowledge that cannon fire against someone flinging cobble stones over the wall was really rather effective.

There was little reprieve for the Belgians as just six years later the European superpowers were at it again, this time fighting out the War of Spanish Succession across the low countries. At the victors' post-war territory handing out party, the Belgians found that their land had been given to the Austrians, who managed to hang on to it for the next eighty years or so until France decided to declare war on Austria by taking the easy and now well-trodden path of attacking Austrian-owned Belgium.

Which brings us back to Napoleon's time and the decision at the Congress of Vienna in June 1815 of who should have

Belgium. The Final Act of the congress, signed just before Napoleon's defeat, saw the ambassadors agree over a dozen European land swaps, as if trading properties in a giant game of Monopoly, and the low lands were handed over to William of Orange, joining the areas of Belgium and Holland together as the 'United Kingdom of the Netherlands'.

No one had asked the Belgians who they had wanted to belong to and just fifteen years later, on the night of 25 August 1830, after listening to the patriotic words of Auber's revolution-inspiring opera, *La Muette de Portici*, the well-to-do Bruxellois ran from the Opera House on to the streets of Brussels, joining the peasants revolting outside and together declared that they would have a go at ruling their Catholic country by themselves, thank you very much Mr Protestant William of Orange King. Supported by the British who welcomed a neutral (i.e. small and boring) country across the water, the Belgians declared independence in October 1830. The gene pool of European royalty was dredged in the search for a suitable monarch, with the final *Who Wants to be a King* winner being Prince Leopold Georg Christian Friedrich of Saxe-Coburg, who had the winning combination of being Queen Victoria's uncle, German, a Freemason and not French. Leopold was crowned as the first king of Belgium on 21 July 1831, and the Belgians still commemorate this happy event with a public holiday every 21 July in the form of a flag-waving Belgian National Day. The Dutch finally agreed to relinquish any claim over Belgium when they signed the Treaty of London with the European superpowers in 1839 and the Belgians looked forward to an eternity of peace and prosperity for their very own, brand-new country.

They managed to clock up an impressive eighty-four years without having been invaded, and were heading for the record books with the longest period of peace ever in the land of the *Belgae*, when in June 1914 some unknown archduke was assassinated over 1,000 km away in Sarajevo. Two months later the people from across the Rhine – the Germans – launched the Schlieffen Plan, aiming to capture the French army in six weeks by taking, you guessed it, a quick short cut through flat and neutral Belgium. But the Germans had not counted on the Belgians putting up a fight and the British honouring the small print of the Treaty of London which included a clause that Britain would defend Belgium if it was attacked. With British Empire, French and Allied troops piling in to support the beleaguered Belgian army, there was nothing quick about the German advance, and battle lines were drawn up and trenches dug across Belgium that would remain more or less in place for four long years of slaughter.

Much of the fighting centred around the town of Ypres – a prosperous linen and lace-making town prior to the outbreak of war with, according to my 1921 *Cook's Traveller's Handbook*, 'much rich gothic architecture' and a municipal museum with two Rubens paintings. The British decided that Ypres was of strategic importance and undertook to keep it at all cost in order to stop the Germans advancing to the Belgian coast. Keeping the town 'at all cost' may have seemed like a good idea in 1914, but as Ypres was surrounded on three sides by the front line and was continually pounded by German guns, by 1918 the entire town and its surrounding villages were reduced to little more than smouldering rubble. The soldiers' daily life for the four years – sitting in a trench waiting to be blown up by a falling artillery round – was interrupted by five major offensives around Ypres during which one side or other would start with a period of intense shelling before going over the top and hurling themselves towards lines of firing machine guns. All this for near certain death and the glorious purpose of shifting a trench a few hundred metres one way or the other.

In the time-honoured tradition of trying out newly-invented killing mechanisms in Belgium, the Germans tested a Zeppelin air ship for the first time with a bombing raid on Liège when the Schlieffen Plan was launched in August 1914. Although they succeeded in creating panic on the ground, the Zeppelins caused little material damage and they came with a fundamental design flaw for military use – being excessively large, slow, and filled with highly flammable gas. Not to be disheartened by this lack of success, the German inventors came up with a far more efficient way of spreading death and terror, and at the Second Battle of Ypres in April 1915 experimented with the first use of poison gas by dropping 168 tonnes of chlorine along trenches held by French, Moroccan and Algerian troops. By 1917 the poison gas experiments had led to the invention of mustard gas which was used in such quantities around Ypres that the French troops referred to it as *Yperite*. The British soldiers were not so literate and simply called it 'HS', short for 'Hun Stuff'. And if poison gas wasn't enough, the Germans had a go with another new invention: *flammenwerfer*, flamethrowers, which were used for the first time in World War One on British positions at Hooge on the outskirts of Ypres. Whether meeting traditional horrific ends, or the newly invented, even more unimaginably horrific means of death, over a million Allied and German soldiers were killed or wounded in the slaughter around Ypres between 1914 and 1918. The Schlieffen Plan of taking a quick short cut through Belgium didn't go down in the history books as a classic military success.

Having declared that visits to mass cemeteries were not at the top of her holiday activity list, Hannah opted to stay at home with her Belgian cousins, while Ruben and I borrowed sister-in-law Betty's car and set out for Ypres – the focus of Belgian World War One memorial activity. Fortunately satnav lady knew the way, as curiously we didn't see a single signpost to Ypres. As we drew near our destination, we started seeing a lot of signs for what Ruben and I took to be some form of leper infirmary. 'Why would so many people want to drive here to see a leper?' Ruben asked. But 'leper', it transpired, or more precisely, 'Ieper', is the Flemish name for what the Walloons, French and most British books refer to as Ypres. The English soldiers were equally perplexed by the different names and made up their own anglicised version, simply referring to the town as 'Wipers'.

My 1921 *Cook's Traveller's Handbook* still waxed lyrical about the wonderful gothic architecture and masterpiece-stuffed museums of Wipers, evidently copying this information across from a pre-war edition, but a hastily added postscript of, '*but this has been destroyed*' had been added after the now redundant descriptions. I was therefore somewhat surprised on arrival in Ypres to find that the town looked remarkably whole and medieval. It transpired that German reparations after the war had paid for the entire town to be rebuilt, stone by stone, with the Cloth Hall only being completed some fifty years later. Perhaps the German money was still being put to use, as we had to circle the Flanders Fields museum building three times in order to find the 'under restoration' way in. Once inside, the euphoria of finding the ticket desk and the museum entrance, quirkily concealed on the second floor of the building, quickly dissipated. The eerie whistle of a bomb falling followed by the sound of an explosion made Ruben jump every few minutes. It was a clever way of showing the permanent terror felt by those sitting waiting in the trenches, although if I could make a suggestion, spraying a bit of trench foot around and tossing the occasional rat across the floor every now and again would make it even more authentic. There was an exceptionally depressing display of the Christmas Eve football match that took place between the Ypres trenches in 1914, showing how the war came tantalisingly close to ending. But after singing Christmas carols, playing football and exchanging German *bratwurst* and McConnachie's tinned stew, they were back to bombing and bayoneting each other on Christmas Day. There was an even more depressing section given over to the short-lived war poets. A reading of John McCrae's *In Flanders Fields* was accompanied by pictures of poppies and the sound of larks singing, while Wilfred Owen's *Dulce et Decorum Est*, recounting the agonising death of a gas attack, was accompanied by the visual aid, in case we needed it, of gas masks filling with smoke. The museum is well worth a visit, but don't expect to come out of it with a spring in your step or a smile on your face. We trudged on to the inevitable gift shop, flicking through books with titles such as *Dark Journey*, *Killing Time* and *Mopping Up*, with black-and-white front cover photographs of mud, dead bodies and cemeteries. A postcard of Manneken-Pis peeing on departing German soldiers was the best we could find to lighten the mood, but the museum could really do with the offer of a screening at the exit of *The Wipers Times* or an episode of *Blackadder Goes Forth*, for those in need of counselling.

Looking for an outdoor activity that might lift the spirits, we drove out to Tyne Cot cemetery on Passchendaele Ridge, home to 12,000 war graves looked after by the Commonwealth War Graves Commission. I missed the car park on arrival and found myself driving through the gardeners' entrance and on to the main cemetery, upsetting visitors and cemetery-keepers alike. Once installed in the right parking lot, and leaving a suitable length of time so as not to be recognised as the person who had just made a U-turn in the graveyard, we followed the track to the excellent Tyne Cot cemetery visitor centre. The voice of a sad lady greeted us from the bushes, reading out names of the dead every seven seconds:

'Egbert Dredge, aged 21.'
'Thomas Hume, aged 23.'
'Cecil Crawford, aged 21.'

And so she carried on, from bush to bush, from little black loudspeakers placed every few metres by the side of the track.

The fighting at Passchendaele in the Third Battle of Ypres had been particularly severe. It followed one of the most ambitious military mining operations in history, with the Allies digging 8 km of tunnels beneath the German front lines along the Messines Ridge and packing them with over one million kg of explosives. The mines were exploded at 3.10 a.m. on 7 June 1917, killing an estimated 10,000 German troops in an explosion that was heard in London. As if this wasn't enough, in July the Allies spent a fortnight firing over four million shells at German positions, and when the bombardment was done the ANZACs and Canadians went over the top. In 100 days the Allies managed to advance the grand total of 8 km, with 245,000 Allies and 215,000 Germans killed, wounded or missing in action.

I'm not sure what I had expected of Tyne Cot cemetery at Passchendaele. I hadn't been to anything near this scale before – I learnt in the visitor centre that Tyne Cot is the largest Commonwealth war cemetery in the world – and I don't know why I had thought that a visit to a war cemetery would be a mood-shifting thing to do after the onset of deep depression caused by the Flanders Fields museum. Row upon row of white tombstones stood in silence, with only the drone of a lawnmower in the distance. It was overwhelming. Incomprehensible. The futility of it all. Young men blown up, mown down, torched, gassed in their prime. And this cemetery of 12,000 graves only represents a tiny fraction of the hundreds of thousands who had perished to move the Passchendaele line just 8 km. Some of the tombstones were inscribed with the occupant's name. Recently visited graves had flowers or a little wooden cross in front, with 'to Granddad' or 'to Great Uncle' handwritten in pen. Most of the stones were just marked, 'A soldier of the Great War – Known unto God'.

There was blue sky overhead, the sun shone brightly, and right on cue a skylark started up, just as we had heard in the recording in the museum. I looked around for a loudspeaker hidden in a flower pot, but it was the real thing – *Alauda arvensis* spiralling skywards on a summer courtship flight. I mumbled what I could remember of the poem to myself.

In Flanders fields the poppies blow
Between the crosses, row on row,
That mark our place; and in the sky
The larks, still bravely singing, fly
Scarce heard amid the guns below.

We are the Dead. Short days ago
We lived, felt dawn, saw sunset glow,
Loved and were loved, and now we lie,
In Flanders fields.

McCrae wrote his poem in Ypres in 1915, and was dead from pneumonia before the war was out. Through McCrae's poem, Belgium has given us the red poppy symbol of the British Legion and Remembrance Day. A useful bit of trivia for those 'there's nothing famous in Belgium' questions, but given the choice, not something the country would wish to be known for. As we left, the haunting voice followed us again from the bushes:

'John Ensley, aged 18.'
'Percy Barber, aged 21.'
'William Edwin Shute, aged 22.'

There are however two things about Ypres that do genuinely lighten the mood and take your mind away from troubled thoughts of the incomprehensible slaughter of World War One. First, there is the *Kattenstoet* – a festival held every three years, dating from the Middle Ages, in which live cats are hurled off the top of the Ypres belfry tower and witches are burnt at the stake. Nowadays health and safety jobsworths have reduced the spectacle to toy cats being flung from the high tower and only effigies of witches are allowed to be burnt, which diminishes the authenticity of this age-old Belgian tradition but nonetheless brings a smile to an otherwise overly solemn place. Secondly, if you are in Ypres, you are just 15 km from St Sixtus Abbey, home and sole purchase point of Westvleteren 12 – repeatedly voted 'the best beer in the world' and the holy grail for anyone who has taken the Belgian beer vow. If you are anywhere near Ypres, there is no excuse; you must visit the St Sixtus Abbey cafe and pile however many bottles they allow you to buy (it will be a very small number) into your pockets, backpack, suitcase, car boot, trailer – whatever you have to hand. While the other five Trappist breweries in Belgium were taken over by the Germans during the war and most of the area around Ypres was flattened by the continual bombardment, the Abbey of St Sixtus remained in Allied hands and miraculously intact. The Germans removed the copper brewing equipment from their captured abbeys to melt down for the war effort, but the Allies left the St Sixtus monks to continue brewing their fine beer in the original copper vessels. The abbey's grounds were taken over to house a large military hospital and I would like to think that many a soldier's last wish would have been granted here – with the world's best beer on tap by his bedside.

After the faith-restoring trip to St Sixtus Abbey, we headed back to Ypres for the final part of the World War One memorial experience – the 'Last Post' being played at the Menin Gate.

Members of the local fire brigade have been bugling the 'Last Post' at the eastern end of the gate every evening at precisely 8.00 p.m. since 11 November 1929, only taking a break, for reasons that should be obvious, between May 1940 and June 1944. No matter what the date is when you are reading this book, a certainty that you can count on is that today at 8.00 p.m. in Belgium the firemen of Ypres will be, or will have been, bugling the 'Last Post' at the Menin Gate.

The restaurants of Ypres emptied promptly at 7.45 p.m. as British, Australian and New Zealand diners headed off towards the gate – a large stone arch crossing the Meensestraat and home to the names of the 54,406 British and Commonwealth servicemen who have no known grave. A crowd of several hundred had gathered beneath the arch: tourists, school groups, ANZAC soldiers, medal-laden veterans and visiting bands. There was a buzz in the air of pre-concert excitement. Musical instruments tuned up, berets were straightened and then all stood still in complete silence. A voice from somewhere in the crowd instructed us in English and Flemish not to applaud as this was an act of remembrance. A group of flag-bearing ANZAC soldiers and sailors marched in to a clearing under the arch and following some very nifty flag twirling (I expect that's not a military term) worthy of any Olympic opening ceremony or Majorettes' championship, an Aussie schoolchildren's choir on their European tour burst into song. These were just the warm up acts for the four Ypres firemen who took centre stage to bugle the melancholy 'Last Post'. The sound of the bugles echoed hauntingly around the stone walls beneath the arch and a ray of light from the evening sun caught the inscription on the wall opposite me: '*Here are recorded names of officers and men who fell in Ypres Salient but to whom the fortune of war denied the known and honoured burial given to their comrades in death.*'

The crowd was silent. Even the Dutch school group who had been chattering during the flag twirling now stood still, with baseball caps in hands and heads bowed as Binyon's *Ode of Remembrance* was read out.

> *They shall not grow old, as we that are left grow old,*
> *Age shall not weary them, nor the years condemn*
> *At the going down of the sun and in the morning,*
> *We will remember them.*

A motorbike roared down the Bollingstraat during the minute's silence and an orderly queue formed for those laying wreaths on the steps to the side of the arch. National anthems were sung and then the Aussies were off, following their marching band blasting out 'Waltzing Matilda'.

The Menin Gate memorial was only completed in 1927 and it took the Commonwealth War Graves Commission a further eleven years to carve over 500,000 headstones, plant 140 km of hedges and build 160 km of walls around their cemeteries before declaring that they had finished the job. Safe in the knowledge that there would be no further call on their cemetery building skills after the Great War, the war to end all wars, they packed up and went home in 1938.

But the War Graves Commission had not counted on the plans of a World War One survivor – an Austrian who had joined the German army after failing to qualify in his own country and who had spent much of the war in the German trenches around Ypres. He took part in the First and Second Battles of Ypres, earning an Iron Cross along the way, was sent across the border to France for action at the Battle of the Somme and was back in Belgium again for the Fifth Battle of Ypres in 1918, where he was temporarily blinded by a British gas attack. This probably didn't make him overly-friendly to the British. The soldier's name was Adolf Hitler. Rather disturbingly, Hitler reminisced in 1941: '*I brought back home with me my experiences at the front; out of them I built my National Socialist community.*' That's not a great advertisement for the 'Made in Belgium' brand.

It can hardly come as a surprise by now to learn that Hitler's plan to wipe out the French army at the start of World War Two consisted not of marching straight into France but of taking a quick short cut through, yes, you guessed it – neutral and inoffensive Belgium. The heavily fortified Maginot Line which the French had built along their border with Germany as an impregnable defence might as well have had large arrows painted on it, pointing north, reading 'Invade here'. On 10 May 1940, German troops poured into Belgium around the northern end of the rather embarrassingly useless Maginot Line. Keeping up the tradition of using Belgium as a test-site for new methods of warfare, the Germans launched their invasion by carrying out the first airborne assault with the innovative combination of military gliders, paratroopers equipped with flamethrowers and specially designed bunker-busting bombs. To maintain the element of surprise, the fifty German gliders came silently across the border at dawn landing on and around the Belgian fort of Eben-Emael which controlled a large section of the Albert Canal and strategic bridges which would be used to bring the German troops into Belgium. It was a brilliant and daring attack in which the fort's guns were silenced and two of the bridges secured. Had the Germans won the war, instead of watching *The Dam Busters* and *The Great Escape* every bank holiday weekend we would be watching endless re-runs of *Segelflugzeug mit Flammenwerfer zum Eben-Emael*.

Attacking from the north had the effect of luring both the French army and the British Expeditionary Force into Belgium. It looked like the Schlieffen Plan all over again but the Germans had learnt their lesson from the disaster of World War One and this time, in Return of the Schlieffen Plan, or the *Sichelschnitt* ('sickle cut') as Hitler called it, the Germans unveiled their cunning plan – to draw the Allies to the north of Belgium and then entrap them by invading with an even larger German force through the Ardennes to the south.

The northern invasion force, coming over the bridges secured by the flame-throwing paratroopers at Eben-Emael, engaged the French army in the Battle of Hannut – the largest tank battle in history up to this point, with over 1,200 German and French tanks facing each other on the flat Belgian countryside to the west of Liège. While most of us are blissfully unaware of the significance, or even the existence of this battle, an American military geek website ranks the Battle of Hannut as number 5 in the 'Ten Most Epic Tank Battles in Military History'. How's that for not being boring? El Alamein only makes the list at number 9. And if you are an avid reader of *Wargames Illustrated*, you will of course remember issue 276 which told you how to re-enact the epic battle with tiny miniature plastic tanks that you can buy for the bargain price of US $1,500 (postage included). However despite its 'epic' status in world tank battle rankings, the Battle of Hannut was rather inconclusive, with the French sort of winning on the first day, the Germans sort of winning on the second day, and then what was left of the French tanks trundling off to the south when they heard about the attack from the Ardennes.

We are all familiar with what happened next – the humiliating defeat of the British and French armies turned into a propaganda coup by Winston Churchill as over 300,000 soldiers were lifted off the beaches a couple of kilometres over the Belgian border, at Dunkirk in northern France. The Allies were quick to blame each other for the disaster. The British and French traded insults with one another, but like two playground bullies in a fight, they soon turned on someone smaller and defenceless to give the full blame – little, neutral Belgium. When asked if Belgian soldiers could join the British and French evacuation from the beaches, the Chief of General Staff of the British forces is reported to have said, 'We don't care a bugger what happens to the Belgians' – hardly a sentiment to engender strong Anglo–Belgian relations. Belgium's King Leopold III didn't help the situation by surrendering on 28 May 1940, just as the evacuation from Dunkirk had started, and the British and French were left to get off the beaches by themselves.

Leopold III decided to stay with his people in Belgium during the war and did not join his government in exile, which fled first to Paris and then to London when the French surrendered less than a month after the Belgians. While Leopold III reputedly had a rather cosy time of it in the Royal Palace in

Brussels, the rest of the country suffered terrible deprivations during the occupation. Conny's grandparents took in orphans and refugees and ended up looking after a family of sixteen. Her grandfather's meagre income to support the family came from his job as an inspector in a coal mine which he cycled to every day. When a group of German soldiers came to the house late one night to demand his bicycle, he said that it had already gone while it stood above their heads in the hay loft. Fortunately they did not find it in their search – if they had, he would have been shot or sent to a concentration camp, joining the 25,000 Belgian Jews who the Nazis deported to Auschwitz.

Four years after the humiliation of Dunkirk, the Allies were back in France with their new partners in Europe, the Americans. Having pushed through from the D-Day landings in June 1944, the Allies liberated Belgium in November. At last, the Belgians thought, they were free. No more wars. The war after the war to end all wars had run across their country, twice. Now, surely, that would be it. Meanwhile in Berlin, Hitler had other ideas. He was facing the problem of fighting the war on an increasing number of fronts and came up with a master plan to bring German victory in Europe: he would launch a devastating attack to the west, knock the Allies back to the sea, negotiate peace with the Western powers and then concentrate all his efforts on the Russian front. But where should he attack in the West? He had the choice of Norway, Denmark, the Netherlands, Belgium and the length of France. Using the same expert logic as General Melchett in *Blackadder Goes Forth*, Hitler decided to launch his massive counter-attack in exactly the same place he had launched the last attack, and therefore, the place the Allies would least expect it.

Astonishingly, this logic appeared to work and the Americans were totally unprepared when five panzer divisions and eight infantry divisions, containing nearly a quarter of a million German soldiers, crossed the Rhine and raced through the Belgian Ardennes on 16 December 1944. *Unternehmen Wacht Am Rhein* (Operation Watch on the Rhine) became known as 'the Battle of Bulge' to the Americans, as the panzer divisions reshaped the Western Front, surrounding the Americans at Bastogne and pushing westwards in the direction of Antwerp. The Battle of the Bulge, immortalised with varying degrees of accuracy in Henry Fonda's 1965 Hollywood blockbuster of the same title and the excellent 2001 *Band of Brothers* series, became the Americans' bloodiest battle of World War Two, claiming nearly 20,000 US lives. Amongst the many thousands of other Allied and German casualties were 3,000 Belgian civilians who happened to be living in the wrong place at the wrong time. Hitler could have benefited from Edwin Starr's fine words on the value of war, as three months after launching his counter-attack his troops were back to their starting positions on the banks of the Rhine, with absolutely nothing to show for it apart from a trail of death, destruction and prisoner of war massacres on all sides. The return to their starting positions followed vicious street fighting through the eastern provinces of Belgium, including the towns that now make up the corners of the Formula One circuit at Spa-Francorchamps. Belgium was, at last, free from war.

The aftermath of two world wars, however, still lingers on and the Belgian army's bomb disposal unit has to deal with an annual total of nearly 200 tonnes of World War One and World War Two munitions which find their way to the surface or are uncovered by farmers, construction workers or gardeners. Pushing a spade into the ground in the back garden of a house around Ypres is a risky hobby. It has been estimated that 1.5 billion shells were dropped on Flanders fields in World War One alone, with a quarter of them sinking into the mud without exploding. The most extraordinary pieces of unexploded ordinance have to be the leftovers of the Messines Ridge mining operation. Nineteen of the giant bombs were exploded under the German trenches, but several were left in place due to tunnel collapses or were abandoned due to discovery by the Germans. An entire set of mines at the south end of the ridge became obsolete when the Germans moved their positions and were never detonated. We are not talking about your average unexploded shell or landmine here, but vast underground caverns packed floor to ceiling with over 20,000 kg of explosives, large enough to blow the side of the hill off. Exactly how many of these mines are left and where they are located is a matter of some conjecture, but in 1955 the location of one of the mines was revealed when a lightning strike detonated it – leaving behind a massive crater and a dead cow. What is thought to be the world's largest unexploded bomb has been identified sitting beneath a barn at the south end of the ridge. With 22,000 kg of explosives beneath his feet, the owner doesn't jump up and down a lot, or particularly enjoy thunderstorms.

So what have we learnt in the 2,000 years since Caesar wrote his report on the troublesome *Belgae* fighting with those people from across the Rhine? Belgium has brought us thoroughly-tested killing machines, the red poppy symbol of remembrance, Adolf Hitler, a number 5 ranking in the 'Ten Most Epic Tank

Battles in Military History', the biggest unexploded bomb in the world and periodic large dents in the size of the human population. That's not a great legacy. In fact with such a tragic history, Belgium has done well to hold the image of being *boring*. After what has been perpetrated on its soil, it could be seen as the sorriest, saddest little country in Europe. The sighs and pained expressions on the faces of your fellow dinner party guests as you tell them that you are spending your summer holiday in Belgium should not be of boredom but of deep sadness. We should burst into tears at the mere mention of Belgium. I will have to press on with my quest, hopefully finding one more item for the interesting list. My best chance may lie in sport – even if chicken-singing drew a blank, there might be one sport that produces heroes, champions, famous people, someone, something of interest. But what is Belgium's national sport?

CHAPTER 14
BELGIUM'S NATIONAL SPORT?

Finding the national sport of Belgium wasn't as easy as I had expected. My initial research drew a blank, and despite the many thousands of pages of no doubt very useful information on the government's official website, not one of them identifies or describes anything as the country's 'national sport'. This is surely a missed opportunity for the EU: each European state could be forced to have its own official sport which would need regulating, supervising, controlling, comparing, contrasting, promoting, subsidising and translating in twenty-three languages – just think of all the tantalising paperwork that could be generated. Something for Herman to consider when he's next scribbling haikus in a bored moment at a European Council meeting.

Football is certainly a worthy contender and depending on your knowledge of the UEFA and various European championships, you may, or may not, have heard of the four main Belgian teams: Anderlecht, Club Brugge, Standard de Liège and Genk. They have all made appearances in the

European leagues, and had occasional wins, although you will need a long memory to recall their strongest years of the 1970s and 80s. The national team, the *Rode Duivels* (Flemish), *Diables Rouges* (French) or *Rote Teufel* (German) – the 'Red Devils', on account of their generally red kit – have not fared much better, achieving at their peak a fourth place finish in the 1986 World Cup. Apart from a minor rise in pulse rate caused by a 1–0 win over Argentina in their 1982 opening game and a disallowed goal against Brazil in 2002, it has been difficult to get very excited by the Red Devils – the only interest being whether they would get to the group stages or not, and if they did, how long could they hold on before being knocked out. Things may be looking up for the Red Devils though, as at the time of writing, twelve Belgian players are in top teams in the English Premier League, from Eden 'I didn't kick the ball boy' Hazard of Chelsea, to hard man Vincent Kompany of Manchester City, who carried on playing a World Cup qualifier for Belgium while suffering from a broken nose, a cracked eye socket and concussion. It's a good try, but football doesn't make it as the national sport.

Tennis can make a good claim to be the national sport of Belgium, and it's not often that a country just half as big again as Wales can rightfully claim to have two of the greatest women players in the world at the same time. Both Kim Clijsters and Justine Henin were winning the Grand Slams between 2004 and 2010 (an astonishing thirteen Grand Slam victories between them), with Clijsters even coming back from maternity leave in 2009 as the first unseeded player ever to win the US Open.

Some would say that one of the peculiar bird-related 'sports' could qualify as the national sport of the country. *Hanenzang,* as related in the first chapter, is rather niche but modern-day pigeon-racing (invented in Belgium in the mid-nineteenth century, with its world governing body centred in Brussels) and *vinkensport* are more mainstream. *Vinkensport,* recently placed on the register of Flemish culture, is a 400-year-old 'sport' related to *hanenzang* in that it is a competition based on the number of times a caged bird sings in an hour. The difference is that *vinkensport* involves caged male chaffinches pointlessly singing for a mate instead of brutish cockerels crowing. Each *vinkenier* (finch owner) sits on a small wooden stool in front of a caged finch singing in a darkened wooden box, in a long row down the middle of a road closed off for the event. They sit bent over listening intently for sound from their bird's cage and mark each call with a stroke of chalk on a metre-long pole that they clutch for the hour-long contest. The winner is the *vinkenier* whose bird sings the most times in an hour. Fascinating stuff and very popular, with an estimated 13,000 enthusiasts who spend their Sunday mornings sitting in the middle of a road waiting for their bird to chirp. With the pressure on to sing upwards of 600 times in the hour in order to produce a winning score, rumours circulate about doping scandals and other tricks to fire up your chaffinch before the competition. Playing heavy metal to your bird during training sessions is allowed, but thanks to a campaign by blinded World War One veterans in the 1920s, poking your chaffinch's eyes out is no longer permitted. Quite understandably, the Flemish bird protection society, *Vogelbescherming Vlaanderen*, is not keen on the sport, but they may have approved of an ingenious form of cheating that is said to have taken place in the 2007 *vinkensport* season – a mysterious bird that chirped precisely

725 times in three consecutive competitions. Suspicious judges opened the blacked out cage, only to find a small CD player in place of the bird.

Another equally bizarre Belgian sport involving birds – or models of birds – is 'vertical archery'. This involves archers shooting at bird-shaped targets up to 20 m above their heads. Although the end of the arrow is flattened, there is still the rather obvious disadvantage of this sport, in that what goes up must come down, and it's generally not advisable to stand directly beneath an arrow that you have just shot vertically above your head. Belgium also leads the way in a safer, horizontal version of this bird-shooting archery and managed to sneak ten events, such as the 'Team fixed large bird' and 'Individual moving bird, 50 m' into the 1920 Antwerp Olympics. The sport took the other Olympians so much by surprise that no one else entered four of the events, leaving the Belgians to win gold, silver and bronze, and overall to claim eight gold medals out of the ten events. Unsurprisingly, long distance bird-shooting with a bow and arrow was dropped from the subsequent Olympic games and is probably a bit too niche to be in the running for Belgium's national sport.

Fishing is a popular sport in Belgium and while I expect there may well be exciting trout fishing streams in the Ardennes, my experience of this Belgian 'sport' is the common sight of a lone man hunched in a folding chair in the rain on the concrete bank of the Albert Canal, rod on the rest, Thermos flask in one hand and fag in the other. Grey skies over a grey canal in a post-industrial landscape – nothing could sum up boredom more than this bleak image, with the only prospect of excitement during the many lonesome hours spent on the canal bank being the unlikely capture of a solitary carp that will need the hook and maggot ball removed from its mouth before being tossed back into the muddy water from whence it came.

While these contenders for the title of the national sport of Belgium can all make a case, there is one sport that is associated with Belgium more than any other. In the absence of any official government stipulation as to what may or may not be classed as the country's official sport, I shall take the word of my father-in-law, an avid follower of all Belgian sports, that *wielrennen* (cycling) should be given the title. One of his many disappointments on visiting Conny in Jersey during the summer (in the pre-Wiggins and Froome days) was the shocking discovery that there was practically no coverage of the *Tour de France* on British television. He was used to sitting in his armchair at home, with the remote control glued to his hand as he flicked through at least six different Flemish, French, Dutch and German channels throughout the day, each with live coverage of the course with their different camera angles and commentaries. Like many Belgians, his diary is dictated by the 'season' and he rarely leaves home while the great races are on. These start in February, with the first of the one-day 'Classics'. The five most prestigious of these, and not to be missed on any account, are referred to as 'Monuments'. These are the Milan–San Remo in Italy, the *Ronde van Vlaanderen* in Belgium, the Paris–Roubaix in France, the Liège–Bastogne–Liège in Belgium and the *Giro di Lombardia* in Italy. Only three cyclists have won all five Monuments – all three of them Belgian. After the Classics and the Monuments come the three 'Grand Tours': the *Tour de France*, the *Giro d'Italia* and the *Vuelta a España*, during which time my father-in-law cannot be away from the television. When the summer season ends, the Belgian bike fans turn to their other great love – *veldrijden* (cyclo-cross) where mud-splattered participants part-cycle, part-run, part-slide across the water-logged fields, hills and bogs of Belgium. The Belgians, and the Flemish in particular, dominate this strange sport, and since the Cyclo-Cross World Championships started in 1950 have produced nearly three times as many winners as any other nationality.

If cycling is Belgium's greatest sport, Belgium's greatest cyclist, is of course the famous *Tour de France* winner, holder of four Olympic gold medals, winner of six cycling World Championships and all round national hero: Sir Bradley Wiggins. Yes, Wiggo was born in Ghent, East Flanders in 1980 to an English mother and an Australian professional cyclist father. If the marriage had worked out, Wiggo would have grown up in Belgium and there would be a display cabinet reserved for him as one of the greatest *Flandriens* in the National Cycling Museum in Roselare. But wedlock was not cycling pro Gary Wiggins' forte, and when marriage number two broke down Linda Wiggins returned to the UK with their two-year-old toddler Bradley. The rest, as they say, is British cycling history.

Both British and Belgian cycling fanatics will be upset with me for having dared to suggest that Sir Wiggo is the greatest Belgian cyclist, as this title, and many would say, the title of the world's greatest cyclist belongs to Edouard Louis Joseph Merckx, aka Eddy 'The Cannibal'. Eddy Merckx is to cycling what Pelé is to football and Muhammad Ali to boxing. He is an icon, a legend. Five times winner of the *Tour de France*, five times winner of the *Giro d'Italia* (winning both in the same year three times). He still has more stage wins in the *Tour de France* than any other rider ever, is three times winner of the World Championship and in his peak year of 1971, he won nearly half of all the races he entered. While Eddy's achievements are well documented in many excellent biographies, something that you don't come across in the books is the startling fact that Eddy Merckx is the secret identical twin of Frankie Howerd. Apart from the small matter of the timings of their births, there can be no doubt about it – just look them up on Google Images.

Eddy was born in the village of Meensel-Kiezegem in Flemish Brabant in June 1945. It was not a happy place to be in post-World War Two Belgium. One of the branches of the Merckx family had sided with the Germans during the war and a Gaston Merckx was shot by the Resistance in August 1944 for collaboration, resulting in the rounding up and deportation of seventy-one villagers – nearly the entire male population – to Neuengamme concentration camp in Germany. Only eight survived and on their return to Belgium in August 1945, vicious reprisals added to the injustice and division in the village. Although Eddy's parents had not been involved, the atmosphere in the village can hardly have been conducive to raising a child and in 1946, a year after Eddy was born, the family moved from their Flemish village across the language divide to the French-speaking Brussels suburb of Woluwe-Saint-Pierre. Unlike many of his cycling contemporaries, Eddy grew up to be bilingual, not seeming to bother if he spoke French or Flemish. Belgian cycling at this time was deeply divided along regional and language boundaries, with the heartland of the 'real' Belgian cyclists – *de Flandarien* – being the Flemish regions of West and East Flanders. Eddy, with his

Bruxellois background, had a unifying effect on Belgian cycling and broadened its appeal from its working-class Flemish routes. Merckx won the amateur World Championship in 1964, the professional World Championship in 1967 and his first *Tour de France* in 1969. He didn't just win the 1969 *Tour*, he annihilated the competition – all the great riders of the day – by making a break on the now legendary seventeenth stage from Luchon to Morenz, where he tore away from the peloton on the Col du Tourmalet and rode alone for the remaining 140 km. He won the green jersey, the yellow jersey and the mountain classification that day, a feat unmatched by any other cyclist before or since, and he went on to win the 1969 *Tour* with a margin of a staggering seventeen minutes and fifty-four seconds. Extra trains were put on from Brussels to Paris for his arrival on the Champs Élysées on the last day of the *Tour*, as Belgium emptied to the French capital to cheer him home. On the same evening that I lay sulking in the caravan in the Netherlands, as man walked on the moon for the first time, Eddy and every Belgian was out celebrating Belgium's first win in the *Tour de France* for thirty years, and the beginning of cycling world domination by Eddy 'The Cannibal' Merckx.

Merckx was unstoppable, indestructible, cycling on after crashes no matter how many bones were broken. There was one incident however that had a lasting impact on Merckx. Just two months after winning his first *Tour de France*, Eddy and his pacer Fernand Wambst were tearing around the Blois velodrome on 9 September 1969, when a pile-up at the head of the pack resulted in Merckx and Wambst flying off the course. Wambst was killed instantly and Merckx suffered a cracked vertebra and broken pelvis, leaving him in pain for the rest of his cycling career. Eddy didn't allow the pain to slow him down and the wins kept coming.

Success on the race track came at a price for Eddy. The French media turned against him as he started to dominate the sport, winning 'their' *Tour* year after year. Races became a competition for second place, summed up by Spanish rider Domingo Perusena who said of Merckx: 'Most of the time you spent looking at his arse'. There were whistles as Eddy crossed the finish line in first place and in the worst case, in the fourteenth stage of the 1975 *Tour de France*, a French spectator gave him a mighty punch in the lower back 150 m from the finish line. Eddy had been on track to win his sixth *Tour* in 1975 but with the punch causing an inflammation around the liver, and a broken cheekbone sustained from a subsequent fall, Eddy limped over the finish line in second place to a Frenchman.

What was it that made Eddy superhuman? I am sticking to Eddy's story that it was a blind determination to win, but there are others who raise questions. Eddy was the first leader of one of the Grand Tours to be disqualified from the race for drug use (in the 1969 *Giro d'Italia*). Eddy has always maintained his innocence, and it is true that the testing procedure was highly dubious – in a car park with no real controls or security, and the test results would not in any way be admissible today. In more recent times, the Belgians have not covered themselves in glory in this area, with Lance Armstrong's US Postal Service team manager, the Belgian Johan Bruyneel, being accused by the USADA (US Anti-Doping Agency) of all kinds of heinous acts involving blood transfusions, human growth hormones and EPOs (the performance enhancing drug of choice of pro cyclists). Not a great day for the Belgians or their national sport. And it wasn't just EPOs that they were taking. Belgian pro cyclist Tom Boonen, the supposed heir to Eddy Merckx and fellow US Postal Service team rider with Lance Armstrong, went a bit off track by testing positive in 2008 – not for a performance-enhancing drug, but for cocaine, and somehow again in 2009.

After the 1969 incident, Eddy had a couple more brushes with the doping police in his career, but I am happy to report that he managed to pass smoothly into retirement still being held out as a national hero. Herman Van Rompuy describes Eddy as 'Belgium's biggest ambassador in the world.' And he is. I am not even a cyclist, or interested in phenylpropanolamines (which I'm sure Eddy isn't interested in either), but I am Eddy's biggest fan. On retirement, Eddy set up Eddy Merckx Cycles, and while I'm not in the market to purchase a pro cycle, I see that the new owners of the company have come out with a range of Merckx footwear. I am going to get myself a pair of Eddys.

Cycling is big business in Belgium, and every weekend the roads and cycle paths are packed with groups of mainly middle-aged men and muscly women clad head-to-toe in matching Lycra. They could cycle the length and breadth of Belgium as the country is blessed with a phenomenal network of cycle paths that criss-cross the flat parts of the country from north to south and east to west, but from what I can see, these middle-aged cycling groups tend to head for a local cafe, where they sit out on the terrace sipping Belgian beers. This would be the ideal sport for me, if it were not for the requirement to be dressed head-to-toe in matching, figure-hugging Lycra.

By the way, if you are confused, as I was, by finding references on the Internet to Belgian Eddy Merckx winning world three-cushion billiard tournaments and thought 'Is there no end to this man's talents?', it turns out that Eddy Merckx the three-cushion billiard tournament champion is a different Eddy Merckx to Eddy Merckx, the greatest cyclist the world has ever seen. Eddy Merckx (billiards) was born in 1968 and named after Eddy Merckx (cycling) won his first *Giro d'Italia* in the same year. According to my father-in-law, Conny, who was born a month after the *Giro d'Italia* win, would also have been called Eddy if she had been a boy. That was a close shave.

I'm not going to give Belgium a score of 'interesting' for three-cushion billiards, but for producing Eddy Merckx and creating a nation of Lycra-clad oldies who clog up the roads in their racing packs and take over local cafes – this is definitely a resounding final 'yes' for the interesting list.

CONCLUSION

So Belgium, how did we do? Amazingly, we seem to have scored more interestings than anything else, with a total of: seven interestings, two borings, two tragics, one odd, one weird and one morally repugnant. Admittedly my quest did take me to a rather random selection of Belgian curiosities, and there are still many more areas that merit attention. For example, Belgium has produced some of the greatest, and weirdest, artists in the world, over 80 per cent of the world's diamonds are traded through Antwerp, and you don't have to be Eddy Merckx (the three-cushion billiard tournament champion) to know that the finest billiard balls in the world are made in Belgium. And pigeon-fancying, which I dismissed without even investigating in the first chapter may not be quite so boring after all, with a record-breaking sale reported recently for a Mr Leo Heremans, a diamond polisher from Antwerp who sold his top bird to a Chinese investor for a staggering €310,000. The entire contents of his loft went for over €4.3 million, giving a whole new take on *Cash in the Attic*. Belgium also has some of the most bizarre street festivals in the world, including the Aalst carnival which has made it on to UNESCO's 'List of the Intangible Cultural Heritage of Humanity'. The carnival takes place every year on the weekend before Lent, and while it may not have the weather of Rio, it has tens of thousands of participants, no-holds-barred political satire, people throwing onions, and men parading down the street in women's underwear – what more does a good festival need?

As I promised in the 'Note from the Author' section at the start of the book, I have spared the reader an investigation into Belgian politics, as that would not have given a positive result for my quest. There is however one story told to me by a Belgian politician concerning a prime minister's visit to the US which does liven up the tedium of Belgian politics. To fully appreciate this story, it is important to know that *fokken* in Flemish means 'to breed', and *paarden* is the Flemish for 'horses'.

US President, making small talk after meeting the Belgian prime minister: 'Do you have any interests back home in Belgium?'

Belgian PM: 'Yes, I *fok* horses.'

US President: 'Pardon?!'

Belgian PM: 'Yes! That's right, horses! You know Flemish? But it's just a hobby – I don't do it for the money.'

US President leaves hastily.

My Belgian friends tell me to hurry up and write this book, as Belgium may not be a country too much longer. It took them a world record breaking 541 days to form a government in 2010/2011, and they may well be capable of holding out for a new personal best whenever they are called to polls in the future. There is even talk of whether the country will eventually break up into its component Flemish, Walloon, Bruxellois and German parts, which would have a certain irony given Belgium's centre stage role in the European Union. I hope not, as my quest has brought me to appreciate the many wonders of this quirky little nation. I have learnt that Belgium is a country of contradictions: of Michelin stars and mechanically recovered meat, where Trappist monks make the best beer in the world and grown men derive pleasure from watching cockerels sing. Its people are modest and humble, seeing nothing special in making the world's finest chocolate or hosting the most exciting race of the Formula One season. I have failed to find any justification for the relentless Belgium-bashing and have to conclude that Belgium is just a small, harmless country, bullied and belittled for no apparent reason by its larger and loutish neighbours.

The next time I am asked where I am going on holiday, I could take a lead from the modest Belgians and say, 'I'm going to Belgium, it's normal, it's how every country should be.' But I'm not, no, I'm going to hold my head up high and shout 'Belgium!', because it's not even half boring – in fact, according to my research, it's above-average interesting. And there is still so much more to discover. Now, where's that billiard ball factory…

TEN FAMOUS BELGIANS

It would not be fair to leave the reader with the unanswered question of the ten famous Belgians. You shouldn't have to name any famous Belgians, but once you start to take an interest in the country it won't be long before someone with an annoying smirk asks you to name ten of them. It won't be a Belgian person asking. They can't understand the point of this question or why it is of any relevance, which of course it isn't. Yet again, it is big country bullies trying to poke fun at little Belgium. The country has a population of 11 million – a sixth smaller pool to pick famous people from than the UK, or a thirtieth smaller than the US. Tell them to pick on populations of their own size. No one asks with a condescending snigger if you can name ten famous Cubans, or residents of Karachi, or Belarus, or ten famous inhabitants of Tianjin. And as it happens, Belgium, despite its small size, has a surfeit of A-listers. Here are over forty famous, or nearly famous, Belgian or part-Belgian, real or fictional characters, which should be enough to wipe the smirk off the face of any Belgium-baiter.

Sports

Jacques Rogge (1942–), former Belgian Olympian and President of the International Olympic Committee

Jacky Ickx (1945–), eight times Formula One Grand Prix winner

Eddy Merckx (1945–), five times winner of the *Tour de France*

Eddy Merckx (1968–), three times winner of the World Bar Billiards championship

Justine Henin (1982–), winner of seven Grand Slam singles titles

Kim Clijsters (1983–), winner of four Grand Slam singles titles

Film

Jean-Claude Van Damme (1960–), 'The muscles from Brussels'

Literature

Maurice Maeterlinck (1862–1949), Nobel Prize winning author of *Blue Bird*

George Simenon (1903–1989), author of the *Inspector Maigret* series, one of the biggest sellers of all time with an estimated 1.4 billion sales

Georges Remi (1907–1983), aka Hergé, author of the *Tintin* series

Pierre Culliford (1928–1992), creator of the Smurfs

Art

Jan van Eyck (*c.*1390–*c.*1441), master medieval painter

Pieter Bruegel the Elder (*c.*1525–1569), Flemish Renaissance artist

Pieter Bruegel the Younger (c.1564–1636), carried on the family tradition

Peter Paul Rubens (1577–1640), Flemish Baroque artist (OK, born in Germany but lived most of his life in Antwerp)

Sir Anthony van Dyck (1599–1641), Flemish Baroque artist

Victor Horta (1861–1947), art nouveau architect

René Magritte (1898–1967), surrealist fond of floating bowler hats

Music

Adolphe Sax (1814–1894), inventor of the saxophone

Jacques Brel (1929–1978), singer-songwriter

Toots Thielemans (1922–), very big in the harmonica-playing world

Salvatore Adamo (1943–), over 100 million record sales (moved to Belgium aged seven where his father worked in the mines)

Plastic Bertrand (1954–), 'Ça Plane Pour Moi' performer (note to Belgians: just go with me on this one)

Science and Business

Gerard Mercator (1512–1594), Europe's leading globe-maker who coined the word 'atlas'

Simon Stevin (1548–1620), inventor of the land yacht, double-entry bookkeeping for the national accounts and decimalisation

Lambert Quetelet (1796–1874), creator of the body mass index

Zenobe Gramme (1826–1901), inventor of the first industrial electric motor

Ernst Solvay (1838–1922), chemist and philanthropist who invented the Solvay process

Leo Hendrik Baekeland (1863–1944), inventor of Bakelite

Jules Bordet (1870–1961), inventor of the first vaccine against whooping cough

Julius Nieuwland (1878–1936), Holy Cross priest, inventor of synthetic rubber that became neoprene

Georges Lemaître (1894–1966), Jesuit priest who came up with the Big Bang theory

Edward de Smedt (18??–18??), inventor of asphalt

Albert Claude (1899–1983), Nobel Prize-winning scientist who discovered chloroplasts in plant cells

Politics

Charlemagne (742–814), perhaps more 'self-declared king' than politician, aka Charles the Great, Founder of the Holy Roman Empire and ruler of most of Western Europe

Paul Henri Spaak (1899–1972), founding father of the Benelux, the EU and all round 'Mr Europe'

Willy Claes (1938–), former Belgian Foreign Minister who became Secretary General of NATO

Jean-Luc Dehaene (1940–), Belgian Prime Minister whose bid to become head of the European Commission in 1994 was blocked by John Major; my father-in-law held me personally responsible

Herman Van Rompuy (1947–), first full-time President of the European Council

Fictional Belgians

Hercule Poirot, Agatha Christie's great detective of thirty-three novels and more than fifty short stories

Dr Evil, the nemesis of Austin Powers

Tintin, chasing baddies, saving friends, and blowing up the occasional rhino in twenty-four adventures

Not really Belgian, but can be used against persistent 'Name ten famous Belgian' questioners:
Bradley Wiggins – born in Belgium
Audrey Hepburn – born in Belgium
Johnny Hallyday – Belgian father
David Guetta – Belgian mother
Ludwig van Beethoven – Belgian grandfather, Lodewijk van Beethoven, from Mechelen
Bob Geldof – Belgian grandfather from Ypres. OK, that's probably stretching it a bit far.

RANDOM BEER NOTES

Piedboef bruin
Strength: 1.2 per cent (that's less than half of an alcopop!)
Type: known as a '*tafelbier*' or '*bierre de table*'
Notes: Like Tizer or a cheap cola without the cola taste. Fizzy, sugary sweet. This makes a non-alcoholic beer positively alcoholic. A glossy brown colour like a supermarket beef stock. Thankfully no signs of beef in the ingredients list, but plenty of E numbers: colouring E150c, antioxidant E300 and sweetener E954. This last E is the number for saccharin, a product described in my dictionary of E numbers as a 'non-nutritive sweetener, 300 to 500 times sweeter than sucrose'. It is also known as *benzosulfimide* and is apparently derived from coal tar. That's not right and it's certainly not pleasant.
Score: 0/10
In a word: eeerrrrr

Jupiler
Strength: 5.2 per cent
Type: Pils

Notes: Very easy to drink. Probably OK if you are very thirsty or at the Belgian Grand Prix in Spa-Francorchamps, where it is the only beer available. Light, low on taste. Wait for a hot summer's day before trying this one again.

Score: 5/10

In a word: easy

Duvel

Strength: 8.5 per cent

Type: Strong blond

Notes: My first 8.5 per cent-er. Weak on flavour, strong on kick. Really might have to break my vow and have another one of these to see if I can find any taste. Surprisingly drinkable for a beer so strong. A 'fatboy' bottle, blond in colour. In fact, effortlessly drinkable.

Conny's friend Marc tells me that Duvel is the downfall of many a visitor. 'They have more than one Duvel and when they stand up, they find they are, how you say, "wasted".' Yes, that would be about right. Despite the temptation, will stick to my vow. It's no coincidence that Duvel is translated in the local dialect as 'the Devil'.

Score: 7/10

In a word: deceptive

Cristal Alken

Strength: 4.8 per cent

Type: Pils

Notes: Cristal, like Jupiler, Stella and Maes, is one of the over-the-counter Pils lagers, sold more usually from the pump than the bottle. Cristal is indeed an ordinary beer. In fact very similar to water, just slightly coloured and with a few bubbles. Really very short on taste. And the bubbles are rather prickly. A faint smell of insecticide which took me back to the time when I worked in the kitchens of a hotel in St Tropez.

Every morning before starting cooking we would pull back the fridges and empty cans of industrial strength insecticide behind them, in a futile attempt to hold back the tide of cockroaches which returned every night. Each sip of Cristal took me straight back to behind those fridges.

I would of course like to point out to the makers of Cristal, and their lawyers, that I am not in any way suggesting that industrial strength insecticide is used in the making of Cristal Alken or any other of their wonderful products. I am just saying that it tastes like it.

Score: 2/10

In a word: St Tropez

Gueuze Belle-Vue

Strength: 5.2 per cent

Type: Gueuze

Notes: The first sip set my mind racing. What was that strange, yet familiar flavour? According to the label it is *amorisé* and it certainly does have a special, scented flavour. The cherries on the label were a clue, and I knew that this is what is known as a 'fruit beer'. But what was that strange sickly taste? It wasn't long before it clicked. Belle-Vue has the same taste as that horrible, treacly cough syrup that is stuffed full of chemical flavours and colourings to disguise the nasty medicine you are taking. The good thing about cough medicine is that you only need to have a spoon or two of it. The bad thing about my

bottle of Belle-Vue is that I still had half a bottle to go. I took it in small sips. It was a long evening.
Score: 1/10
In a word: sickly

Jessenhofke
Strength: 7 per cent
Type: a 'Belgian double brown beer'
Notes: Brewed by the son of the hairdresser who lives across the road. It says on the label in Flemish and French that it is 'to pass the dark days'. Can you say that? It also says to 'drink moderately but regularly'. I'm really not sure about the PC nature of the health warnings, but for such a strong beer it is remarkably drinkable and has more taste than a Duvel. And it gets an extra point for being organic. Looking forward to being able to have this one again.
Score: 8/10
In a word: yes

Tripel Karmeliet
Strength: 8.4 per cent
Type: Tripel
Notes: I had always been put off this beer by the name and the strength. It sounds more like an armour-plated assault vehicle than something you would want to sip leisurely on a warm afternoon in the market square. Quite a nutty, flavoursome drink. In fact surprisingly enjoyable. Tastier than a Duvel which is becoming my benchmark for these more than 8 per cent beers. And no desire to vomit as you approach the end of it, which is always a good sign with

a beer in this category. Definitely going on the list to retry when the vow is complete.

Score: 7/10

In a word: nutty

Oude Gueuze

Strength: 7 per cent

Type: Lambic beer

Notes: My first real lambic beer! I had been looking forward to having one of these after reading about these 'spontaneous fermentation' beers in the *Good Beer Guide Belgium*. The landlord of the Egel in Hasselt released the champagne-style cork with a pop. 'These can be dangerous,' he says with a chuckle. 'It's my first one,' I reply, 'are they any good?'

'Everyone has their own taste,' he says diplomatically, which I take to be a 'No'. 'They can be sour,' he adds. Ouch, he is right. This is rough. Sandpaper rough, fighting-back-at-you-with-every-sip rough. Curiously cider-like. It reminds me of the infamous scrumpy night at university, when Clive's friend was sick down the back of the radiator and it was still there when we came back after the summer holidays. Wish I hadn't remembered that thought now. This is a very odd beer but somehow, against all my usual taste preferences, I am enjoying it to the last drop and look forward to when I can try another one.

Score: 8/10

In a word: prickly

Kwak

Strength: 8.4 per cent

Type: Speciality beer

Notes: Everybody has to try a Kwak at least once in their life, if only for the bizarre contraption that it comes in. The glass, looking like a stunted 'yard of ale' glass with a thin neck and rounded bottom, is held upright by a wooden stand that acts as the handle with which to hold it by (although I am told that purists remove the glass from the stand to drink its contents). There is a great story behind the Kwak glass and its wooden stand. It dates from Napoleon's occupation of Belgium and the law that he brought with him forbidding coach drivers from joining their passengers for a drink. Innkeeper Paul Kwak devised this special glass which could hang on the side of the carriage by the driver's seat without spilling a drop of ale as the coach sped away. Ingenious – good for beer sales to thirsty coach drivers, but not so good for nineteenth-century drink-driving casualties.

The blurb on the label of the present day bottle says that Kwak is 'incomparable'. That's a silly thing to say, as of course it can be compared with anything. Ruben thought the smell was comparable to disinfectant, and at a strength of 8.4 per cent it may just kill off 99 per cent of all known germs. I would say that the flavour doesn't compare that well with some of the other more than 8 per cent beers. But getting to the end of the glass, although tricky from a practical sense, was easy.

Based on the amusing glass alone, this is one to retry when the vow is up.

Score: 6/10

In a word: showy

Cuvée de Noel St Feuillien
Strength: 9 per cent

Type: Abbey Christmas Ale
Notes: Occasionally the time and place where you have a beer are as important as the beer itself. Sitting on Christmas Eve in the Poechenellekelder, a bizarre cafe in Brussels with manky puppets hanging from the ceiling and vintage Manneken-Pis prints on the walls, I asked the barmaid for her recommendation. The result was a glass of their beer of the month, the Cuvée de Noel St Feuillien. At 9 per cent this is the strongest beer I have had to date, yet it is also one of the smoothest and easiest to drink. Subtle flavours and silky smooth to the last drop. Perhaps it's the creepy puppets, mannequins and stuffed things that are affecting me. Perhaps it is Christmas Eve. Perhaps it is the 9 per cent.
Score: 9/10
In a word: when can I have this again? (Yes, I know that is more than one word.)

Hoegaarden Speciale
Strength: 5.7 per cent
Type: White beer
Notes: Consumed in the family's Belgium home on Christmas day in my very own Hoegaarden Speciale glass. I have to admit that I love this beer. I don't care what the purists say about it being industrially produced by InBev; as far as I am concerned, Hoegaarden Speciale is a delicious beer. It has a very distinctive spicy flavour which I find quite hard to pinpoint. I passed the glass around the table for suggestions. Conny thought it smelled of freesias and orange peel. Hannah said the smell reminds her of the cleaning products used to clean the tables at her school. This led to an unwelcome story from Ruben about his history

lesson, where he follows a room of fifteen-year-old boys who leave the room filled with pungent BO which apparently smells like a pizza topping.

It took me a while to focus again on the Hoegaarden. It's really very spicy. I can see that it wouldn't be to everyone's taste. I wonder if I can get hold of some of Hannah's school's cleaning product?

Score: 9/10
In a word: heaven

Sloeber
Strength: 7.5%
Type: Strong blond
Notes: Worth trying just so that you can ask the barman for 'a pint of your finest slobber'. This will of course be lost on him, as Belgians do not serve pints and find nothing amusing in the word 'slobber'. I had my Sloeber instead from a bottle. A 'fatboy' Duvel bottle which boded well, but on closer inspection the illustration on the label of a dancing Sloeber bottle wearing a bow tie and white gloves, doffing its *chapeau à la* Maurice Chevalier, did not inspire confidence. Quite a chunky taste, heavier than a Duvel, and unfortunately one of those which induces a heightened sense of nausea towards the end of the glass. Not helped by the onset of the aroma of moth repellent accompanied by a whiff of the *urinoir*.

Score: 2/10
In a word: whiffy

Maes Pils
Strength: 5.2 per cent

Type: Pils

Notes: The message on the can tells me to '*Volg je dorst*' ('Follow your thirst'), and that Maes is the beer of the music festivals. I must therefore be young and cool to drink this, and there is a good chance that I will be excessively spotty and smelly too. I'm sure it's fun to drink in a sweaty tent at a summer rock festival, but I was trying to enjoy it in the cafe at the Plop gnome theme park and the Plop classic hit, '*Eeh Oh, Eeh Oh, Sloebi Doebi Dabi Dee*' was blasting out of the loudspeakers at me and messing with my brain. You try not to sing along – you know it's wrong, but it grinds you down and after a while you find that you are tapping your feet and mumbling '*Eeh Oh, Eeh Oh, Sloebi Doebi Dabi Dee*' under your breath, hoping that no one will hear. Notwithstanding Plop, the Maes was fairly pleasant to start with, although rather flat by the end of the glass. I think you are meant to drink it quickly. Perhaps that's the idea of the Plop mind-music – to get you to drink up and go.

Score: 5/10

In a word: *tentsletje*

Vedett Extra Blond

Strength: 5.2 per cent

Type: Pils

Notes: A surprise to find a lager in the same 'fatboy' bottle as a Duvel, but in a bright green glass. Not so surprising when the label reveals that it is from the same Moortgat brewery. Unlike Duvel, it is extremely light, almost tasteless. Better than the run-of-the-mill Pils as it stays good to the end. Served in a fancy high champagne-style flute from a bottle with a smart white, black and red-striped label. As I have already confessed, I am a sucker for good marketing and no doubt real beer aficionados will tell me that it is just water. However, it looks good, I feel good and I am impressed that it is so extra blond that it is practically tasteless. Really light and refreshing, nearly as good, say, as a glass of cold water.

Score: 6/10

In a word: water

Corsendonk Agnus Tripel

Strength: 7.5 per cent

Type: Tripel

Notes: The wonderfully named 'Corsendonk' manages to encompass a heavy beer with the thirst-quenching properties of a light lager. The unusual glass has an ice-cubed shaped chunk for the stem. Quite heavy and yeasty, like a tasty Duvel. Having had one of these at lunch time I discovered that Corsendonk has soporific properties and spent an enjoyable Sunday afternoon asleep with my father-in-law on the sofa, 'watching' the Amstel Gold cycle race on the television.

Score: 7/10

In a word: zzzzz

Deus Brut des Flandres

Strength: 11.5 per cent

Type: Speciality beer

Notes: this is a grand beer that comes in a champagne-style bottle looking as though it is a bottle of Dom Pérignon. It is served in champagne flute glasses. Impossible to fill up without overflowing, unnaturally foamy – like someone has squirted

Fairy Liquid into the bottom of each glass when you weren't looking. It has a kick, as you would expect with a beer of this strength, but it's not impossible to drink and there is no growing nauseous feeling. The label around the neck of the bottle continues the packaging hype, describing its labour-intensive production – first in the Belgium brewery and then hand-finished in France. Here it is bottled and undergoes *remouage* – the turning by hand of the bottle each day to encourage the yeast sediment to drop to the neck of the bottle where it is frozen and removed. That's a lot of work just for a bottle of beer. Is it worth it? To be honest, if someone approaches you with a bottle that looks like Dom Pérignon – better hope that it is Dom Pérignon.

Score: 4/10

In a word: foamy

Black Albert

Strength: 13 per cent

Type: Black beer

A warning on the label reads 'VERY STRONG BEER'. This is probably unnecessary, as you would think that picking up a bottle of beer that is clearly marked as 13 per cent would let the consumer know that this is not going to be a can of watery pils. It is black, jet black, and pours into the glass like motor oil. Even the very thin layer of foam darkens. The label lists 'candy' in the ingredients and I am worried that it is going to be a sickly-sweet treacly concoction. Fortunately nothing could be further from the truth – it turns out to be a black stout, like Guinness on steroids. At 13 per cent this is an evil drink, but unbelievably I can drink it to the end seemingly

without any after-effects (although I notice the handwriting of my beer notes deteriorates, and I can no longer read my last comments or remember the beer I tried after this one).
Score: 6/10
In a word: evil

Westvleteren 12
Strength: 10.6 per cent
Type: Trappist beer
I am holding the Westvleteren glass in my hand, looking at the 'I helped build an abbey' inscription and feeling good about myself. I was expecting not to like this beer, not to fall for the hype, but I can't help it. Is it the best beer in the world? Without having tasted every last one of the world's other beers I don't think I'm in a position to suggest that, but I can say that it is really very, very good. The beer has a rich dark chestnut colour, with a small head of creamy foam, asking me to try it. Sip after sip. It is silky to drink, sweet even and good to the very last drop. This is why I took my vow. There may be more on the list to try but this is spiritual beer heaven.
Score: oh go on, I'll join the hype: 10/10
In a word: enlightenment

BEER CHECKLIST

If you have taken the Belgian beer vow, I hope this checklist of nearly 500 beer types that you are likely to come across proves useful to you in recording the beers that you taste along the way. Before I started using such a list, I found that I kept inadvertently breaking the vow by forgetting which I had previously sampled. The list will help you keep track, and serve as a reminder of those to try again, or avoid, once you have completed your vow and reached your own nirvana.

Take the vow: *No beer shall be consumed for a second time, until all other Belgian beers available have been tried.*

Beer	Dubbel/ Tripel, etc.	Date	Location	Score	In a word
3 Schténg					
Aardmonnik					
Abbaye d'Aulne					
Abbaye de St Martin					
Abbaye des Rocs					

BEER CHECKLIST

Beer	Dubbel/ Tripel, etc.	Date	Location	Score	In a word
Abbaye de Forest					
Achel					
Achelse Kluis					
Adelardus Trudoabdijbier					
Adler					
Adriaen Brouwer					
Affligem					
Alpaide					
Altitude 6					
Alvinne					
Amarante					
Ambiorix					
Ambrio					
Angelique					
Antiek					
Apple Lindemans					
Arabier					
Archiduc					
Arend					
Artevelde					
Aubel					
Augrenoise					
Augustijn					
Authentique					
Bacchus					
Balthazar					
Barbar Bok					
Barbe d'Or					
Barbe Rouge					
Barbiot					

BOTTOMS UP IN BELGIUM

Beer	Dubbel/ Tripel, etc.	Date	Location	Score	In a word
Bavik					
Beersel					
Bel Pils					
Belgoo					
Bella Mère					
Belle-Vue					
Bellegems					
Bersalis					
Betchard					
Bie					
Bieken					
Bière de Miel					
Bière des Ours					
Bière du Corsaire					
Bink					
Biolégère					
Bios					
Black Albert					
Black Hole					
Blanche d'Ardenne					
Blanche de Bruxelles					
Blanche de Namur					
Blauw					
Bloemenbier					
Bock					
Bockor					
Boerke					
Bokkereyer					
Bokrijks					

BEER CHECKLIST

Beer	Dubbel/ Tripel, etc.	Date	Location	Score	In a word
Bon Homme					
Bon Secours					
Boneffe					
Bons Voeux					
Bornem					
Bos Bier					
Bosprotter					
Boteresse					
Boucanier					
Bouillion					
Bourgogne des Flandres					
Brabançonne					
Brasserie de Bellevaux					
Bravoure					
Brice					
Brigand					
Broeder Jacob					
Brugge Tripel					
Brugs Tarwebier					
Brunehaut					
Brussels Fruit Beer					
Buffalo					
Bush					
Cambrinus					
Campus					
Canaster					
Cantillon					
Captain Cooker					
Caracole					

BOTTOMS UP IN BELGIUM

Beer	Dubbel/ Tripel, etc.	Date	Location	Score	In a word
Carolus					
Caulier					
Celtic Angel					
Cervesia					
Chapeau					
Chimay					
Ciney					
Cnudde					
Colère Rouge					
Contra Pils					
Cookie Beer					
Coq Hardi					
Corsendonk					
Couckelaerschen Doedel					
Crianza					
Cristal					
Cuvée Angelique					
Cuvée des Trolls					
Cuvée du Chateau					
Cuvée St Antoine					
De Graal					
De Koninck					
Delirium Nocturnum					
Delirium Red					
Delirium Tremens					
Den Bras					
Den Drupneuze					
Den Haene					
Den Herberg					

BEER CHECKLIST

Beer	Dubbel/ Tripel, etc.	Date	Location	Score	In a word
Dendermonde					
Dentergems Witbier					
Deus – Brut des Flandres					
Dikke Mathile					
Domus					
Double Enghein					
Druide					
Ducassis					
Duchesse de Borgogne					
Duivels Bier					
Dulle Griet					
Dulle Teve					
Duvel					
Echt Kriekenbier					
Edel Bräu					
Eerwaarde Pater					
Egmont					
Embrasse					
Ename					
Equinox					
Estaminet					
Eupener					
Ezel					
Fantôme					
Faro Boon					
Faro Lambic Lindemans					
Fasso Blond					
Felix Speciaal					

BOTTOMS UP IN BELGIUM

Beer	Dubbel/ Tripel, etc.	Date	Location	Score	In a word
Femme Fatale					
Festina Lente					
Floreffe					
Floris					
Forestinne					
Framboise Lindermans					
Framboise Max					
Framboise Oud Beersel					
Freaky					
Gagaleer					
Gaspar					
Gauloise					
Gentse Strop					
Gentse Tripel					
Gueuze Girardin					
Gordon Finest Gold					
Gouden Carolus					
Gouyasse					
Gribousine					
Grimbergen					
Grisette					
Grottenbier					
Gruut					
Gulden Draak					
Guldenberg					
Hanssens					
Hapkin					
Hector					

BEER CHECKLIST

Beer	Dubbel/ Tripel, etc.	Date	Location	Score	In a word
Hellekapelle					
Helleketelbier					
Hercule					
Herkenrode					
Heylissem					
Hik					
Himelein					
Hoegaarden					
Hoeve Bier					
Hof					
Hoogstraten Poorter					
Hop Ruiter					
Hopus					
Horse-Ale					
Houblon					
Houten Kop					
Ichtegem's					
Iris					
Itters Bruin					
Jacobins Gueuze					
Jambe-de-Bois					
Jan De Lichte					
Jessenhofke					
Joseph					
Joup					
Judas					
Jupiler					
Kalle					
Kameleon					

BOTTOMS UP IN BELGIUM

Beer	Dubbel/Tripel, etc.	Date	Location	Score	In a word
Kapel van Viven					
Kapittel					
Kastaar					
Kasteel					
Katje					
Keizer Karel					
Kempisch Vuur					
Kerasus					
Kerelsbier					
Kerkomse					
Kerst Pater					
Kerstbie					
Kerstlicht					
Kessel					
Keyte					
Kira					
Klevertien					
Kloeke					
Koekelaring					
Koempelbier					
Kortrijk-d'Utsel					
Kriek Boon					
Kriek de Ranke					
Kriek Fantastiek					
Kriek Girardin					
Kriek Mariage Parfait					
Kriekedebie					
Kwak					
Kwibus					

BEER CHECKLIST

Beer	Dubbel/ Tripel, etc.	Date	Location	Score	In a word
La Binchoise					
La Botteresse					
La Bouillonnaise					
La Chèvenis					
La Chouffe					
La Cré Tonnerre					
La Divine					
La Grelotte					
La Gorgnarde					
La Guillotine					
La Hervoise					
La Mac Vertus					
La Médiévale					
La Mère Vertus					
La Merveilleuse de Chèvremont					
La Moneuse					
La Poiluchette					
La Rulles					
La Sambresse					
La Trompeuse					
La Wambrechies					
Lam Gods					
L'Ambrasse-Temps					
Lamme Goedzak					
Lamoral					
L'Angelus					
L'autruche bière des Gilles					
Lambicus					
L'Enfant Terrible					

BOTTOMS UP IN BELGIUM

Beer	Dubbel/ Tripel, etc.	Date	Location	Score	In a word
Le Pavé de l'Ours					
Leeuw					
Leffe					
Leireken					
Lesage					
Leute					
Liefmans					
Limburgse Witte					
Lindermans					
Livinus					
Loterbol					
Lucifer					
Lustem					
Ma Mère Spéciale					
Maes					
Malheur					
Manten					
Maredsous					
Martens Pils					
Martin's					
Mea Culpa					
Melchior					
Moeder Overste					
Moinette					
Mongozo					
Montagnarde					
Morpheus					
Mort Subite					
Mug					

BEER CHECKLIST

Beer	Dubbel/ Tripel, etc.	Date	Location	Score	In a word
'n Toeback					
Nen Uts					
Netebuk					
Newton					
Noblesse					
Noir de Dottignies					
Nondedju					
Nostradamus					
Oerbier					
Oesterstout					
Omer					
Ondineke					
Ops-Ale					
Orval					
Oudbeitje					
Oude Gueuze					
Oude Gueuze Boon					
Oude Kriek					
Oxymore					
Palm					
Pannepot					
Pater Lieven					
Patersvat					
Paulus					
Pax Pils					
Pee Klak					
Père Noël					
Petrus					
Pick Up					

BOTTOMS UP IN BELGIUM

Beer	Dubbel/ Tripel, etc.	Date	Location	Score	In a word
Piedboef					
Pilaardbijter					
Piraat					
Pissenlit					
Plokkersbier					
Poorter					
Poperings Hommelbier					
Poperings Nunnebier					
Postel					
Primus					
Prior Tongerlo					
Queue de Charrue					
Quintine					
Rochefort					
Rodenbac					
Romy Pils					
Rose de Gambrinus					
Saint Lamvinus					
Saint-Monon					
Saison					
Sara					
Sas					
Sasbräu					
Satan					
Saxo					
Serafijn					
Sezoens					

BEER CHECKLIST

Beer	Dubbel/ Tripel, etc.	Date	Location	Score	In a word
Silly					
Sinpalsken					
Sint Canarus					
Sint Gummarus					
Slaapmutske					
Slag					
Sloeber					
Smiske					
Speciale 1900					
St Benoît					
St Bernardus					
St Feuillien					
St Idesbald					
St Louis Gueuze / Kriek					
St Paul					
St Sebastiaan					
Stella Artois					
Steenbrugge					
Stille Nacht					
Stouterik					
Straffe Hendrik					
Strangaper					
Strubbe					
Struise					
Super 64					
Super Acht Export					
Super des Fagnes					
Sur-les-Bois					
Taras Boulba					

BOTTOMS UP IN BELGIUM

Beer	Dubbel/Tripel, etc.	Date	Location	Score	In a word
Taurus					
Tempelier					
Ter Dolen					
Timmermans					
Titje					
Tongerlo					
Tonneke					
Toria					
Tournay					
Tripel Karmeliet					
Triple Moine					
Triverius					
Troubadour					
Troublette					
Tseejes					
Tumulus					
Tuverbol					
Uitzet					
Ulricher Extra					
Ultra					
Urchon					
Val-Dieu					
Valeir					
Vapeur					
Vedett					
Vicardin					
Vicaris					
Vichtenaar					
Vieux Temps					
Villers					

BEER CHECKLIST

Beer	Dubbel/ Tripel, etc.	Date	Location	Score	In a word
Viven					
Vlaamsche Leeuw					
Vlaskop					
Vleteren					
Voisin					
Vuuve					
Waase Wolf					
Waaslander					
Waterloo					
Watou Tripel					
Watou's Wit Bier					
West Pils					
Westmalle					
Westvleteren					
Wevelgemse Tripel					
Wildebok					
Wilderen					
Winterkoninkske					
Witkap					
Witterkerke					
Wostyntje					
XX Bitter					
Yperman					
Zeezuiper					
Zinnebir					
Zonderik					
Zottegems					

ACKNOWLEDGEMENTS

I didn't write an acknowledgements page for my book on Tibet, as I was concerned at the time that I might get some people into trouble if the book didn't receive approval from the authorities. I have always regretted this, but as I might have inadvertently mentioned the 'invasion' of Tibet once or twice instead of referring to China's takeover as the 'peaceful liberation' (something that really doesn't go down well with Beijing censorship boards), it was probably the right decision at the time. Hopefully, writing a book on Belgium will not give rise to the same concerns and no one thanked here is going to be taken away for Belgian thought re-education. Thanks to Jennifer Barclay for commissioning the manuscript in the first place and believing that something of interest may lie within. And to Anna Martin of Summersdale, who has been an exemplary editor throughout, suggesting helpful structural changes and correcting an embarrassing array of what I like to call 'typos' but which were really spelling mistakes and poor grammar. I have also been incredibly lucky to have worked with Justine Gore-Smith as my copy editor, bringing

ACKNOWLEDGEMENTS

her forensic attention to detail to the final drafts. Thanks go to my Dutch friend Erik for sending me quirky Belgian beers, through the post no less. Some of them arrived in one piece. I am indebted to Patrick Mertens of Boon who gave his time freely to explain the mysteries of Belgian chocolate. Thanks to my brother Richard for giving advice on the first draft, and to my new friends at CAMRA and the *Good Beer Guide Belgium*, Simon Hall and Tim Webb for permission to use a few quotes from their excellent book. Most of all, Conny's family and friends – to cousin Hilde for more odd beers and transport, to brother-in-law Jan and his friends Joel and Herman for even more beers and a fine day out in Spa-Francorchamps, to Pa for introducing me to rooster-singing and for cracking the code to secure me a case of Westvleteren 12, and above all, to Conny's sister Betty who has been hugely supportive throughout, despite her constant worry that my research would lead to an embarrassing conclusion. Hannah and Ruben, thanks for putting up with my excursions to Belgian 'places of interest' (none more bizarre than the trip I insisted on taking to the extraordinary CasAnus – an 'art' hotel outside Antwerp in the shape of a giant colon) without complaining too much and for cajoling me to 'get on with the book' in the subtle way that teenagers do. And finally, thanks to Conny, for everything really.

Have you enjoyed this book?
If so, why not write a review on your favourite website?

If you're interested in finding out more about our books,
find us on Facebook at **Summersdale Publishers** and
follow us on Twitter at **@Summersdale**.

Thanks very much for buying this Summersdale book.

www.summersdale.com